PAGES FROM CHURCH HISTORY

Also by the Author

Jonathan Edwards: A Guided Tour of His Life and Thought
Martin Luther: A Guided Tour of His Life and Thought
J. Gresham Machen: A Guided Tour of His Life and Thought
An Absolute Sort of Certainty: The Holy Spirit and the Apologetics of Jonathan Edwards
The Legacy of Jonathan Edwards: American Religion and the Evangelical Tradition (coeditor)
Heaven on Earth: Capturing Jonathan Edwards's Vision of Living in Between

PAGES FROM CHURCH HISTORY

A Guided Tour of Christian Classics

STEPHEN J. NICHOLS

PUBLISHING
P.O. BOX 817 • PHILLIPSBURG • NEW JERSEY 08865-0817

Illustration 7.5 is used by permission and is taken from Martin Luther, *Dr. Martin Luther Der kleine Katechismus* (Munich: Müller, 1933); Illustration 7.6 is used by permission and is taken from *ABC und Namen Büchlein für Kinder* (Belleville, PA: Joseph E. Peachey, n.d.); Illustration 8.2 is used courtesy of Montgomery Library, Westminster Theological Seminary, Philadelphia; Illustration 9.4 is used by permission and is taken from John Bunyan, *The Pilgrim's Progress* (Cincinnati: H. M. Rulinson, n.d.), 133; Illustration 10.3 (also on front cover) is used courtesy of Beinecke Rare Book and Manuscript Library, Yale University; Illustration 10.4 is used by permission of Forbes Library, Northampton, Massachusetts; Illustration 10.5 (also on front cover) is used courtesy of First Church, Northampton, Massachusetts.

Page design by Lakeside Design Plus

Printed in the United States of America

Library of Congress Cataloging-in-Publication Data

Nichols, Stephen J., 1970-
    Pages from church history : a guided tour of Christian classics / Stephen J. Nichols
      p. cm.
    Includes bibliographical references and index.
    ISBN-10: 0-87552-636-5 (pbk.)
    ISBN-13: 978-0-87552-636-2 (pbk.)
    1. Church history. 2. Christian biography. 3. Church history—Sources. I. Title.

BR150.N53 2006
270—dc22

                              2006046020

For my teachers of church history:
William S. Barker
D. Clair Davis
D. G. Hart
Gary L. W. Johnson
with appreciation

CONTENTS

Part Four: The Modern Age

LIST OF ILLUSTRATIONS

Acknowledgments

I am grateful to the many friends who have contributed to this book. Some of these chapters bear my debt to specific people. My thanks to Will Barker, who first opened up the world of the early church to me; the chapters on Polycarp and Augustine are for you. Clair Davis, in his inimitable way, illuminated the middle ages; Anselm, à Kempis, and even Aquinas are for you. A very warm thanks to Sean Lucas, my good friend since seminary days; Calvin is for you. Lester Hicks has become a trusted friend and a valued colleague; Luther is for you. And I am very thankful for my close friend and constant encourager, Dale Mort; Bonhoeffer is for you.

This book would have been a lot more work for me were it not for the expert and timely assistance from my student, Eric Brandt. His meticulous research paid off again and again throughout this book, for which I am most grateful. I am also thankful to the administrators at Lancaster Bible College for supporting my work.

Finally, I am grateful to Heidi. She's always willing to listen to me talk of church history and of books. As Charles Wesley wrote to Sarah, "My heart is with you."

INTRODUCTION:
CONNECTING WITH OUR PAST

Langston Hughes's "The Negroe Speaks of Rivers," in merely nineteen lines, poignantly depicts the meaningful connections with our past that shape our identity in the present. The rivers that Hughes speaks of flow back to "when the dawns were young"—the great Euphrates, the Congo, the Nile. Then he speaks of the more recent past, recalling the Mississippi, whose "muddy bosom" he had watched "turn all golden in the sunset." These rivers portray the flow of human history, with both the distant and recent past taking shape as the rivers flow on, carving out their contours. "I've known rivers," Hughes muses, "Ancient, dusky rivers," adding, "My soul has grown deep like the rivers." Standing along the banks of these rivers, Hughes becomes aware of the past that has gone before, humbling and encouraging him at the same time. He is made deeper; his life is enriched because of these connections to his past.

But perhaps the reverse is also true. Without meaningful connections to the past, the soul does not grow deep, but constricts, growing more and more shallow. As many have observed, our age tends to be consumed with the present, the new, and even the future. In some ways, this tendency proves helpful. Medical advancements, ease of communication, and travel are all direct benefits of such forward thinking. There also lurks, however, a downside, as this tendency can lead to a certain *ahistoricism*, a sentiment that tells us the past is of little relevance and may be handily brushed aside. "Newer is better," the saying goes. As evangelicals, especially as American evangelicals, we are not immune to the *ahistoricism* infecting our age. Perhaps, in light of this cultural atmosphere, it is worthwhile to offer an apologetic for this book, and for the value of church history in the present life of the church.

Of course, one can always find substantiation for an argument by quoting Charles Haddon Spurgeon. And it was Spurgeon who said, "I find it odd that one who thinks so highly of what the Holy Spirit teaches him, thinks so little of what the Holy Spirit teaches others." In context, Spurgeon was arguing for the use of commentaries. Yet his point has broader application. If the Holy Spirit works in us, then (paraphrasing Spurgeon) how much more work has he been doing in the lives of countless others who have gone before us over the past two millennia? Another voice from the past, Martin Luther, declares in his famous hymn "A Mighty Fortress Is Our God": "The Spirit and the gifts are ours." Consequently, because of the gift of the Spirit, we are equipped for all things pertaining to life and godliness. But the Spirit is not our unique, solitary gift. The Spirit is a corporate gift, given to a long train of past generations and, Lord willing, given to many generations to come. We, like the narrator of Hughes's poem, are merely a part of a river. In fact, we are part of *the River*, flowing through the pages of history.

Studying the past offers meaningful connections with our legacy. We are enriched through our study of the past, simultaneously humbled by testimonies of courage and emboldened by reflections of God's grace and faithfulness. This is the primary reason why I have written this book:

to enable readers to get better acquainted with those who have preceded us. It's a way to get in touch with our roots.

Church history not only inspires, it also instructs. Among his many books, John R. Stott wrote one intended for pastors entitled *Between Two Worlds*. His thesis, as reflected in the title, is that the pastor lives between two worlds: the world of the Bible on the one hand and the particular world, or his point of time and cultural context, on the other. The pastor's task is to bring the world of the Bible to bear upon this world, the world of his audience. While a helpful model for understanding the task of preaching, Stott's vision applies to far more than pastors and preaching. In fact, all Christians are tasked with bringing the world of the Bible—and all its demands—to the world in which they live, to speak the Bible faithfully and truly in their "world." No small task, to be sure. Examples abound in the pages of Scripture of individuals who did this well and also of those who did not. We can learn from both. We can also widen the net, adding to the mix the many figures from church history who sought to bring the Bible to bear upon their times. Through the stories of church history, we can observe others who tried to live between two worlds. We have many models, some successful, some not so, but from all of them we can learn. We can learn from the specific things they teach. Augustine's understanding of the doctrine of sin and humanity skillfully brings together a great deal of the Bible's teaching on the subject. Luther's ethic is not simply a model; it is one that can directly apply. Jonathan Edwards's understanding of God's redemptive work in history helps one to understand the big picture of what God is accomplishing in the world. And the list could go on.

Taken together, these reasons clearly point to the value of church history. But, books on church history, from one-volume to multivolume works, abound. So the question naturally arises: why this particular book on church history? Two principles drive this book. The first is the principle of selective attention. This means that in order to grasp a rather large and complex subject, like that of church history over the last two thousand years, one is best served by focusing on key elements that anchor the myriad details. This focus enables one to navigate the grand current of church history. Rather than get lost in a sea of facts, dates, and information, this approach helps us to see the big picture and catch the flow of events.

The second principle concerns the notion that reading *about* church history is no substitute for reading church history. Now, of course, this needs modification. This book, after all, fits the category of reading about church history. Its aim, however, is to do more, and to leave the reader not satisfied with simply retelling the story of the past. By focusing on some key texts that have significantly contributed to the Christian tradition and that continue to shape our identity in the present, this book is a means to an adventurous journey of reading not about church history, but reading the actual texts that constitute it. These texts, however, can be daunting. Simply thumbing through Augustine's *Confessions* can be intimidating. This book offers help by providing a context, walking through the text, and pointing the way for further exploration.

The greatest challenge of this selective approach concerns what to include and what to leave out. I fully anticipate that my list will not meet with approval by all readers or reviewers. Rather good cases could be made against some of my selections and for the inclusion of others. I welcome such disagreement—it reveals that we all have texts that are meaningful to us. Nevertheless, there are reasons for the twelve that I have selected. Some are household names and, I suppose, would make it onto just about everyone's list. On this point, Augustine, Luther, Calvin, Edwards, and the Wesleys all come to mind. Others are included because they stand at the fore of a significant movement or have left us a significant legacy. For example, the modern missions movement owes much to the efforts of William Carey. Other figures are included because they so well typify their age. Polycarp, one of the more well known of the martyrs, gives us an intriguing window into the challenges faced by the early church. Anselm, Aquinas, and à Kempis help us understand the crucial and often-overlooked medieval period. Dietrich Bonhoeffer offers an inspiring account of courage in the face of Nazi Germany in the twentieth century.

Before these figures and their writings are explored, a chapter briefly surveying church history provides the backdrop for these individuals and their contributions to the Christian tradition. In the next twelve chapters, we'll look at the lives of these significant figures and discuss their major works. A conclusion offers guidance for further exploration. These lives and texts from church history are just a sampling of the many rivers that have been flowing over the past two millennia that continue to shape our identity. And like the narrator in Hughes's poem, as we make meaningful connections to our past, we just might find our souls growing deeper.

1

A Quick Look at the Big Picture: A Brief Survey of the Last 2,000 Years

History, said Ralph Waldo Emerson, is biography. So it is with church history. It is simply the collective stories of people, some gifted and privileged, some common, and still others from the margins. This story of the church resembles in many ways the story of biblical history, a story of kings and shepherds, complete with triumphs and foibles. Each is a collection of intensely human stories. Unlike the legends from ancient Greece and Rome, or Egypt, or Persia, these people are not heroes possessing superhuman qualities. If anything, their faults shine through too clearly. So it is with the stories of the dozen lives that follow. In order to make sense of the individual stories in the next chapters, we'll first take a step back and look at the grand story of church history, a look at the forest before a look at the trees.

This grand sweep of church history conveniently breaks down into four major groupings. We begin with the story of the first generation of the church after the apostles and the completion of the New Testament. This period, the ancient church, stretches on to the fall of Rome and the onset of the Middle Ages. The medieval church, though often slighted by Protestants, covers a great deal of time, one thousand years roughly from the end of the fifth century until the sixteenth. Next follows the Reformation, corresponding with the Renaissance and covering the sixteenth and seventeenth centuries. Finally, there is the ambiguous Modern Age, spanning from the later years of the seventeenth century until the twentieth century. Many speak of our own generation's move from a modern to a postmodern era. Perhaps that is so—a little historical distance from our own age will more than likely offer the final word on the subject. Our story, as far as the lives in this book are concerned, ends rather abruptly in the middle of the last century. Clearly, as we look at the current landscape, major cultural shifts have recently and rapidly occurred, leaving the church with significant and complex challenges. Looking back over the previous centuries might not offer all of the answers, but it can offer much-needed perspective. We begin our grand tour with the ancient church.

The Ancient Church

The story of the early church is a story of growth under pressure. It was the church's incubation and early years, a time of growth spurts, awkward and painful, as the church grew in numbers and in its understanding of the gospel and its task in the world. Yet the growth came at a tremendous cost. Getting a sense of the culture and world in which Christianity developed leads to a deeper understanding of the particular pressures early Christians felt and the struggles they faced. The Greco-Roman world afforded unique opportunities and challenges both for good and for ill. The Roman Empire brought about benefits of travel both by the advanced road system and through navigation on the Mediterranean Sea, ease of communication through Greek as the universal language, and stability and peace to a region of divergent nations embroiled in war during previous eras. All of these advantages had the cumulative effect of easing the spread of the gospel and facilitating the travels of the apostles and other early Christians. Yet there is a double edge to this sword: the Roman world also brought with it a great deal of hostility to the early Christians. The first pressure the church faced came from without as the Roman world, hostile to the church, initiated wave after wave of persecution.

Mistakenly, we have the impression that the early church faced constant and empire wide persecution under Roman rule. In reality, the persecutions were more sporadic, often at the whim of the local proconsul or Roman official. There were, however, those moments when the persecution reached intense proportions. The first of these occurred during the decades of the writing of the New Testament under the Emperor Nero. Legendary for his cruelty, Nero engaged in barbaric and grossly inhumane treatment of Christians. The incident that apparently set off his persecutions concerns the burning of Rome. Historians today largely attribute the great fires of Rome to Nero, as his attempts to remove areas of the city to make way for his redevelopment plan soon got out of control, causing massive devastation. Nero needed a scapegoat, so he turned to the Christians. His logic was simple: the Romans, through their toleration of the Christians, had angered the gods, who in turn brought about judgment of the city. Christians were arrested en masse, tried, and found guilty. The Roman historian

Tacitus records the result: "Mockery of every sort was added to their deaths. Covered with the skin of beasts, they were torn by dogs and perished, or were nailed to crosses, or were doomed to the flames and burnt, to serve as a nightly illumination, when daylight had expired."

FIG. 1.1

Creeds of the Ancient Church

These creeds engage heresies regarding the person of Christ. The first creed, stemming from the Council of Nicaea in 325 and affirmed at the Council of Constantinople in 381, emphatically declares that Christ is fully God and fully human. The second creed is from the Council of Chalcedon, which countered false teachings about the union of the divine and human natures in the person of Christ. This creed affirms the orthodox statement that Christ is two natures, fully divine and fully human, in one person. It was unanimously formalized—"all with one consent"—by over four hundred bishops, a near-miraculous feat given the complexities of the language and the stakes of the discussion.

The Nicene Creed, 325

We believe in one God, the Father Almighty, Maker of heaven and earth, of all things visible and invisible.

And in one Lord Jesus Christ, the only-begotten Son of God, begotten of his Father before all worlds, God of God, Light of Light, very God of very God, begotten, not made, being of one substance with the Father; by whom all things were made, who for us and for our salvation came down from heaven, and was incarnate by the Holy Spirit of the virgin Mary, and was made man; and was crucified also for us under Pontius Pilate; he suffered and was buried; and the third day he rose again according to the Scriptures, and ascended into heaven, and is seated at the right hand of the Father; and he shall come again, with glory, to judge both the living and the dead; whose kingdom shall have no end.

The persecutions occurred from then on throughout the next centuries until the time of Constantine and the curious event of the Battle of Mulvian Bridge in 311. Just prior to Constantine, one of the most intense persecutions occurred under the Emperor Diocletian. His edict in 303

And we believe in the Holy Spirit, the Lord and giver of life, who proceeds from the Father and the Son; who with the Father and the Son together is worshiped and glorified; who spoke by the prophets; and we believe in one holy catholic and apostolic church; we acknowledge one baptism for the remission of sins; and we look for the resurrection of the dead, and the life of the world to come. Amen.

The Chalcedonian Creed, 451

We, then, following the holy Fathers, all with one consent, teach men to confess one and the same Son, our Lord Jesus Christ, the same perfect in Godhead and also perfect in manhood; truly God and truly man, of a rational soul and body; consubstantial with the Father according to the Godhead, and consubstantial with us according to the manhood; in all things like unto us, without sin; begotten before all ages of the Father according to the Godhead, and in these latter days, for us and for our salvation, born of the virgin Mary, the mother of God, according to the manhood; one and the same Christ, Son, Lord, Only-begotten, to be acknowledged in two natures, inconfusedly, unchangeably, indivisibly, inseparably; the distinction of the two natures being by no means taken away by the union, but rather the property of each nature being preserved, and concurring in one Person and one Subsistence, not prated or divided in two persons, but one and the same Son, and only begotten, God the Word, the Lord Jesus Christ; as the prophets from the beginning have declared concerning him, and the Lord Jesus Christ himself has taught us, and the Creed of the holy Fathers has handed down to us.

effectively declared open season on Christians. The church historian Eusebius, who lived before and after Constantine, records that the prisons were so full of Christians during Diocletian's persecution that there was no room for common criminals, launching a crime spree.

The early church responded to this external pressure in two ways. First, there were the martyrs. A seemingly passive response at best, martyrdom proved effective nevertheless in responding to Rome's attempts to stamp out Christianity. As Tertullian explains, "The blood of the martyrs is the seed of the church." Intended by Rome to extinguish Christianity, the persecutions and the resultant testimonies of the martyrs won the Christians a sympathy vote from the populace and also led to converts to Christ. One such testimony is that of Justin Martyr. A philosopher from Samaria, Justin enjoyed the thought and writings of Plato. One day he witnessed a martyrdom and the thought occurred to him that, while he liked Plato, he certainly would not be willing to die for him. This caused him to take a close look at Christianity and biblical teaching. He became not only a convert, but also one of the early church's prime spokespersons as an apologist. He, too, was martyred for his faith in 165.

The church also responded more actively through the activities of the apologists. The Greek word *apologia* means nothing like its apparent English counterpart, *apology*. Instead, the term means to speak to or to get oneself free from a charge. It is a legal term, understood best in a legal setting. When one is accused of a crime, he or she has the opportunity to give an answer, to speak to the charges. This is how many English translations of the Bible treat the Greek word, as in 1 Peter 3:15. So the early apologists, such as Justin Martyr and Athenagoras, among others, devoted much energy to answering the false, even ludicrous, claims levied at the early Christians. As seen in the martyrdom of

Polycarp, ironically the early Christians were accused of atheism because they denied the gods of the state. They were also accused of cannibalism, a clear misunderstanding of the practice of communion as the early Christians gathered to eat the body and drink the blood of Christ. Equally preposterous, they were accused of incestuous practices and even orgies because of their loving their brothers and sisters and the practice of the love feast.

From our perspective these charges all seem rather far-fetched, to say the least. Given certain elements of Roman culture during the first few centuries A.D. and given the rather bizarre practices of some of the so-called mystery religions of the time, however, these charges stuck. It was the task of the apologists to answer them. In the end, they had to show that Christianity was not subversive to the empire, that Christians were not bad citizens, and that quite the opposite was in fact the case. They were not, however, all that successful in their apologetic attempts. For example, Athenagoras wrote his apologetic books for the emperor, but there is no evidence that he ever saw them.

Once Constantine came into power, however, the empire changed almost overnight from a culture that was hostile to Christianity to one that was friendly if not favorable toward it. Constantine, in a response of gratitude for the overwhelming victory at Mulvian Bridge, issued a series of edicts in the years 312 to 314 that overturned earlier edicts that led to persecution. The stage was set for the Christianizing of the empire and the onset of the Holy Roman Empire. Now the church faced a whole new set of challenges. Paraphrasing Paul, the church had learned to live during times of want. The new challenge would be to live during times of plenty.

One of the benefits of this newfound relationship with the empire was that the church, no longer running for its life, could devote time and energy to establishing some significant doctrines, doctrines that we tend to take for granted, unaware of their historical origins. Much of this doctrinal development derived from yet another pressure the church faced: pressure from within by heresies. Even before we get out of the pages of the New Testament, John, among others, warns us that those will come who will deny cardinal doctrines such as the humanity and the deity of Christ. And they did come. Consequently, much of the theologizing of the early church centered on the doctrine of the Trinity, and specifically on the doctrines of the person and work of Christ. As a result of these struggles, one of the most treasured legacies of the early church has come down to us: the Nicene and Chalcedonian Creeds.

As the fifth century began, the old empire began to break apart and a new era was soon setting in. Precisely at this time, one of the most celebrated figures of church history lived his eventful life, Augustine, the Bishop of Hippo. He serves well as a conclusion to the early church because during his lifetime he witnessed the fall of the Roman Empire. He also stands at the fount of the debates over the biblical teaching on humanity, sin, and salvation. These debates carried on through the centuries of the Middle Ages and took center stage at their conclusion during the Reformation. Augustine's shadow looms large as a hero in both Protestant and Catholic traditions, and an in-depth look at his life and thought well repays the effort.

With Augustine's passing, the era of the early church came to an end. During this time the church had faced intense challenges, from both within and without. It was a time of difficulty, trial, and dark days. Yet it was also a time of victory and triumph, and a time that witnessed God's faithfulness in building the church's foundation. The ancient church had learned to live out a Christian worldview in a cultural environment that was first hostile, before

Constantine, and then favorable. Both times had occa-sioned a different set of challenges and opportunities. The church was learning firsthand the complexities of Christ's prayer in John 17, of living as Christians in the world, but not of it. This challenge would not be uniquely theirs; it would also be that of the church throughout the ages down to the present day. The church during the Middle Ages would not escape the challenge, either.

The Medieval Church

One's view of the Middle Ages largely depends on reli-gious affiliation. For Roman Catholics, the medieval church means one thing; for Protestants, it means quite another. The typical Protestant view understands the Middle Ages largely as a decline, the retreat of the Bible as the church's authority and the eclipse of the gospel. These one thousand years serve largely to set the stage for the Reformation of the sixteenth century and the recovery both of God's Word and the glorious gospel at its center. To be sure, this era is marked by the unfortunate demise of the faithfulness of the church to the truth of Scripture. The church's response to Martin Luther and his attempts at reform would reveal how far afield the church had moved. When he sought to restore the gospel, he was painted as the very enemy of Christ. Yet the medieval age is not entirely a story of decline. There are many bright spots. And while much of the legacy of the church today derives from the era of the Reformation (which, among other things, marked the reversal of certain medieval developments), there is much that comes from this era that shapes us and much that we can still benefit from.

The most far-reaching development of the Middle Ages concerns what historians refer to as the *medieval synthesis*, or what commonly goes by the name "Christendom." In the words of church historian Mark Noll, the medieval synthesis is the bringing together of all of life under the sphere of the church. To illustrate this, it is conservatively estimated that the Roman Catholic Church owned at least one quarter of the land of Europe and England. With this ownership of land came great wealth and power. The use of the interdict, a powerful tool in the hands of the church, furthered this power. The pope could issue an interdict for a certain region or country, which would invalidate any of the sacraments practiced in that region, effectually stripping the people of any hope of grace. Without the validity of the sacraments, no baptisms could be performed and no last rites could be offered. The lifeline to grace in the Middle Ages, the Mass, would also be severed. The pope typically used this power as a bargaining chip in negotiations with civil rulers. The cry from the populace would be so great that the ruler would more than likely give in to the pope's demands.

But the connection of church and state is only part of the medieval synthesis. Another major element concerns the bringing together of the fields of philosophy and theology. Students of medieval philosophy will find themselves studying the same people as students of medieval theology. That is simply not the case for any other time. Anselm and Thomas Aquinas illustrate this bridge perfectly as they made significant contributions to both fields. One key issue of this synthesis of philosophy and theology is the relationship of faith to reason, a subject that gets right to the heart of different approaches to apologetics.

The medieval synthesis further encompasses the church's role in daily life. The sacraments loomed over one's entire life, from the cradle (by baptism) to the grave (by last rites). And in between, there was the Mass. The church, to which the sacraments solely belonged, played the role of the indispensable mediator of grace. While ultimately grace came through the work of Christ on the cross, that grace was not immediately imparted to the sinner. Instead, it was mediated through the church and the sacraments. We will suspend this discussion until the time of the Reformation and the retrieval of faith in Christ alone as the means of grace.

The outstanding feature of the medieval synthesis is the absolute prominence of the church in all of life. The church extended itself into all of life through the two institutions of the papacy and of monasticism. The papacy represented the hierarchy of the church and included the papal see in Rome, as well as the system of cardinals, bishops, and priests that extended throughout Europe and beyond. One of the curious developments of the medieval church is how the Bishop of Rome, from the era of the early church, had risen over the other bishops to become the pope. Much of the development is owing to the strong leadership of Gregory I, or Gregory the Great, who, among other things, is the namesake of the Gregorian chant. Quite capable as a leader, Gregory was able to appeal to various events and ideas of the past five centuries that seemed to imply the prominence of Rome and its bishop. Consequently, he emerges as the first pope, although he argued that he merely stood in the line of apostolic succession extending back to Peter, the first bishop or pope of Rome.

The other institution, monasticism, also has a rich history. Key developments include the early monastic life of Antony, admired by both Athanasius and Augustine, and the work of Benedict, the namesake of the Benedictine order. The monastic movement provides another perspective on the church's challenge to live in the world. On the one hand, monasticism can be characterized as promoting withdrawal from the world, perhaps an unhealthy move. On the other hand, monastic communities were quite engaged in life outside the convent and monastery walls. They served as educational institutions and hospitals, provided safe havens for pilgrims and travelers, pioneered agricultural practices like terrace farming and crop rotation to increase productivity, and could be counted on to care for the sick and the dying, the hungry and the displaced. Of course, corruption seeped in from time to time, springing up reform movements and the establishment of new monastic orders and communities. One need only think of the exploits of the characters of Chaucer's *Canterbury Tales*, fictional accounts of all-too-nonfictional occurrences. Nevertheless, in many ways, the monastery or convent was truly a lifeline for those living in the Middle Ages.

From monasticism also came the divergent traditions of scholasticism (represented in such figures as Anselm and Aquinas) and mysticism (represented in the work of Thomas à Kempis). Just as the papacy and monasticism represent the two institutions of the Middle Ages, so mysticism and scholasticism represent the two approaches to living the Christian life or two methodologies of the Middle Ages. Though the nuances are complex, one can see the difference by an illustration of how one comes to know God. The scholastic would respond by hitting the books, looking to past experts and teachers on the subject. No stone would be left unturned as painstaking and meticulous research would search out source after source on the subject, concluding in the careful and systematic arrangement of the material.

The mystic would not be so troubled. Instead, he or she would simply wander off, preferably to a quiet and serene location. Eventually the mystic would get the answer in the form of an experience. But in the spirit of the ineffability of religious experience, the mystic would not be able to communicate it, only approximate it through, in most cases, meditative or visionary literature. In other words, for the mystic, in order to know God, one must experience him, and that experience must be personal.

The thousand years of the Middle Ages do in many ways represent a decline in the doctrine and practice of the church. Nevertheless, there are many shining moments and there are those figures who have left us a treasured legacy. Additionally, the events and movements of the Middle Ages, while complex, are far too important to be ignored because they are quite crucial to understanding trends in our own day. Grasping the flow of the Middle Ages also proves crucial to understanding the Reformation. Not all members of the medieval church accepted the status quo. Long before the Reformers, many offered criticism of the church's practice—and some did so at great personal cost. These "pre-Reformation Reformers" include such figures as Peter Waldo, Jan Hus, and John Wycliffe, the "Morning Star of the Reformation." Even Thomas à Kempis aimed at reforming the church by his focus on piety. But these pre-Reformation reform movements stopped short of stemming the tide of the decline.

The Reformation

In order to understand the Reformation, we need to overcome two typically held but not entirely accurate perceptions. The first is that the Reformation occurred overnight and came out of nowhere. The second is that all of the Reformers were on the same page. Both of these perceptions contain truth, but they also miss some nuances that, when in place, reveal the full picture of the era of the Reformation.

In response to the first perception, it is true that, especially in the case of Luther, the Reformation was a cataclysmic event. In fact, the Reformation occurred during a time of great upheaval and change in the world. The printing press, invented by Gutenberg in 1450, led to a virtual revolution of learning that made books and ideas available to the masses that far exceeded the painstakingly long process of the scribes and bookmaking in the Middle Ages. Indeed, Luther's ideas spread quickly, facilitated by the easy and broad circulation of his writings coming off the new presses. The pioneering work of Copernicus and Galileo also brought about a revolution in the field of science that sparked further explosion of learning in many fields. Explorers such as Christopher Columbus were opening a rather insular Europe to the far reaches of new worlds. And the great Holy Roman Empire was beginning to break apart and the modern nation state was rising in its place. The saying "May you live in interesting times" (wrongly characterized as a Chinese proverb) was certainly true for those witnessing the sixteenth century.

At the heart of the sea change that caused such interesting times was the young Augustinian monk Martin Luther. Like a thunderbolt, Luther's criticisms of the Roman Catholic Church as it had evolved over the Middle Ages struck a decisive and timely blow. Yet even for Luther, while the first wave of his reforming work took merely three years—from the posting of the Ninety-Five Theses to the Diet of Worms—the work of establishing the fledgling church required the remainder of his life. Luther would also be the first to admit that his work greatly built upon the preceding efforts at reform from the likes of John Wycliffe and Jan Hus. Additionally, the Conciliar Movement, a movement intending to return the church's power to councils as opposed to its central location in the pope, while not all that successful, nevertheless managed to significantly weaken the pope's power base in northern Europe and the German Rhinelands. Luther's protector, Frederick the Wise, refused to grant the pope's request to send the outlaw monk to Rome, which most certainly would have resulted in Luther's death. Frederick's refusal would perhaps not have been possible had it not been for the Conciliar Movement. Again, the Reformation was not overnight, and it was not without precedent.

The Reformation in England further exemplifies the long process of reform. Beginning under Henry VIII in 1534, many more decades verging on centuries passed, with ups and downs as the balance tipped between Protestant and Catholic monarchs, before the Reformation came into full flower. Even under the Protestant monarch Elizabeth I, there were many who felt that the present state of affairs was not contributing to a pure church. So it was during her reign that the Puritans emerged. The seventeenth century in England witnessed further ups and downs, much related to the intrigues of the monarchs. Consequently, the British Reformation has a long and variegated history spanning two centuries. From this era comes one of the best-loved classics of all time, John Bunyan's *The Pilgrim's Progress*.

The second misconception of the Reformation is that all of the Reformers were on the same page. While there was much agreement among the Reformers, especially concerning the essentials of Christianity and the gospel, disagreements abounded. It often occurs that, when various parties respond to a common enemy, they soon find out that the only thing they have in common is what they are against. They quickly realize that they have very different pictures of what the new program should look like. So it is with the Reformation. Various wings of the Reformation soon emerge from the common cause. First, there is Luther and the Reformation in Germany, bringing about the Lutheran Church. Next follows Ulrich Zwingli at Zurich and John Calvin at Geneva, constituting the Swiss Reformation and bringing about the Reformed churches. In the geographical regions of Germany and the Swiss Confederacy, not all lined up with either movement. These various parties form the Radical wing of the Reformation, so named not because of their extreme ways, but rather from the Latin word *radix*, meaning "root." The Radical Reformers, also referred to as the Anabaptists, viewed the other Reformers as not getting to the root of the problem with the Roman Church—namely, the confusion of church and state. The Anabaptists called for the complete separation of these two institutions.

Moving off the continent, the British Reformation also takes on unique characteristics. In fact, the British Reformation may be best seen as a rather large umbrella sheltering various camps under it. First there is Anglicanism, started under Henry VIII and shaped by Thomas Cranmer, the first Archbishop of Canterbury. Next follows the Puritans, who advocated a congregational form of church government and, in response to both Anglicanism and Catholicism, held to the autonomy of the local church. They were for a *pure* church. In their day, they were referred to as dissenters or nonconformists. This group encompassed such theologians as John Owen and William Perkins, and included those who, at first, migrated to the Netherlands before crossing the Atlantic and arriving in New England. The term *Puritans* functions well as an umbrella term, entailing the Congregationalists, Baptists, and, especially in Scotland under the leadership of John Knox, the Presbyterians.

These various groups held much in common. In fact, the first Baptist statement of faith, the *London Baptist Confession of Faith*, 1677, follows the *Westminster Confession of Faith* rather closely, differing only on the issue of believer's versus paedo (or infant) baptism. Shortly after the Puritans made it to New England, they met and issued the *Cambridge Platform*, 1649. This document affirmed the Westminster Standards, only differing on the issue of church government.

Finally, the Reformation's widespread impact even included the Roman Catholic Church itself, as evidenced in the Counter-Reformation. Under the leadership of Ignatius of Loyola, the founder of a new order, the Society of Jesus or the Jesuits, this movement resulted in the Inquisition, an attempt to purge the church. It also led to the Council of Trent in the 1560s. Trent became a significant council in Roman Catholicism's history in which the reforms of Luther—namely, justification by faith alone (*sola fide*) and Scripture alone (*sola Scriptura*)—were solidly denounced and pronounced anathema.

The makeup of the contemporary church finds its origin in these various wings of the Reformation. This rings true both of the church's practice, as we see in different denominations, and of the church's doctrine. The so-called *solas* of the Reformation clearly mark out the doctrinal boundaries of evangelicalism. Yet over many theological issues substantial differences remain.

All of us who call ourselves Protestant owe a great debt to Martin Luther. Yet, only a fraction of the readers of this book are most likely Lutheran. In fact, the readers of this book, like evangelicalism more broadly, more than likely represent a variety of denominations. And there we can see the legacy of the Reformation. Luther spawned more than a singular alternative to the Roman Catholic Church. Yet, while there are alternatives, to be sure, at the heart of these various Protestant groups who remain faithful to the gospel there is a common core: a theological center that consists of the authority of Scripture alone and insists that salvation comes by faith alone through God's grace alone—and that this salvation comes through the work of Christ alone. This is the lasting legacy of the Reformation—not the discovery of the truths, but their recovery and their return to the heart and center of the church.

The Modern Age

"Bliss it was in those days to be alive," a line from the poet Percy Bysshe Shelley, captures well the sentiment of the Modern Age. Marked by progress and revolution, the Modern Age closely wed itself to the Enlightenment, *Aufklärung* in German. Yet the Modern Age is deeply laced with irony. As an era, more is known about the world and humanity than ever before, all the while the true knowledge of both is perhaps more obscure than ever. The Modern Age has produced advances in medicine that have eliminated plagues and diseases that threatened whole swaths of people in the past, all the while creating weapons of mass destruction capable of destroying the world multiple times over. Charles Dickens expressed this irony best in his portrayal of the French Revolution with the famous first lines from *A Tale of Two Cities*, "It was the best of times, it was the worst of times." That, however, stops Dickens in midsentence. Finishing the quote is instructive:

> It was the age of wisdom, it was the age of foolishness, it was the epoch of belief, it was the epoch of incredulity, it was the season of Light, it was the season of Darkness, it was the spring of hope, it was the winter of despair, we had everything before us, we had nothing before us, we were all going direct to Heaven, we were all going direct the other way.

These ironies, as Dickens points out, directly touch religion and the church. In each era, the church finds itself in some way or another impacted by the culture and age. The worldview of any given culture surrounds it like the atmosphere. Consequently, we tend to be children of our age almost reflexively or unconsciously. So it is with the church in the Modern Age. The culmination of modernity's impact, with its belief in science and the inevitable progress if not ultimate perfectibility of humanity, may be seen in the religious responses of deism, primarily flowering in England, and old-fashioned liberalism, primarily originating in Germany. Deism, marked by a generic belief in God that views him as starting things but then removing himself from the picture and letting nature take its course, soon became the quintessential gentleman's religion. It enabled one to be with the times and current, while maintaining a semblance of Christianity and upholding the value of religion for the good of society. In the end, however, deism domesticated God and succeeded in minimizing the Bible's authority, subordinating it to the laws of science and human rationality. In fact, looking at the history of ideas, deism is not all that far from rationalism, the belief in the superiority and ultimate authority of human rationality.

Moving across the English Channel to the continent, one finds the rise and prominence of liberalism. In order to understand liberalism, one needs to see the context of the erosion of biblical authority. This occurred on two fronts: the challenge of authorship of the books of the Old Testament and the separation of the so-called historical Jesus from the Jesus of the gospel accounts. In other words, liberalism directly attacked the authenticity of the biblical texts; showing them to be human in their origin, not divine as the previous, less-enlightened generations had supposed them to be. In response to this, German theologian Friedrich Schleiermacher wrote his crucial text *On Religion: Speeches to Its Cultured Despisers* (1799). The cultured despisers were those of his own generation who were simply too intellectually sophisticated for the mere child's play of religion. So Schleiermacher advanced an apologetic for religion. Though his argument is much more complex, in short, he replies that religion is valuable not because of its truth, but rather because it enriches one's life. He exchanged the criterion of truthfulness for that of experience. He was trying to help, but his cure, proverbially, was worse than the disease. From the pages of Schleiermacher's book emerges liberalism, which subordinates religion to experience and sentiment.

The two movements of deism and liberalism manifest themselves rather diversely and prominently in religion in the past few centuries and even currently, revealing that while the Modern Age has made incredible advances in many fields, Dickens was right: it is an age of foolishness, of darkness, of incredulity, and it is a winter of despair. Yet not all is bleak, as the Modern Age has also produced many celebrated figures in the church who, in various ways, opposed the currents of the age. Most well known for his famous sermon "Sinners in the Hands of an Angry God," Jonathan Edwards was the premier figure in the Great Awakening in the colonies and has been hailed by many as America's greatest theologian and philosopher. His legacy runs deep as he left an indelible mark both on his own age and on future generations down to the present day. Born the same year as Edwards, John Wesley also left his mark on the eighteenth century and continues to make an impression. He and his brother Charles were prodigious, to say the least, racking up miles on horseback, preaching, writing hymns, and organizing churches—all at staggering statistics.

The Modern Age is also marked by a continuing sense of globalization. For some, an expanded world is seen in terms of economic opportunities; for others, it shouts the world's need for the gospel. And so emerges one of the church's shining moments in the Modern Age: the age of world mission endeavors. At the forefront of this movement are the missionary pioneers David Livingstone, C. T. Studd, Amy Carmichael, and noted founder of modern missions William Carey.

Finally, the Modern Age, especially in the twentieth century, offers occasion after occasion to live as a disciple in a culture running counter to the biblical worldview. As with the ancient church, this consists of both times of want and times of plenty. For some in the Modern Age, the challenge has been to live in a culture that is favorable to Christianity; for others, the challenge has been to live in an environment that is hostile. It has been said that there have been more martyrs in the twentieth century than in all previous centuries combined. One such martyr, a Lutheran minister, theologian, and author of the classic text *The Cost of Discipleship*, Dietrich Bonhoeffer, offers a moving example of courage in the face of the Nazi regime. Perhaps we have come full circle, as we started with Polycarp and his courageous stand for Christ in his day. Polycarp and Bonhoeffer, as well as the many generations stretching in between, remind us that in the end we are all pilgrims, called to travel through this world as faithful witness-bearers to the gospel and called to our true home, Zion, the city of our God and King. This task is now undertaken by the twenty-first-century church.

This survey of church history only scratches the surface of our rich and enduring legacy. In the chapters to follow, we go beneath the surface to take an in-depth look at the lives and classic texts of a dozen or so significant figures who have made a significant impact on the Christian tradition.

A Note on the Sources

Mark Noll offers an enjoyable and informative summary of church history in *Turning Points: Decisive Moments in the Shaping of Christian History* (1997). Indispensable reference works include Walter Elwell, ed., *The Evangelical Dictionary of Theology* (1984); J. D. Douglas, ed., *The New International Dictionary of the Christian Church* (1974); and F. L. Cross, ed., *The Oxford Dictionary of the Christian Church* (1997). A singular source for primary readings may be found in John Leith, *Creeds of the Churches* (1982), and online at www.ccel.org, the home page of the Christian Classic and Ethereal Library.

PART ONE

THE ANCIENT CHURCH

2

POLYCARP
THE MARTYRDOM OF POLYCARP

"The blood of the martyrs is the seed of the church."
Tertullian

"O, blessed and valiant martyrs . . ."
The Martyrdom of Perpetua and Felicitas

Eighty-six years I have been his servant," declared Polycarp, "and he has done me no wrong. How can I blaspheme my King who saved me?" These bold words, proclaimed by the octogenarian Bishop of Smyrna, came in response to the Roman proconsul. Polycarp was offered a choice. If he merely recanted his Christian profession, he would go free. If not, he would be set before the gladiators and the beasts. Without hesitation, he declared his allegiance to Christ, the least he could do in light of what Christ had suffered for him. And for his allegiance he was martyred. Or, as his contemporaries preferred it, he attained his day of victory, demonstrating that he was a faithful disciple, following his Master even to the point of death.

Polycarp's martyrdom reminds us that the church began in a hostile environment. We sometimes have the impression that the persecutions in the first centuries of the
church's life were always empire wide and always at full
tilt. That's not necessarily the case. At times it was true as
certain emperors made it their chief ambition to persecute Christians in futile attempts to stamp out Christianity. More often than not, however, the persecutions were
sporadic, driven by the whims of particular local and regional leaders, and tended to target the church's leaders
or a select few in order to prove a point. But persecution
comes in a variety of forms. And it is right to view the
early Christians as taking a great risk for their faith. Their
profession of faith was a bold move, and for most of them
it came at a cost. For some, that cost was their very lives.
Estimates of the numbers of martyrs in the early church
vary from the hundreds to the many thousands. But far
from squelching this new movement within the empire,
the persecutions led to a fortified and secure church. By
the time the persecutions came to an end in the early
decades of the fourth century, the church had grown
strong in numbers, deep in its resolve, wide in its influence. Tertullian, a church father from around the turn of
the third century, got it right—the blood of the martyrs
had become the seed of the church.

Among the early martyrs, perhaps none was better
known than Polycarp. He was the Bishop of Smyrna, a
city just north of Ephesus in which a church was established during the days of the apostles (Rev. 1:11). Curiously, the letter to the church at Smyrna, recorded in
Revelation 2:8–11, mentions the suffering of the members of the church there and exhorts them: "Be faithful,
even to the point of death" (2:10). It is believed that Polycarp was personally discipled by John while a young man

at Ephesus. Consequently, Polycarp became one of the most prominent figures in the early church and one with a decisive link to the apostles and the New Testament era. Not only influential in life, Polycarp was perhaps (and mostly) influential in death. The story of his martyrdom, popularly called *The Martyrdom of Polycarp* and also known as *The Epistle of the Church at Smyrna*, was widely circulated and known throughout the early centuries, bolstering other Christian communities that faced persecution. For the church throughout the centuries, *The Martyrdom of Polycarp* offers a window into the challenges faced by the early church. Though not as widely read today, this classic text continues to remind contemporary Christians that being a Christian can sometimes mean taking a costly stand, and that sometimes those whose commitment and allegiance goes first to Christ may find themselves at odds with the world and culture in which they live.

Around the middle of the sixteenth century, Christians in Britain faced intense persecution when Mary, a devout Roman Catholic, ascended to the throne after the Protestant monarchs Henry VIII and Edward VI. Mary put Christians in the Tower of London, beheaded them, and forced others into exile. When her bloody reign came to an end, one person in particular determined that the testimonies of those who had suffered during her reign, as well as those who had suffered persecution through the centuries, would not be forgotten. John Foxe wrote his classic text, his *Book of Martyrs*, so that the church would remember. Such a memory is important, even crucial. *The Martyrdom of Polycarp* was written so that we would not forget, but that we would remember. In the pages that follow, we will bring this memory to life as we explore Polycarp's work, writings, and martyrdom.

2.1 Map of Roman Empire. Smyrna is located on the east coast of Asia Minor.

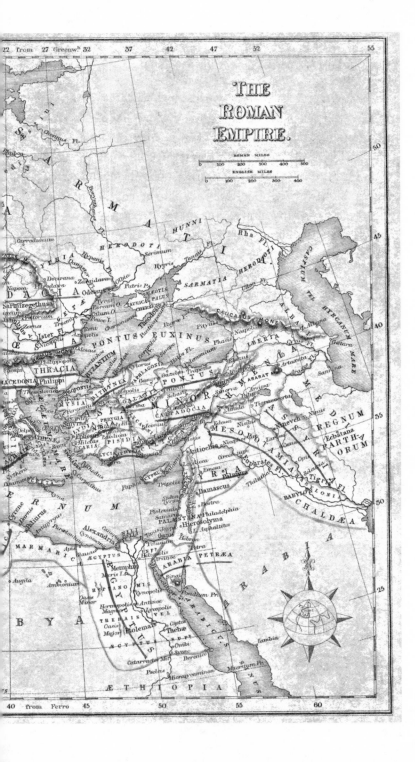

THE
ROMAN
EMPIRE.

ROMAN MILES
0   100   200   300   400   500

ENGLISH MILES
0   100   200   300   400

Polycarp's Life and Times

In some ways, Polycarp's world was a very different one from ours. Besides the obvious differences of language, customs, and geography, this was a world with a different set of philosophies and schools of thought, of economies and governments, and of religions and myths. Great debates raged over the merits of the philosophy of Plato versus that of Aristotle. Slaves made this empire run, and mystery cults were the religion in vogue. Due to the nature of the Roman Empire, a conglomerate of formerly independent city- and nation-states, a certain pluralism prevailed. To be a Roman was the glue that held everything together, but underlying this was a great pantheon of gods and religions and worldviews.

To accommodate these differences, the empire dubbed certain religions as acceptable—*licitas religio*, "legal religion." These religions tended to be pluralistic or at least polytheistic, so to simply bring them into the already expanded fold of gods mattered little. Some of them observed secretive rites and rather bizarre practices. They were accepted, however, because these religions did not preclude their members from participating in the civil cult, or offering sacrifices to the gods of Rome.

FIG. 2.2

Timeline of Polycarp and other Early Church Fathers

Ignatius	?–c. 107
Polycarp	c. 70–155
Justin Martyr	c. 100–165
Athenagoras	?–190
Irenaeus	c. 130–202
Tertullian	c. 155–220

But not all religions fit so well. Judaism, for instance, claimed as its distinguishing feature that there is one true God. For some reason, the Roman Empire allowed an exception in this case. Christianity, however, did not fare so well. Not only did Christianity affirm that there is one God, it also made the point that there is only one way to God. For Christians, other religions do not simply provide alternatives; they are false. All of this resulted in Christianity's being designated an illegal religion. In fact, reflective of Rome's disdain, Christianity was dubbed an *illicita superstitio*, "illegal superstition."

We gain some insight into this tension by a letter exchange between the Emperor Trajan (98–117) and Pliny the Younger (Plinius Secondus), a governor in Asia Minor and a historian of ancient Rome. The Christians in the region were plentiful and had abandoned the pagan cults and temples, making for economic difficulties, curiously similar to the fallout of Paul and the church at Ephesus just a century earlier (Acts 19:21–41). Pliny knew the Christians were to be executed, but he was puzzled as to the exact nature of the crime. He failed to see how they were enemies of the state. Trajan assured Pliny that they were in fact enemies of the state and were to be executed, though he did not seem to indicate that doing so should be Pliny's top priority. The main reason for their treatment, Trajan affirmed and Pliny consented, was that they failed to offer a sacrifice to the images of the gods or to the images of the emperor.

Consequently, and quite ironically, the early Christians were accused of atheism; they did not recognize the gods of the Roman state, and they certainly could not offer sacrifices to them. This gave Nero, emperor during the martyrdoms of Peter and Paul—as church tradition has it—his reason to persecute them, as well as Diocletian, Trajan, Hadrian, and the long line of emperors to follow. Nero and the others bootstrapped the accusation that the Christians denied the gods of the state (which was true) to the charge that the Christians were the enemy of the state (which was not true). In reality, Christians made great citizens, as the exchange between Trajan and Pliny concedes. Christ and the New Testament teach that Christians are to honor the government and its officials. Christianity practiced compassion for the less fortunate and practiced a high ethic concerning social relationships in the marketplace and in the home. Christians were law-abiding and peaceful. Yet they were hated and viewed as the very enemy of the state. As mentioned in chapter 1, perhaps the real reason for the persecution is that the Christians were a convenient scapegoat. Tertullian reveals this ulterior motive: "They consider that the Christians are the cause of every public calamity and every misfortune of the people. If the Tiber rises as high as the city walls, if the Nile does not rise to the fields, if the weather will not change, if there is an earthquake, a famine, a plague—straightway the cry is heard: 'Toss the Christians to the lions!'"

These persecutions tended to be sporadic and regional. This is the case in the persecution facing Polycarp at Smyrna. Perhaps due to his prominence, Polycarp was arrested and brought to the stadium for his trial and eventual martyrdom. Asia Minor, owing to the lasting effects of Paul's missionary work there, was home to a rather large Christian population. The very public martyrdom of Polycarp, not to mention the cruelty of martyring such an aged person, was clearly intended to halt the growth. A few decades later, the Christians at Vienne and Lyons, cities in Roman Gaul and modern France, met with intense hatred and persecution. In 177, sanctioned by the philosopher-emperor Marcus Aurelius, officials rounded up the Christians and tortured them, intending for them to abandon their faith. While some were released, many held firm and eventually were mass-martyred. Their story is preserved for us. Blandina, Ponticus, Attalus, Maturas, Sanctus, and many others, all forgotten names, were martyred for the crime of professing, "I am a Christian." In addition, there is the account of the martyrdom of Perpetua and Felicitas, early heroines of Christianity. Perpetua was a nursing mother who withstood not only the challenges of the proconsul but also the manipulations of her father as he tried to get her to recant her faith for his sake and for the sake of her young child. And to these accounts, many unrecorded and unknown names could be added.

All of this would change in 312 at the Battle of Mulvian Bridge and the so-called conversion of Constantine to Christianity. Whether or not Constantine became a believer, he did change the way the empire treated Christians. Through a series of edicts, Christianity went from an illegal superstition to a legal religion, eventually emerging as the favored religion. Paul's autobiographical statement that he had learned how to be content both in times of want and in times of plenty (Phil. 4:11–12) became the test for the early church. Could it be content and faithful and true both in times of hostility and in times of privilege?

The church did take advantage of its newfound freedoms to develop doctrines that today we hold central to Christian orthodoxy. At the councils of Nicaea (325), Constantinople (381), and Chalcedon (451), the church hammered out the truths that Christ is fully man and fully God and that these two natures are conjoined in one person. And these councils were all funded by emperors—no small token as the Council of Chalcedon consisted of over five hundred bishops and numerous attendants. The early church further developed the doctrine of the Trinity, establishing the orthodox view not only of the deity of Christ, but also of the deity of the Holy Spirit, and the teaching that God is three persons in one substance or essence. The church, also during this era of political freedom, turned its attention to the recognition of the canon: the authoritative and definitive list of the books of the Bible.

In the end, it may be best to see both pros and cons at work during the two eras of the early church. During the times of persecution and the pre-Constantine era, the church was strengthened in its resolve, and a committed community of believers resulted. During the times of privilege and the Constantinian era, the church developed its theology, resulting in a crucial and well-defined doctrinal core and identity. This is not to suggest that the church prior to Constantine did not give attention to theological matters. It, too, had its share of theological developments. And in these, we can also see Polycarp's influence.

Little is known of Polycarp's actual life. His martyrdom recounts only the last days of his life, and only a few contemporary references to him survive. One of the most fascinating of these accounts comes from Irenaeus, who like Polycarp also came from Smyrna and the region of Asia Minor and eventually became Bishop of Lyons, rebuilding the church there after its intense persecution in the last decades of the second century. Well known for his writings against various heresies, he was first taught by Polycarp. In those writings, entitled *Against the Heresies*, Irenaeus records that Polycarp was a pupil of the apostle John while he was at the church in Ephesus before his exile to the island of Patmos. Irenaeus further notes, "Polycarp also was not only instructed by the apostles, and conversed with many who had seen Christ, but was also, by apostles in Asia, appointed Bishop of the church in Smyrna."

Irenaeus proceeds to recall Polycarp's stringent stands against heretics, a trait he learned directly from the example of John. One such encounter came between Polycarp and Marcion. Marcion instigated the teaching, among other things, that much of the Old Testament, as well as some of the books of the New Testament, is not indeed the Word of God. He was overly influenced by Plato—specifically by the Platonic doctrine that matter is bad. God would not be so concerned with such mundane and earthly matters as much of the record of the Old Testament and some books of the New Testament have it. Further, Marcion denied that Christ was truly human; God, he reasoned, would never stoop so low as to take on flesh. Marcion also thought quite highly of himself. Irenaeus records the famous encounter of the heretic Marcion with Polycarp: "Do you know who I am?" Marcion asked, assuming that since he was so famous, Polycarp would be awed to be in his presence. Irenaeus records Polycarp's response: "I do know you," inflating Marcion's ego before puncturing it with the quip, "[You are] the first-born of Satan." Elsewhere in his letter to Florinus, Irenaeus speaks of Polycarp as an eyewitness to the apostles, the eyewitnesses of Jesus.

In addition to the writings of Irenaeus, Polycarp also shows up in the writings of Eusebius (c. 265–340) and Jerome (347–420), for his teaching on the date of Easter. Polycarp traveled to Rome to discuss this with the Bishop of the church at Rome, Anicetus (martyred 168). Polycarp, representing the churches in Asia Minor, held that the church should celebrate Easter on the fourteenth day of the Jewish month of Nisan, called the *Quartodecimen* date, from the Latin word for "fourteen." Anicetus disagreed, arguing that the church should not observe a special Easter day but instead should observe the celebration of the Lord's resurrection every Sunday. They agreed to disagree and parted on good terms, taking communion together to signify their unity despite their differences.

This event, though dealing with a seemingly trivial matter, has significant implications. First, contrary to later Roman Catholic dogma, the fact that Polycarp still held and practiced his view after he left Anicetus shows that the Bishop of Rome did not exercise authority over other churches in the early centuries of the church. Secondly, the meeting reveals that while the early church was in agreement over many elements of polity, practice, and doctrine, areas of disagreement remained. Lastly, the event reveals the prominence of Polycarp as he spoke for the entire church of Asia Minor and the east when he went to Rome.

One final reference to Polycarp comes from Ignatius of Antioch, who died in 107. Ignatius was arrested for his faith and, like Paul, was taken to Rome for his trial. His journey took him from Antioch through Asia Minor before he made it to Rome. Along the way he met Polycarp, and the two apparently spent some time together. Ignatius refers to him as the Bishop of Smyrna, and the two exchanged letters. These fleeting references to Polycarp are all that survive as evidence of his life. In summary, we know that he was born in either the year 69 or 70 and that he died in 155. In between, he was likely mentored in the faith by John, served for well over fifty years as Bishop of Smyrna, and left a lasting legacy for the church in his death.

Polycarp's Thought and Writings

One significant piece of Polycarp's writing survives. Like Paul, Peter, and John in the New Testament, the bishops in the early church wrote letters to the churches to address questions and solve problems, offering encouragement and guidance in living the Christian life. Of course, unlike the epistles of the New Testament, these writings are not inspired or authoritative. They are, however, instructive. Such is the case with Polycarp's *Epistle to the Philippians*. The letter by Polycarp, written early in the 100s, seems to be occasioned by the Philippian church's request to have the letters of Ignatius. In putting the letters together, Polycarp affixes his own short letter in which he exhorts the church to a virtuous life, discusses the function of church offices, warns against heresy and apostasy—mentioning specifically the fall of Valens, an elder at Philippi—and ends with his prayer that they remain steadfast in the faith.

Much of the letter is not original. In fact, the majority of the letter consists of quotations from New Testament epistles. This is significant because at this point there is not a general consensus on the constitution of the New Testament. The churchwide agreement on the twenty-seven books would not come until much later, at the end of the fourth century. That Polycarp quotes from Paul's letters shows that the early church had and was familiar with a core of the New Testament almost from the very beginning. That he views the citations as authoritative indicates that the early church viewed these writings as the inspired Word of God. Further, by citing these books, Polycarp contributes to the argument that Paul was indeed the writer of these books, contrary to the contentions of later liberal scholarship that the books were not written by Paul.

Polycarp's letter also reveals the role of the bishop in the early church. Significant differences exist today regarding church government and polity. There are those who hold to a hierarchy of bishops, those who hold to a presbyterian form, those who argue for congregational rule, and so on. What we learn from Polycarp's letter, though this does not serve to settle the question based on the biblical teaching, is the practice that emerged early on in the church. Cities and towns tended to have house churches. Actual church buildings were not built until the second and third centuries, although, as we learn from Paul's missionary endeavors in Acts, some Christian communities sprang from Jewish communities where the synagogue then served as church. These various house churches were served by elders and deacons, each of those offices with distinct functions. Over these local officers were bishops, largely responsible for all the various house churches under their care. Hence, Polycarp is Bishop of Smyrna, Ignatius of Antioch, Anicetus of Rome, and so on.

A crucial stop along the way of this development includes Ignatius's teaching, from right around the year 100, that the church is to follow the teaching of the bishop. Polycarp fits in here as well. First, while he was Bishop of Smyrna, he also felt compelled to instruct and advise the church at Philippi. Again, he finds the authority of his teaching not in himself, but in what would become the New Testament. Nevertheless, he instructs them on what to do both generally and specifically, as in the case of treating the lapsed elder Valens. Polycarp also shows the structure of offices in the early church when he writes of bishops, elders, and deacons.

Finally, the letter from Polycarp reveals that the early church had a full-orbed view of living the Christian life. Polycarp calls on the church to be faithful in doctrine and to the apostolic teaching. He equally calls upon it to live ethically and to stand for social justice. Far from fostering insurgency against the anti-Christian Roman regime, Polycarp, like Paul and Peter before him, calls on the church to "Pray for the Emperors, and for the potentates, and princes, and for those who persecute you and hate you, and for the enemies of the cross that your fruit may be manifest among all men, that you may be perfected in him," quoting or referring to numerous biblical texts. He calls on Christians to be subject to one another (Eph.

5:21), and in quite a few places reminds the church of its obligation to widows and orphans, the marginalized members of society.

Though a short epistle, containing the equivalent of roughly forty verses, Polycarp's *Epistle to the Philippians* offers a great deal of insight into life in the early church and crystallizes for us the thought of Polycarp. He, however, has left a much more lasting legacy for the church in his death and in the letter that records it, *The Martyrdom of Polycarp*.

The Martyrdom of Polycarp

A large debate looms over the date and exact circumstances of *The Martyrdom of Polycarp*. Earlier scholarship fixed the date at around 167, following the lead of Eusebius, the fourth-century church historian. More recent scholarship, based mainly on reconciling the time and place references in the epistle with the historical record, dates it to 155. The text of the *Martyrdom* refers to the date by month and as occurring on the Sabbath. This further enables scholars to pinpoint the exact date, February 23, 155 (a few dissenting scholars argue for February 22, 156). The beginning of the letter, written by members of the Church of Smyrna, reveals the intention to encourage "the Church of God that sojourns in Philomelium, and to all the congregations of the holy and catholic church sojourning in every place." It was intended, in other words, for the whole church. The book consists of twenty-two short chapters of but a few short paragraphs each. The first four chapters speak of martyrdom in general. Chapters 5 to 7 chronicle Polycarp's capture, while chapters 6 through 15 detail his day in the stadium and his martyrdom. Chapters 16 to 18 record how the Christians at Smyrna attempted to recover

Polycarp's remains. The final four chapters return to a discussion of martyrdom in general, recount the exact date and time of Polycarp's martyrdom, and offer a concluding exhortation. Consequently, the epistle not only re-creates in vivid detail Polycarp's martyrdom, it also offers insight into the view of martyrdom in the early church, and we'll touch on both of these.

First, we find that when Polycarp received the news of his arrest warrant, he wanted to turn himself in but was counseled by the church to go into hiding. He went from farmhouse to farmhouse, eluding the contingent of Roman soldiers dispatched to arrest him. Finally, two slaves of the Christians were arrested, and under threat of torture one of them revealed Polycarp's location. After catching up with Polycarp "in an upstairs room in a small cottage," the soldiers responded in bewilderment as they "wondered why there was so much eagerness for the arrest of an old man like [Polycarp]" Polycarp responded by having a meal prepared for his captors, since it was late in the evening and they had spent the day tracking him down.

Chapter 8 records many overt allusions to Christ. Polycarp came into the city of Smyrna from the countryside riding on a donkey, under the watch of a captain of the guard named Herod. He was then brought before the proconsul, Philip the Asiarch, in the stadium and given a chance to recant. "Have respect for your age," he was told. All that Polycarp had to do was simply say, "Away with the atheists," meaning that he was to turn his back on his fellow Christians. Exploiting the irony and reflecting, perhaps, his sense of humor, Polycarp turned to the "crowd of lawless heathen who were in the stadium" and then, with a grand, sweeping gesture toward them, said, "Away with atheists!" Not amused, the proconsul gave him another chance to recant, which Polycarp followed with his testimony cited earlier: "Eighty-six years I have been his servant, and he has done me no wrong. How can I blaspheme my King who saved me?"

The proconsul persisted, showing his reluctance to persecute such an innocent person. To all of his attempts, Polycarp replied, "Listen carefully: I am a Christian. Now if you want to learn the doctrine of Christianity, name a day and give me a hearing". The proconsul was not about to offer Polycarp a debate, so he threatened him with the wild beasts, to which Polycarp replied, "Call for them." The crowd took over at this point, demanding the lions be set upon this teacher of the Christians, "the destroyer of our gods, who teaches many not to sacrifice or worship." Philip told them that he couldn't since he had already ended the animal hunts, so they demanded that Polycarp be put on the pyre.

Polycarp refused to be nailed to the stake, telling his executioners that God would enable him to endure. Polycarp then offered a prayer, one last testimony to God. He blessed God, who had "considered me worthy of this day and hour, that I might receive a place among the number of martyrs in the cup of your Christ." When he said "Amen," the fire was set.

The epistle also reveals the early church's view of martyrdom. This text is actually the first case in which the Greek word *martyrion*, which means "witness" or "testimony," took on the technical meaning of a blood witness, or a witness to Christianity in the sacrifice of one's own life. In a few places the text further refers to martyrdom as being "in accord with the gospel." This reflects an idea in the early church that to be a true disciple of Christ, one must follow Christ to the point of death. Now this view was held to varying degrees within the church. Obviously, one needs to take into account that Polycarp himself didn't walk right into his martyrdom, for he first attempted to elude capture. Further, not even all of the Christians in Smyrna were martyred along with their bishop. Nevertheless, many in the early church exalted the martyrs to a level nearing a special place of sainthood. In fact, that practice eventually morphed into the Roman Catholic doctrine of saints during the medieval era. A further legacy of this extreme view concerns the way in which martyrdom was transformed once the empire turned favorable to Christianity. Since martyrdom was no longer an option, those who truly wanted to be Christ's disciples literally made their entire lives a living sacrifice by entering the monasteries and convents.

Further, the persecution caused a significant problem in the early church. Not all had the fortitude of Polycarp. When some were put to the test, they recanted. Then, after the season of persecution subsided, some of those who had recanted sought to rejoin the church. This desire to return to the church was not always welcomed by the ones who remained, who had suffered because of their stand, and who had lost loved ones. This was especially the case on a grand scale after Constantine and the legalization of Christianity, but through the early centuries of the church, the problem presented itself. Those who recanted Christianity were called *traditors*, or those who handed over their Christianity and the Scriptures; in English they would be called *traitors*. This controversy in the early church is referred to as the Donatist controversy, named for Donatus (270–355), the Bishop of Carthage. He not only refused the *traditors* reentry into the church, he forbid his parishioners even to associate with them. In the process, he used the phrase *Extra ecclesium nulla salutis* ("Outside of the church, there is no salvation"). Perhaps no other phrase from the early church would play such a prominent role in the Middle Ages and Reformation. Not all, however, took such a hard line as Donatus, but the issue certainly caused problems in the early church. All of this, of course, extends beyond the single example of Polycarp. It reveals, nevertheless, the discussions spurred in the early church by the martyrdoms.

One final item worthy of mention in *The Martyrdom of Polycarp* concerns the perspective this text offers. The account of Perpetua and Felicitas refers to their day of martyrdom as the "day of victory." Thus, the early church inverted the event. It was not a defeat; it was a victory. They were not at the mercy of the particular emperor or proconsul or Roman soldier; they were under the dominion of Christ and the sovereignty of God. As *The Martyrdom of Polycarp* summarizes the whole affair: "[Polycarp] was arrested by Herod, when Phillip of Tralles was high priest during the proconsulship of Statius Quadratus, but while Jesus Christ was reigning as King forever." Then it adds, "To Him be glory, honor, majesty, and the eternal throne, from generation to generation." The reference to Christ as the true King was intended to remind other Christians who might very well find themselves standing before a Roman soldier or a proconsul or even the emperor himself that they should not fear the one before them. It also reminded them there was a reality that was true and firm and real, all appearances to the contrary notwithstanding. The martyrdoms were victory, not defeat.

Polycarp's Legacy

It has been said that there are more martyrs from the twentieth and early years of the twenty-first centuries than from all of the previous centuries of the church's existence combined. In fact, many Christians in various parts of the contemporary world find themselves in exactly the same spot as Polycarp and the early church: in a hostile environment, facing persecution. For them, the words of Christ in John 15:18 ring all too true. "If the world hates you," Christ tells the Twelve, "keep in mind that it hated me first." Christ proceeds, however, to inform the disciples that this is precisely the world that he is sending them into.

Perhaps the most telling lesson we learn from Polycarp concerns the way he experienced being a disciple in the world. Polycarp's world required of him the sacrifice of his life. And so he went boldly to his death, remaining faithful to the end. Consequently, his martyrdom had a great impact on his contemporaries and on Christians in the ensuing centuries. The account of his martyrdom became well known to the early church and bolstered those who would face their own persecution and, in some cases, martyrdom. Eventually, the tide changed and Christians enjoyed the favor of the Roman Empire for many centuries. Today the church lives in both worlds as some Christians enjoy the favor of government while others are persecuted for their faith. Both groups can learn from Polycarp that regardless of who sits on the various thrones and seats of power in governments, Christ is the eternal Emperor, and in that Emperor's steps we are to follow.

A Note on the Sources

There are many English translations of *The Martyrdom of Polycarp*, as well his *Epistle to the Philippians*. One of these is J. B. Lightfoot and J. R. Harmer, eds., *The Apostolic Fathers*, which also includes a great deal of other writings from the early church. A fuller English collection of these writings is the thirty-two-volume set *The Anti-Nicene and The Nicene Fathers*. Much of what we know about the early church is chronicled by one of the later church fathers, Eusebius, Bishop of Caesarea (c. 265–340), in his *Church History*, which may also be found in these sets. For more recent histories of the early church, see Henry Chadwick, *The Early Church* (1967) and Everett Ferguson, *Backgrounds of Early Christianity* (2003).

3

AUGUSTINE
THE CONFESSIONS

> The less you allowed me to find pleasure in anything that was
> not yourself, the greater, I know, was your goodness to me.
>
> Augustine, *Confessions*

> If Augustine had written only the *Confessions*, he would have to
> appear on anyone's list of great writers and great books.
>
> Jaroslav Pelikan

Augustine shows up just about everywhere and in some rather curious places. He is one of the most commonly referred-to figures from a variety of traditions. Few Roman Catholic university campuses do not have a building with his name. He is a founding father to evangelicals of all stripes. He shows up historically, as well. Thomas Aquinas never even had to refer to him by name, as he was always "The Theologian." He sparked Martin Luther to read Paul, and the Protestant Reformation ensued. When someone was looking for an apt title for Jonathan Edwards's place in history, "America's Augustine" won out. When T. S. Eliot wanted the supreme example of one in need of salvation in *The Wasteland*, he turned to Augustine. Speaking for him, Eliot renders:

> To Carthage then I came
>
> Burning burning burning burning
> O Lord Thou pluckest me out
> O Lord Thou pluckest
>
> burning

Augustine shows up in literature, in theology, in history, in the church. He shows up just about everywhere. And he deserves to.

If we were to look in on Augustine's life at certain times, however, we would be quite surprised to find out that the one we were observing would become the towering figure of church history. In his early adulthood, he's running from God. The Scriptures lack rhetorical punch for him, the work of the theologians leaves him intellectually unsatisfied, and a Christian ethic imposes far too much restriction on him—especially when he looks upon his mistress. Christianity is both too much and not enough for Augustine. This despite the lifelong prayers and pleas of his saintly mother, Monica.

Augustine himself would agree with our surprise. In fact, he would state it much more starkly. In his clear-eyed view, he would see his rebellious heart, tempting him at every turn to run from God. He would see the futility of all his efforts. As for his take on our assessment of him as the towering figure in church history, he would likely blush. Not unto us, he would say alongside of the psalmist, but to your name give glory. Herein is Augustine's story. It is the story of the Hound of Heaven—Augustine applied that term to

God with the utmost reverence—tracking him down, and it is the story of his classic work, *The Confessions*. This work beckons us, and has done so throughout the ages, to pause and consider the essence of a life. It is Augustine's autobiography, but as he tells his story it becomes the story of every Christian.

Augustine's Life and Times

Augustine is a central figure in the sweep of church history for a number of reasons, his incredible literary output and his role as a pivotal figure among them. He died at a crucial point in world history. The Vandals had already sacked Rome in 410, which incidentally prompted the writing of his other classic, *The City of God*. As he lay dying, with the text of the psalms written across the ceiling and the walls of his chamber, the Vandals were at the city gates of Hippo, the place of his bishopric. This was the end of the Roman Empire, the end of the flourishing of Greco-Roman civilization, the end of the robust centuries of Greek philosophy and Roman law. In turn, it marked the dawning of the medieval era. Perhaps no other figure stands so central in this epochal shift. Versed in all that the Greco-Roman world had to offer, Augustine shows the impact of that world on the early centuries of the church and Christian theology. He knew his way around Plato and Aristotle, and he matched, in terms of both style and substance, the greatest the empires of Greece and Rome had produced. Shortly after his life, and even during it, his thought was the topic of debate. As the church entered the medieval era, there was no question that the thought of Augustine would dominate. The only question was how deep the commitment would run. And so from the latter fifth century on through the time of Luther, all debates swirled around Augustine,

entailing those fully committed to his line of thinking, those
partially so, and those merely resembling it faintly.

Augustine's Thought and Writings

That Augustine would come to be such a central figure
is due to the fact that he wrote so broadly and so early. He
did not coin the term *Trinity*. Tertullian takes that honor.
But Augustine was the first, apart from the revelation of the
Trinitarian doctrine by Scripture's authors, to offer the

FIG. 3.1

Timeline of Augustine's Life

354	Born at Thagaste, North Africa
370	Studies at Carthage
371	Son Adeodatus is born to mistress
376–383	Teaches at Carthage
383	Sails to Rome
384–388	Teaches at Milan; hears Ambrose preach
386	Conversion; dismisses his mistress
388	Returns to North Africa; settles at Hippo
390	Son dies
391	Receives ordination as priest
395	Becomes Bishop of Hippo (holds post until death)
400	Writes *Confessions*; altogether, will write manuscripts for 396 books of varying length
412	Starts *City of God*; completes it in 425
430	Dies at Hippo, August 28

---

fullest treatment of it and the most enduring arguments for it. He expressed this in his work *On The Trinity*, ten years in the making. He also offered one of the first fully developed and truly Christian philosophies of history and of society. This shines through in his work *The City of God*, another lengthy project that entailed thirteen years. This was not supposed to take so long to write—fortunately it takes much less time to read. The sacking of Rome, as mentioned already, prompted the book. Some Romans were blaming the Christians (again) for this misfortune. Like times past, Rome's downfall could be traced to the Christians indirectly. The gods, so the logic goes, were angered by the tolerance of Christianity in the empire and withdrew their protective hand. Others blamed Christians more directly: the Christian ethic of turning the other cheek does not necessarily make for a suitable world-conquering empire. Augustine decided he would write an apologetic for Christianity in light of these charges. The result went far beyond the bounds of the sack of Rome and the question of Christian guilt and responsibility. Augustine unravels a tale of two cities: the City of God and the City of Mankind.

In his tale, Augustine addressed two major issues, a philosophy of history and a political philosophy. On the first topic, he countered the in-vogue view of history as merely cyclical. Represented in the Phoenix myth or in the Atlantis myth from Plato's *Timaeus*, this view held that history repeated itself, again and again and again. The question of origins becomes murky at best, and the question of the future leaves one with not much to go on. Future life is little more than reorganization, and the upshot for the individual is that life has little meaning. Augustine instead charted a philosophy of history that has a beginning and an end, with a great deal of purpose and meaning to the middle. Here he put forth the doctrine of creation *ex nihilo*, that is to say, God created all things out of nothing; he brought this world into being through his speech. Augustine also argues that there is a definite end for this world: the end determined by God and resulting in everlasting life or judgment. In between, Augustine eloquently argued, the guiding hand of God's providence governs the activities of the city of humanity and he governs the human heart. History is not cyclical but linear and, consequently, purposeful. Long before writing about being purpose-driven in life became popular, Augustine showed that it alone had merit as a philosophy of history on the grand scale and as a meaning of life on the much smaller one.

He also set out a political philosophy. For Augustine, these two cities of God and humanity are distinct spheres and shouldn't be entangled. Thinkers in the medieval era wrestled deeply with this idea. The consensus soon came to drop Augustine's sharp demarcation, opting instead for the virtual union of the two as Christendom emerged. We will see later how that came to be, as well as how Luther responded with an alternative direction. Suffice it to say that the ideas in *The City of God* cast a long shadow. Augustine's view, however, does not preclude him from having a great deal to say about politics and society. Just as one example, Augustine may be credited with offering the fullest development of the just war (*jus causi bellum*) theory, a topic that continues to make headlines and garner interest.

A philosophy of history and a political philosophy were not the only two things Augustine discussed in his book. He also put forth his take on the doctrines of humanity, sin, and salvation, making himself a central figure in the much-debated issue of the human will and God's sovereignty in salvation. *The City of God* was not the first place Augustine tackled these topics. He had previously written briefly on them, sparking disagreement with Pelagius. A full discussion of this would be a book unto itself. The salient points of Augustine's view may be sketched out, however.

Augustine held that Adam was born with a free will, that he was able not to sin. Through the fall, his will is now bound to sin, and he is unable not to sin. Augustine does not deny humanity freedom; we sin freely, he would say. We act freely in concert with our nature. This freedom should not, he argues, be the type of freedom that we would want to celebrate, as it is in reality bondage. At redemption, we are restored to our pre-fall state and once again free, as in having the ability not to sin. But we are not truly free yet, he would quickly add. That comes as we enter eternity in our glorified state, entirely free from the bondage of sin and entirely free to be the creatures that God intended us to be. This teaching is not without its dissenters in the history of the church. In fact, these few sentences in this paragraph have been the topic of debate after debate, book after book.

Again, the point stands, Augustine, probably more than any other, left his mark. Yet we have not even mentioned his most widely read and perhaps his most intriguing work, *Confessions*. As R. S. Pine-Coffin, who has produced one of the most popular modern translations of *Confessions*, remarked, this work has special appeal as the story of a great sinner who became a great saint—and, we might add, it is all owing to a great God.

Augustine's *Confessions*

"You made us for yourself," Augustine declares in the closing lines of the book's first paragraph, "and our hearts are restless until they rest in you." As the book unfolds, he takes us along as he recounts the long journey of his restless life. His was not much of a normal childhood, especially against today's standards. He enjoyed Latin, but could not much enjoy Greek. He learned "to have a horror of faulty grammar," all the while opining that he was squandering the brains that God had given him. He's interested in deeper things than languages and grammar as he looks at his young life. He sees that he responded foolishly to all that God had given him, confessing directly to God, "I should have owed you gratitude." He should have seen God in all and returned to him due praise. Instead, he turned to himself and to other creatures. Augustine is simply applying Paul's indictment of humanity in Romans 1 to himself. Augustine puts it rather straightforwardly: "My sin was this, that I looked for pleasure, beauty, and truth not in him, but in myself and his other creatures." Quite insightfully he adds, "And the search led me to pain, confusion, and error." Rather than honor God or give God thanks, as Paul notes in Romans 1:21, Augustine looked within, to the creation, and to creatures. And again as in the case of Romans 1, futility followed.

Book 1 contains all of the broad strokes of the first half of Augustine's theological autobiography. As the next books unfold, he simply adds more detail. In these first seven books, the lion's share of the work, he sketches his attempt to run from God and he sighs over its hollowness. While labeled "books," these segments are more like chapters, and by the time he gets to books 7, 8, and 9, Augustine begins to transition to the second half of his theological autobiography. Moving through book 7, we see the intellectual barriers to Christianity begin to crumble, and as we reach the end of book 8 the Hound of Heaven prevails and, as Augustine recalls, "the light of confidence flooded into my heart," and he passed from the kingdom of this world into the kingdom of God. Book 9 recounts the events immediately after his conversion. Tellingly, it begins with Augustine offering praise to God, the very thing he should have done from the beginning of his life. He declares that God has broken the chains that bound him, and he now desires to praise God with his heart and with his tongue, and let that praise be the cry of his whole being.

Then Augustine does something unique for an autobiographer. This should not surprise us. His autobiography, so focused as it is on theology, has already proved to be unique. But here he outdoes even himself as he turns to offer a commentary on Genesis 1 in the last three books of *Confessions*. Augustine scholars enjoy debating the purpose and role of these last three chapters. Some see in them the beginning of another work. Augustine, it is argued, was going to move from his autobiography, which is the story of all humanity, to offer the story of the world. He started with Genesis 1, and, as that alone filled the space of three books, he gave up on the project. Others see that he turns to Genesis 1 to show how he resolved some of his intellectual struggles with Christianity. The question of origins ranked quite high among the philosophical issues that plagued Augustine before his conversion, and in his commentary on Genesis 1 he reveals the resolution to those struggles. Others see a return to book 1 and Augustine's statement that all things come from God and therefore we must praise and serve him—the lesson that Augustine finally learned after his long and painful journey. That being the case, Genesis 1 is a fitting conclusion. While the debate continues over these final three books, just about all of his interpreters agree on Augustine's aim in the first ten books: portraying the restless one finally finding rest in God.

The poet T. S. Eliot understood this quite well. As alluded to earlier, Eliot uses Augustine, quoting directly from *Confessions*, in his epic poem *The Wasteland*. Augustine becomes a quintessential character for Eliot, portraying one wallowing in the wasteland and in need of God. Eliot's characterization of Augustine as "burning" fits. Augustine himself describes this period as a time when he "was aflame with desire for this world's empty show." But as Eliot concludes *The Wasteland,* he borrows a term from the Hindu Upanishad, *shantih.* In his own notes, Eliot tells us, " 'The peace which passeth understanding' is our equivalent to this word." While the pluralistic overtones give us pause, Eliot nevertheless captures the journey of Augustine. Once Augustine is plucked out of the wasteland by God, he finds peace and rest. The wasteland is made new, restored.

It might help to summarize these first nine books. As already mentioned, against today's standards, these books constitute a rather curious autobiography. At various places, Augustine interjects into the narrative extensive discourses on Platonic philosophy and on a quite popular movement in his day, Manicheism. This philosophy, named for a third-century Persian philosopher named Mani, was a strange mix of Christianity, Judaism, Platonism, and Gnosticism. "Platonism" refers to the ideas of the Greek philosopher Plato, in this case primarily the nature of matter. "Gnosticism" (from the Greek word *gnosis,* which means "knowledge"), a prevalent heresy in the early church, tried to marry Plato and his ideas with select elements of Christianity. In fact, Manicheism may be best viewed as one of the many manifestations of this larger Gnostic movement. It is a complex system of thought that sees the powers of Light and Darkness as locked in an eternal battle. Before the world began, Light deceived Darkness, causing the Darkness to consume some of the Light. The purpose of the world and creation is to overcome this Darkness, to redeem the Light.

Like Plato and his followers, the Manichees saw that matter and physical existence was in the hands of Darkness. The way of salvation is to transcend matter; for human beings this meant focusing on the soul, which is trapped in a sinful body. They believed in Jesus, who simply appeared to be a human being—such a divine being could never take on human flesh. Jesus was one of a number of redeemers who pointed the way to salvation. As this cursory explanation shows, while Manicheism was a mixture of Christianity and Plato, it was not very Christian at all. Interestingly enough, however, the church suffered a great deal from the Gnostic heresy, as it is called. The Gnostic heresy was felt in overt ways, in sects like the Manichees, and in the heresy of *docetism*. This heresy (which got its name from the Greek word *dokeow*, which means "to appear") held that Christ only appeared to be a human; he did not really come in the flesh. Even during the time of the apostles, this heresy posed problems. John had to counter it in his epistles, especially in 1 John.

The heresy also maleffected to the church in subtle ways. It undermined the world and life in the flesh. It led people to think that this world matters little and that only the blissful life to come counts. It led to thinking of human beings as merely "souls" to be saved from their bodies and from this evil world. In Augustine's case, he fell prey to the Manichean and Gnostic heresy, but eventually he came to see its errors and shortcomings. In fact, he found it to be very intellectually dissatisfying. A parallel that might help us better understand these portions of *Confessions* is to think of the initial power that a cult or even a world religion promises. It offers the secret key to unlock the universe and provide a well-worked-out system that appears so profound. In reality, it is a house of cards, with no more compelling insight than a bad science-fiction novel. Readers may at first be a bit confused by Augustine's discussions of Manicheism and his tenuous relationship to it. But it offers a great deal of insight into Augustine's world and the heresies facing the church.

Most of the elements of *Confessions* are not all that confusing. In fact, the book offers an intensely human portrait. *Confessions* should be read as literature, as a narrative of life. This entails paying attention to the setting, the plot, and the characters. As for setting, *Confessions* traverses the Roman world. Augustine is born in Thagaste, in Roman-controlled North Africa. He then is a student at Carthage, still on the African coast. Next he travels to Rome, eventually making his way to Milan, where he comes to Christ. He lives out his new life back in his home territory as he becomes the Bishop of Hippo, a region on North Africa's coast in modern-day Algeria. His metaphorical journey is also a literal one.

As for plot, *Confessions* is the story of Augustine's conversion. It begins with the conflict. He is born into sin, and as he grows that sin becomes more and more evident in his life. In fact, he has himself demonstrating his rebellion even as an infant. His story is the classic taking of two steps back before taking any steps forward. He finds the Bible to be less than rhetorically satisfying. He finds apparent solace in the arms of a mistress, against the directives of the Christian ethic. We've already mentioned that he was sidetracked by Manicheism. But one by one, the barriers came down and Augustine came to Christ. And so the plot reaches the climax at the end of book 8 as he is converted by reading a passage from Romans in the garden in Milan. Again the setting is important. In the garden paradise was lost, and in a garden it was, for Augustine, regained. Then there is the denouement, where there is a final resolution to the twists of the plot and the narrative, in books 10 to 13.

A most intriguing way to read *Confessions* and one that proves quite helpful concerns the final element of literature, the characters. Here is where Augustine's intensely human story shines through. The main character is not, as we might at first suspect, Augustine. It is better to see the main character as the Hound of Heaven, the one who oversees the twists and turns of the plots and subplots. The Hound of Heaven directs Augustine's journey. From the human standpoint, however, Augustine is the main character. *Confessions* is, after all, his story. Yet there are others who play crucial roles. Chief among them is his mother, Monica. She is the ever-present human instrument of the Hound of Heaven. As Augustine travels in pursuit of a professional career, Monica is not far behind. She constantly prays for her son; she arranges for others to talk with him, such as Ambrose the Bishop of Milan; and she herself prods and nudges as only mothers can do. When Augustine is converted, he immediately seeks her out. Overjoyed, she praises God, extolling him as the one who is "powerful enough, and more than powerful enough, to carry out your purpose beyond all our hopes and dreams." Throughout all of the turns and twists, against all the barriers and roadblocks, Monica never let up in her prayers and never lost hope in God's power to save.

Augustine was converted in 386 and baptized the following year in Milan. His mother was there for it all, and as if her life's mission were now complete, she died that same year. In her last words she told her son that she had longed to remain alive to see him become a Christian. Now that God had granted her wish, as well as "more besides," she was quite content. Her mission accomplished, she asked rhetorically, "What is left for me to do in this world?" Grief-stricken, Augustine wept, realizing that this precious handmaid of God was now lost to him. He was overwhelmed with memories of her devoted love and patience and tenderness. And so he recalls, "The tears which I had been holding back streamed down, and I let them flow as freely as they would, making of them a pillow for my heart."

Augustine's father, Patricius, played a different role. He was a town councilor, a minor public official, in Thagaste, and of modest means. He ensured that his son was well educated, indicating his ambitions for Augustine and for the family name. He was not a Christian but a pagan, and countered Monica's influence in Augustine's home life. Augustine admired his father's sacrifice and devotion to him in sending him to study. Yet he recognized that while his father wanted Augustine's tongue to be fertile, meaning that he make a significant career in rhetoric, he "took no trouble at all" to see that his son was growing in God or cultivating a heart for God.

When Augustine turned sixteen in 370, he went to Carthage to study rhetoric. There he took a mistress to whom he was faithful for seventeen years, but never married. Curiously, he never names her. She went along with Augustine all the way to Milan. There, Monica arranged for Augustine to marry a Christian woman—one of her zealous attempts to get him converted. He dismissed his mistress and became betrothed to this other woman. He, however, never married her. Even twenty years after he had dismissed his mistress, Augustine wrote that the wound never healed. He more than likely loved her deeply, but saw his relationship as an impediment to coming to Christ, and once he was a Christian, he saw marriage as an impediment to his service of God. He consequently never married. It strikes me that he did care for her, perhaps so deeply that he was unable to even speak her name as he recalled his life with her.

They had one son together, Adeodatus, which literally means "gift from God." He was born in 372, the same year Augustine's father died. After Augustine dismissed his mistress, his son remained with him, and the two were baptized together in Milan in 387. Adeodatus went with Augustine back to the coast of North Africa. Adeodatus died in 389, just after they arrived—another wound that, for Augustine, would never heal.

Other characters in the narrative include friends of Augustine and others who, even unknown to themselves, factor in the divine drama. Faustus is the bishop of the Manichees who does not answer Augustine's questions, eventually leading him away from that movement. In Milan, he encounters Ambrose (339–397). A gifted theologian and eloquent speaker, Ambrose comes into Augustine's life just as he is becoming dissatisfied with non-Christian philosophies. When he first hears Ambrose, he becomes convinced that he owes it to himself to take another look at the Bible and at Christianity. The Milan Cathedral still stands today, as does the baptismal font, from which Ambrose baptized Augustine, his mother looking on.

As for his various friends, two stand out in particular. Augustine, as with his mistress, never gives a name to one of them. This was a friend from childhood, and they were cut from the same cloth and pursued the same dream. His friend took gravely ill and for a moment recovered. This shook Augustine with horror and he pleaded for his friend to be baptized, even though Augustine himself was at this time unconverted. The friend refused Augustine's pleas, and within days the fever returned and he died. Again, Augustine's reluctance to name him points to the deep impact this had on Augustine, and it was one of those points along the way that eventually led him to Christ.

The other friend that stands out among the many mentioned is Alypius. Alypius was from Augustine's hometown and was one of his first students. He, too, found himself traveling along with Augustine and happened to be present at the precise moment of Augustine's conversion in the garden at Milan. He was baptized with Augustine and

taocto:addendo tredecim vt fiant nonaginta vnum: ad/
dendo quattuordecim vt fiant centum quinq̃: addendo
quindecim vt fiant centum viginti: addendo sedecim vt
fiant centum triginta tres: addendo decem ⁊ septem effici
untur centum quinquaginta tres:inuenies ingentem nu/
merum omnium sanctorum pertinere ad hunc numerũ
piscium paucorum.
Quomodo autem in quinq̃virginibus in numerabiles virgines
quomodo in quinq̃ fratribus illius q̃ tor quebatur apud infe/
ros milia populi in deorum: quomodo ĩ numero
centumquinquagintatrium pisciũ milia mili
um sanctorum: sic in duodecij sedibus non.xij.homines
sed magnus est numerus perfectorum. Sed video quid
cõsequenter requiratur a nobis:quomodo de quinq̃ vir
ginibus reddita est ratio:quare ad quinq̃ multe pertine
ant:⁊ quare ad quinq̃ illos multi iudei: ⁊ quare ad cen/
tum quinquaginta tres multi perfecti. Ostende quare ⁊
quomodo ad.xij.sedes:non.xij.homines: sed multi per/
tineant:quid sibi volunt.xij.sedes que significant omnes
vndiq̃ qui tam perfecti esse potuerunt:q̃ perfectio dicti
est: sedebitis super.xij.sedes iudicantes duodecij tribus
israel. Et quare omnes vndiq̃ ad duodenarium numer̃
pertinent.Quia ipsumvndiq̃ q̃ dicimus de toto mundo
dicimus. Orbis aute; terrarum quattuor designatis par
tibus continetur:oriente occidente:meridiano: ⁊ aquilo
ne. Ab his omnibus partibus vocati in trinitate ⁊ perfe/
cti fide:⁊ precepto trinitatis:quoniam per quaterni duo/
decim fiunt: agnoscetis quare ad totum orbẽ pertineant
sancti:qui sedebunt super.xij.sedes iudicaturi.xij.tribus
israel:quia ⁊ duodecim tribus israel totũq̃ israel.xij.tri
bus sunt. Sicut.n.iudicaturi ex toto mundo:sic ⁊ iudica
ti ex toto mundo. Apĩs de se Paulus dum argueret fide
les laicos:q̃ iudicia sua non deferebant ad ecclam:sj ad
publicum pertrahebant eos cum quibus habebant:ait:
Nescitis q̃ angelos iudicabimus?Uidete quemadmo
dum iudice se fecit: non solũ se sj ⁊ omnes qui recte indi
cant in ecclesia. Cum ergo manifestum sit multos qui do
mino iudicaturos: alios vero non tamen ex equo sj pro
meritis iudicandos:cũ omnibus angelis suis veniet:qñ
ante eum congregabuntur omnes gentes:⁊ inter omnes
angelos deputandi erunt illi qui taq̃ perfecti fuerint vt se
dentes super.xij.sedes iudicent.xij.tribus israel.Etenim
homines dicti sunt angeli.Apostolus de se dicit: Sicut
angelum dei suscepistis me.de Johe baptista dicit. Ec
ce mitto angelum meum ante faciem tuam:qui prepara
bit viam tuam ante te.Ergo cum omnibus angelis veni
ens:simul secum habebit ⁊ sanctos. Aperte.n.dicit ⁊ Esa
ias: Ueniet ad iudicium cum senioribus populi. Isti q̃
sunt seniores populi:isti iam angeli nominati:ista milia
multorum perfectorum de toto orbe venientium celum
vocantur. Illa vero terra sed fructuosa:que terra fructuo
sa in dextera ponenda cui dicetur:Esurivi ⁊ dedistis mi
bi mãducare. Uere terra fructuosa cui gaudet apostolus
quando ei miserunt ad necessitates eius:nõ q̃ quero da
tũ inquit:sed requiro fructum. Et gratias agit dicens: q̃
tandem aliquando repulluraistis pro me sapere. Repullu
laistis vt arboribus dicit:que sterilitate exaruerant qua ⁊
dam. Ueniens itaq̃ ossis ad iudicium vt iam plenam fra
tres audiamus:quid facturus est? a Aduocauit ce
lum sursuq̃.Celũ omnes sanctos pfectos iudicaturos:ad
uocauit eos sursuq̃:sessuros secuq̃ iudicaturos.xij.tribus
israel.Quomodo.n.aduocauit celum sursum: cum semp
sursum sit celum?Sed quos b celus dicit:eosdẽ celos ali
bi appellat.Quos celos?Qui enarrant gloziam dei.Celi
n.enarrant gloziam dei:de quibus dicitur:In omne ter/

Aduocauit celum sur
sum.] Et terram vi/
scernere populum su/
um.] Congregate illi
iustos ei°.[Qui° di/

numero centumquinquagintatritm pisciũ milia mili
um sanctorum: sic in duodecij sedibus non.xij.homines

ram exiuit sonus eorum: ⁊ in fines orbis terre verba eoq̃
Uidete.n.discernentem deum in iudicio.Aduocauit ce
lum sursum.   b   Et terram discernere populum suũ.
A quibus nisi a malie:De quibus hic postea non fit mẽ
tio:iam tãq̃ diiudicatis ad penam. Istos bonos vide ⁊
diistingue.Aduocauit celum sursum:⁊ terram discernere
populum suum.Uo
cat ⁊ terra:non tamẽ
concernenda:sed di/
scernendam. Primo
enim commixtos vo
cauit:q̃ido locutus
est deus deorum ⁊ vo
cauit terram: A solis
ortu vsq̃ ad occasum

sponunt testamentuz
eius super sacrificia.]
Et annunciabunt celi
iusticiam eius.] Quo/
niam deus iudex est.]

nondũ discreuerant serui illi qui missi erant inuitare ad
nuptias:qui congregauerunt bonos ⁊ malos.Cum vero
deus deorum manifestus veniet ⁊ non silebit:sic aduoca
uit celum sursum vt iudicet cum illo.Quo d.n.celum ipsi
celi:sicut que terra ipse terre:sicut que ecclesia ipse ecclie.
Aduocauit celum sursum: ⁊ terram discernere populum
suum. Jam cum celo terram discernit.i.celum cũ illo ter
ram discernit. Quomodo discernit terram?Ut alios po
nat ad dexteram:alios ad sinistram.Terre autem discre
te quid dicit:Uenite benedicti patris mei:pcipite regnũ
quod vobis paratum est ab origine mũdi:Esurivi em̃
⁊ dedistis mibi manducare.Et cetera. Illi autem. Quan
do te vidimus esurientem?Et ille: Cum vni ex minimis
meis fecistis mibi fecistis. Celũ terre ostendit minimos
suos iam sursum vocatos:⁊ ab bumilitate exaltatos. Cũ
vni ex minimis meis fecistis mibi fecistis. Aduocauit q̃
celum sursum:⁊ terraj discernere populum suũ.   c   Cõ
gregate illi iustos eius.Uox diuina ⁊ prophetica videns
futura tãq̃ presentia:exhortatur angelos congregantes.
Mittet.n.angelos suos ⁊ congregabuntur ante eũ oẽs
gentes. Congregate illi iustos eius. Quos iustos nisi vi
uentes ex fide:facientes opera misericordie:Etenim ope
ra illa iusticie opera sunt. Habes euangelium:Caue te iu
sticiaj vestram facere coraj bosbus:vt videamini ab eis.
Et quasi quereretur quã iusticiaj:cuj q̃ facis elemosynaj
inquit.Ergo elemosynas opera iusticie esse significauit.
Jpsos congregate iustos eius:eos congregate qui cum o
passi sunt inopi:qui intellexerunt super egenum ⁊ paupe
rem. Congregate illos:confer eat eos illis ⁊ viuificet eos
Congregate illi iustos eius.   d   Qui disponunt ⁊c. Jd
est qui cogitant de promissis eius super illa que operan
tur. Jpsa sunt enim sacrificia deo dicente:misericordiam
volo plus q̃ sacrificium.Qui disponunt testamentũ cius
super sacrificia.   e   Et annunciabunt ⁊c.Uere hanc iu
sticiam dei celi nobis annunciauerunt: euãgeliste pdixe
runt. Per illos audituntus futuros quosdaj ad dexteraj
quibus dicet paterfamilias:Uenite benedicti patris mei
pcipite.Quid percipite?Regnuj. Pro qua re?Esuriui ⁊
dedistis mibi manducare.Quid tam vile:quid tam rere
num q̃ frangere panẽ esurienti?Tanti valet regnũ celoq̃.
Frange esurienti panẽ tuuj:⁊ egeni fine tecto induci do
mum tuũ:Si videris nudũ vesti.Si non babes facultatẽ
frangendi panẽ:non babes domuj quo inducas:non ba
bes vestẽ quo coopias:da calicẽ aque frigide: vn̄te duo
minuta in gazophylatii. Tantũ emit vidua duobus mi
nutis:quantũ emit Petrus relinquẽs retia:quantũ emit
zacheus dando dimidium patrimonii. Regnũ dei tan
ti valet quantũ habueris:Annunciabit celi iusticiã eius.
f   Qui deus iudex est. Uere iudex:non concernens sed
discernens. Nonit.n.ossis qui sunt eius.Et si grana latent
in palea:agricole nota sunt. Nemo timeat esse granuj et
inter paleam:non falluntur oculi ventilatoris nostri. No
li timere:ne illa tempestas que erat in circuitu eius cõcer
nat te cum palea. Certe valida erit tempestas: nullũ ta
men granum tollet a parte tritici ad paleam : q̃ non qui

3.2 Page from Augustine's *Commentary on the Psalms.* His commentary surrounds the
text inset near the top.

returned to the coast of Africa with him. Eventually, Alypius became the Bishop of Thagaste, the region next to Hippo, the site of Augustine's bishopric. They each became bishops in the same year, 395, and they both died in 430. They not only remained friends, but also became great allies as they worked for the church, establishing firm doctrine, handling disputes, and battling heresies. Augustine liked to quote the Roman poet Cicero on friendship: "Friendship is agreement, with kindliness and affection, on things human and divine."

Confessions tells a very human story on a very human plane. But that is not all. It also tells a story on the divine plane. Against the backdrop of the setting, behind all of the twists and turns of the plot, and through the various characters of the drama, Augustine reveals that God was all the while directing his circuitous journey straight to himself. Immersed as Augustine was in the Greco-Roman world, the exact episodes of his journey and the exact nature of his challenges may very well be different from those faced in the world of the twenty-first century. Even though they may look different, the underlying struggle connects. Augustine is the quintessential seeker—long before the term becomes vogue. His story does indeed become that of every Christian. Consequently, Augustine's *Confessions* truly is a classic work.

Augustine's Legacy

Augustine wrote *Confessions* in 400, slightly over a decade after his baptism. He would live another thirty years. He was ordained a priest in 391 and appointed Bishop of Hippo in 395, a post he held until his death. By now the Catholic Church, which was yet to be the Roman Catholic Church with its thoroughly developed papacy, was firmly established. The centuries of persecution were now over, and the church had enjoyed one long century of peace and even privilege within the Roman Empire. All was not well, however. Heresies of many stripes, such as the Gnostic heresy, threatened the church. Augustine devoted a great deal of his time and his sharp intellect to combating them. He was involved in the debates in just about every heresy plaguing the church. His writings continued to be the source for church councils in the ensuing centuries as they engaged new heresies. When Martin Luther was following his own journey as a seeker, it was in reading Augustine that he was led to Paul and the Bible and eventually led to the cross of Christ. It would be hard to overestimate Augustine's impact.

He had an impact on monasticism, himself joining the monastic community at Thagaste before becoming a priest and overseeing the monastery at Hippo. Additionally, he wrote quite a few texts on monastic discipline and practice. Eventually, there was a monastic order named for him in the eleventh century. The Augustinian monks were known as the theologians of the day. Perhaps it's fitting that Luther was an Augustinian monk.

Augustine's published writings include about 130 works of differing lengths. He wrote volumes of lengthy letters, often enjoying the "stolen moments" from his preoccupations. In addition, there are almost 400 sermon manuscripts, a number of which were published. His main subject matter included theology, especially refutations of heresies. He also wrote on philosophy, on the *trivium* of ancient learning: grammar, rhetoric, and logic. He even wrote a significant work on music. His literary accomplishments are all the more impressive when one considers that they were largely compressed into a thirty-year period during which he was an extremely busy church administrator. So extensive are

Augustine's writings, thought, and legacy that a group of scholars has recently produced a rather lengthy (almost 900-page) encyclopedia devoted solely to him.

Sometime in the winter of 430, Augustine was invited to the dedication of a church. He declined the offer, on the grounds of the harsh winter and his old age. "I might have scorned the winter, had I been young," he wrote. He survived the winter, but in the summer months of his seventy-sixth year, his age prevailed. That summer, the Vandals invaded the North African coast, making their way to Hippo. As a forti-fied city, Hippo became home to flocks of refugees seeking shelter within its walls. Augustine, its aged bishop, orches-trated the valiant defense. In mid-August during the siege, he caught a severe fever, which took his life in ten days. In those final days, because he could no longer get out of bed or hold his beloved books, he had his attendants write the psalms across the walls and ceiling of his chamber. As he died, the city was overrun. Along with it, the great Roman Empire passed its full ebb. Yet Augustine's shadow would loom large across the landscape of the emerging medieval world.

A Note on the Sources

Numerous English editions of *Confessions* are in print. Two well-known ones are R. S. Pine-Coffin, ed., *Confessions* (1972), and Henry Chadwick, ed., *Confessions* (1998). A helpful reader of Augustine's thought is N. R. Needham, *The Triumph of Grace: Augustine's Writings on Salvation* (2000). For a recent and compelling biography, see Gary Wills, *Saint Augustine* (1999). The definitive scholarly refer-ence work is Allan D. Fitzgerald, gen. ed., *Augustine Through the Ages: An Encyclopedia* (1999).

PART TWO

THE MEDIEVAL CHURCH

4

ANSELM
WHY THE GOD-MAN

Come then, Lord my God, teach my heart where and how to
seek you, where and how to find you.

Anselm, *Proslogion*

Sinful man owes God a debt for sin which he cannot repay.

Anselm, *Why the God-Man*

I n the city of Bayeaux in Normandy, France, hangs a
tapestry that runs 270 feet, measuring 20 inches
wide—originally it ran longer still. Commissioned, in
all likelihood, as part of the dedication of the Cathedral at
Bayeaux in the final decades of 1000, the tapestry tells the
story of the Battle of Hastings in 1066. Tapestries and battles were commonplace in medieval times. But this particular tapestry and this particular battle stand out for their
singular importance. Historians have been so bold as to say
that what happened in 1066 changed the face of Europe
and the rest of the Western world forever. This revolutionary event would have a far-reaching impact, of which the

significant players were only minutely aware and of which most alive at the time were not at all cognizant. Among this latter group was a monk named Anselm at Bec, also in Normandy. He had just entered the monastery in 1060 and by 1063, at the age of thirty, was serving as the monastery's prior. But largely because of the events of 1066, his path would eventually lead him from Normandy across the English Channel to Canterbury. He would become the archbishop of the famous cathedral there, find himself in the halls of kings and popes, and eventually emerge as one of the most prominent figures in the Middle Ages. Like the Bayeaux Tapestry, Anselm stands out for his singular importance. And also like the Bayeaux Tapestry, Anselm belonged to a world far removed from our own, the world of the Middle Ages.

The times of referring to the era between the collapse of the Roman Empire in the 400s until the time of the Renaissance and Reformation in the 1500s as the "Dark Ages" have long passed. Much about the era, however, remains in a fog for most people, and especially when it comes to Protestants, the history of the church in that era is largely viewed as a mere preface to Martin Luther and his actions at Wittenberg in sparking the Reformation. And while it is true that from a Protestant perspective much of the theology that comes from the Middle Ages took a downward turn, Protestants and contemporary evangelicals do a disservice by ignoring this era. And this is especially the case in ignoring the life and legacy of Anselm of Canterbury. In the pages that follow, we will explore this mysterious era and this little-known monk and archbishop. In the process, we will see that he has much to offer us almost a full millennium later.

Anselm's Life and Times

Born in 1033 in Aosta, Italy, Anselm, like so many figures in church history, was the object of his mother's
prayers and impacted by her devout life. In his teens, he
desired to enter the monastery, but was denied, leading him
to follow other pursuits. Later, after the death of his
mother, he decided to leave the region of his youth in Bur-
gundy, traveling across the mountains to Normandy. There
his desires to enter the monastery rekindled, and in 1060
he became a monk under the respected and scholarly Ab-
bot Lanfranc (1010–1089) at Bec. As a young scholar himself, Anselm came under the spell of Lanfranc's abilities

FIG. 4.1

Timeline of Anselm's Life

1033	Born in Aosta at Piedmont
1056–1059	Crosses Alps; travels to Normandy
1059	Arrives at Bec
1063	Appointed Prior at Bec
1078	Appointed Abbot at Bec
1093	Appointed Archbishop of Canterbury
1098	Trip to Rome
1098–1100	Exiled from England by King William II
1098	Completes Why the God–Man
1100	Returns to Canterbury, following William II's death
1103–1106	Exiled from England by King Henry I
1109	Dies at Canterbury, April 21

and soon surpassed his mentor. In a few years Lanfranc was promoted elsewhere and Anselm replaced him as prior in 1063. Then in 1066, as William of Normandy ascended to the throne in England after his victory at the Battle of Hastings, Lanfranc was called to the post of Archbishop of Canterbury. Again, Anselm would follow his mentor, becoming Archbishop of Canterbury in 1093 after Lanfranc's death. Anselm remained at the post, a few exiles from the English king notwithstanding, until his death in 1109.

While serving in these various posts, Anselm represents much of the medieval era in miniature. He belonged to the two significant institutions of the church: monasticism and the hierarchical establishment of the bishopric. As a cleric, he found himself as a pawn between the power struggles of pope and king that so marked the Holy Roman Empire of the Middle Ages. Through his associations with Pope Urban II (1042–1099), Anselm played a role in the First Crusade in 1095. And as a theologian and philosopher, he produced a classic text in each respective field. His main area of reading was the Bible (in the Latin Vulgate version) and Augustine, aided and undergirded by the philosophy and method of Plato and Neoplatonism.

First, as a monk, Anselm's life offers insight into this significant institution in medieval life. Making an assessment that might come as a surprise to most evangelicals, church historian Mark Noll has observed that the impact of monasticism has been largely for the good. Like any institution made up of human beings in all of their foibles and frailty and sin, monasticism is not without its faults, and there were certainly abuses within it. Yet Noll's thesis is worth considering. The monasteries were for most peasants and even the nobility of the Middle Ages a true lifeline. In times of famine, food could be found within their walls; for the weary traveler, shelter would be provided; and for the so-called marginalized of society, monasteries would always offer a refuge. They also, and this especially came into play with Anselm, served as educational institutions. Monasteries were the originators of the modern university, and their efforts in preserving the great texts of Rome and Greece have not gone unnoticed. A few years ago, Thomas Cahill's *How the Irish Saved Civilization* climbed on to the *New York Times's* bestseller list. Cahill provocatively argued that scribal efforts at copying the manuscripts of the ancient world, quiet labors within monastery walls largely going unnoticed by an illiterate public, not only preserved the literature of classical culture, but also provided the basis for the revival of that culture that fueled the Renaissance and the Reformation. Anselm not only benefited from this rich academic world of the monastery, he also became one of its leading lights.

Not only known for its social work and educational endeavors, the monastery was also a place of spiritual devotion. Theoretically, monasticism, marked by its vow of poverty and seclusion, could be less distracted in its devotion to God, free from some of the trappings that plagued the clerical hierarchy throughout the Middle Ages. In fact, many of the attempts at reform of the medieval church had their beginnings in the monasteries, and it should not go without notice that Martin Luther began his career as a monk. This devotion came to its fullest expression in the mystical tradition, as will be seen in chapter 6 and the discussion of Thomas à Kempis. For Anselm, this may be seen in one part of his literary legacy, his prayers and meditations. Though clearly an academic theologian, a deep spirituality permeates Anselm's work. As a theologian who started as a monk, Anselm thinks and writes differently from what we may be accustomed to.

But Anselm, like so many of his contemporaries, made the move from the monastery to the other significant institution within the medieval church: the hierarchy of bishops and the papacy. As mentioned in the earlier chapters, by the beginnings of the second century, a well-established bishopric was underway in the church. Once Christianity became legalized under Constantine, the hierarchy and bishopric developed further. Protestant and Catholic historians disagree, however, as to exactly how this system of bishops developed, specifically how the Bishop of Rome grew to such prominence as to become the pope. From the Catholic side of things, since the days of Peter, there has always been a prominent Bishop of Rome, who is nothing less than the vicar, or representative, of Christ on earth. This line of succession, referred to as *apostolic succession*, may be traced straight from Peter on to the present day. Protestants find this view tenuous, and the evidence lacking. Instead, Protestant historians point to Gregory the Great, or First (540–604), as beginning the institution of the papacy. Further, they credit him with rethinking the history of the Bishop of Rome and trumping up the position's prominence. While the stages in the history of the papacy are disputed, it remains clear that by the time of Anselm, the papacy was a deeply entrenched institution. As Archbishop of Canterbury, though responsible for many people and separated by a great distance from Rome, Anselm answered to the pope.

A power play between pope and king dominated the medieval era, catching just about everyone in the conflict. Anselm was not immune. Kings William II and then Henry I of England each exiled Anselm from his post at Canterbury, both times as the pawn in the kings' harangues with Pope Urban II and then Pope Paschal II. When Henry I exiled him, the king also intended to take over the lands owned and revenues generated by the church and administered by the Archbishop of Canterbury's office. Anselm countered by threatening Henry I with excommunication; wielding a portentous weapon as excommunication from the church in the medieval era amounted to the damning of one's soul. Eventually, Henry I and Anselm negotiated an arrangement each side could live with, and Anselm returned to Canterbury.

The exiles were not unwelcome by Anselm. He had taken the post of archbishop reluctantly in the first place. Cut of a scholarly cloth, he was not made for the intrigues of diplomacy required of the position. His exiles then enabled him to follow his scholarly pursuits, and during those times he did some of his best writing.

Anselm also came into contact with one other feature of the medieval era, the Crusades. As part of his efforts to reform the church, Pope Urban II sent out the clarion call to reclaim the Holy Land. Anselm's personal view of the Crusades is at best ambiguous; in one letter he advised someone to join a monastery instead of joining the Crusade and so earnestly fight for the heavenly Jerusalem instead of the earthly one. But as Archbishop of Canterbury, he joined in the efforts of drumming up support. He, alongside of King William II and the king's brother, Duke Robert, raised money for the Crusades and commissioned Duke Robert, who personally joined in the Crusade himself. Though the First Crusade was marginally successful, the remaining seven or so Crusades resulted in utter failure. One of the saddest moments in this dark episode of the Crusades concerns the Children's Crusade, led by a young boy named Nicholas in 1212. Literally hundreds of children left France with the belief that God would miraculously lead them to victory. Most died along the journey, and those who did

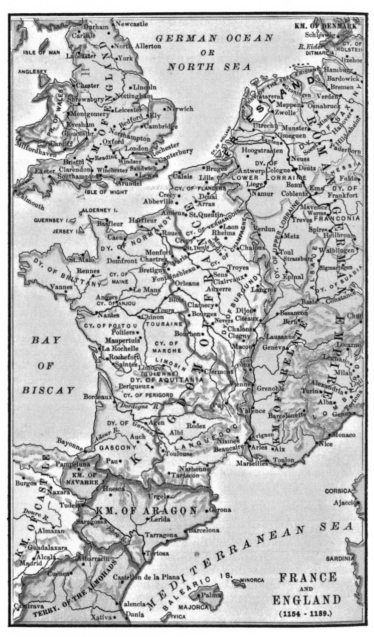

4.2 England and France in the Twelfth Century

reach the Mediterranean shores were tricked into slavery. Only a few made it back to France to chronicle the tragedy.

Amidst all of the strife and bickering and challenges of his professional life, Anselm quite frequently enjoyed the solace and respite of the monastery. He was at his best, withdrawn from the conflicts and, surrounded by his books, contemplating and theologizing. Consequently, Anselm has left a double legacy, one as a churchman involved in the conflicts of his era and one as a theologian leaving his mark on the history of the Christian tradition. His most significant contribution came in his work *Why the God-Man*. But it was far from being his sole contribution.

Anselm's Thought and Writings

Anselm was a product of his era and rose above it at the same time. In the field of scholarship, originality was trumped by a dogged recitation of authority. The great minds and councils of the past circumscribed one's own work. When Anselm completed his first major philosophical work, entitled *Monologion* (1076), he sent it to Lanfranc for review. One can imagine Anselm's anxiety in submitting his thoughts to his mentor. He waited at length for a reply. Eventually Lanfranc rendered his assessment. Don't be original, he informed the upstart, adding, stand aside and let the fathers of the past do the talking. Anselm was among select company: the likes of John Wycliffe, Jan Hus, and Martin Luther all met with the same criticism. Undeterred, Anselm plowed ahead. After *Monologion*, which advances a philosophical argument for the existence of God, he quickly followed up with another piece on the same subject entitled *Proslogion* (1077–1078). Meaning simply "to say a word before," *Proslogion* offers the ontological argument for God's existence. The most philosophical of the so-called classical proofs or arguments for God's existence, the ontological argument begins with the idea of God, or what Anselm initially refers to as a being that is greater than can be thought. From here, Anselm reasons out to the absolute necessity of God's existence. Though complex, the argument may be broken down into three steps.

The ontological argument is so named from the Greek word for "being," *ontos*. The three steps move from the idea of God to the being of God. First, there is the idea of a being that is greater than can be conceived of or thought. In other words, we can have the idea of a perfect being. This, Anselm notes, must be conceded even by "the fool," referring to Psalm 14:1. The second step requires one to see that existence in reality is greater than existence in the mind. This may be illustrated simply by asking if you would rather have the idea of a thousand dollars or have a thousand dollars. So again, existence in reality is greater than existence in the mind. Now, Anselm reasons, if we have the idea of a perfect being that exists only in our minds and not in reality, then this being is less than perfect. That leads to the third step, namely, since we have the idea of a perfect being (first step), and existence in reality is greater than existence in the mind (second step), then it follows that this perfect being exists in reality (the third and final step of the argument). It's not foolproof, and thinkers from Thomas Aquinas to Immanuel Kant have picked it apart. Nevertheless, the argument has a certain staying power that is hard to deny.

One of the things that Anselm is doing in the argument is playing off of Augustine's idea that all of humanity has an undeniable, unmistakable internal testimony of God—an idea that Augustine developed from reflecting on Romans 1:18–23. The second thing that he is doing is betraying his own methodology. Anselm professes to rely solely upon reason in his argument. Yet he was writing in a world that was permeated by awareness of God and of religious sensibilities. The medieval world was a deeply religious and Christian world, bearing the imprint of God just about everywhere. What Anselm sees as philosophically axiomatic, the various steps to his argument, may be nothing less than the furniture of his and his contemporaries' particular worldview. The steps to the ontological argument may very well have been part of Anselm's atmosphere as a monk in the Middle Ages, but that atmosphere is not universal. As mentioned, however, Anselm denies in methodology that which he professes in theory.

The ontological argument comes in chapters 2 through 4 of his book (though referred to as chapters, they are quite short, consisting in some places of a single paragraph). It is interesting to note both the preface and the first chapter. These opening paragraphs essentially amount to a prayer, noting that if humanity (which Anselm refers to as *humoncio*, literally translated as "little man" and best translated as "insignificant man") is to know God at all, it is only because God reveals himself in the first place and that knowledge is grasped by faith. This is all due, following Augustine, to sin and humanity's impaired intellect and reasoning capacity. In chapters 2 through 4, Anselm lays out the argument. Here, in chapter 3, he makes a rather significant leap from the perfect being that everyone conceives of to the God of the Bible, again revealing how his presuppositions and context shaped his argument. Theologically or biblically speaking, it's not a great leap from the notion of the perfect being to God; philosophically speaking, however, it is. The bulk of *Proslogion*, chapters 5 through 26, explores the attributes of God and the Trinity, again assuming a rich biblical and theological framework.

This digression on Anselm's *Proslogion* and the ontological argument, though lengthy and confusing—it usually takes a few passes before the argument begins to make sense—is significant to understanding Anselm's thought. As a theologian in the Middle Ages, Anselm reflects the distinctly philosophical nature of the era. Those who study medieval theology and medieval philosophy find themselves studying the exact same figures and works. This simply isn't true of any other era. This path was started by Augustine, who laid considerable stock in the question of faith and reason. Augustine concluded, as we saw in chapter 3, that faith is primary. Nevertheless, he held strongly that reason played a role. Anselm followed, asserting that faith is necessary and primary, but that reason plays a role. His thoughts in the preface and chapter 1 of *Proslogion* capture this well as he desires a faith that seeks understanding. As he puts it, "For I do not seek to understand that I may believe; but I believe that I may understand." He takes this approach because he realizes that his sin effaces his intellectual abilities. Again, he pleads with God, "Teach me to seek you, and reveal yourself to me as I seek, because I can neither seek you if you do not teach me how, nor find you unless you reveal yourself."

This discussion extends beyond philosophy and speaks to the various approaches to apologetics, even relating to debates of the present day. As will be seen in the next chapter's discussion of Thomas Aquinas, not everyone in the medieval era followed Anselm and Augustine's approach to subordinating reason to faith. Some put the two more on par with each other, others subordinated faith to reason, while still others focused on one to the utter exclusion of the other. Today, the discussion tends to focus on the role of evidences or on the role of the classical arguments for the existence of God in apologetics, rather than on debating the exact relationship between faith and reason. These different apologetic schools of today—referred to as evidentialism, presuppositionalism, and the classical school—all stem from this long discussion stretching back to Augustine and running through the Middle Ages.

In addition to his writings on philosophy, Anselm also authored a number of prayers and meditations, as well as numerous and sometimes lengthy letters engaging most aspects of church life and theology. In his letters, mostly to fellow monks, Anselm extols the virtues of the life devoted to God. "You have begun," he writes to Herluin, a monk at Canterbury, "to taste that the Lord is sweet. Beware, therefore, that you are not so filled with the savor of the world which flows abundantly over you that you are emptied of the savor of God which flows quickly and secretly away from the careless." Fleeing "worldly entertainments," as Anselm often extols, was one of the reasons for the monastery in the first place. In his letters he constantly sounds the alarm to be on guard against the pulls of the world and of the flesh.

Anselm also left his mark on theology. At the pope's request, he wrote a treatise defending the so-called double procession of the Holy Spirit. One of the more curious events of church history is the split between the church in the West (Roman Catholicism) and the church in the East (the Orthodox Church). The split came in Anselm's lifetime in 1054, though it had been centuries in the making, over the issue of whether the Holy Spirit proceeds from the Father alone or from the Father and the Son. One word in Latin, *Filioque*, meaning "and the Son," split the church. That, however, is a little deceptive. Like an iceberg, the tiny surface betrays the great mass that lies beneath. Beneath the fight over this single word, there was a great deal of difference theologically, culturally, and otherwise. In reality, since the early centuries, there had been two epicenters of the church, one in Rome and the other in Constantinople or Byzantium. Nevertheless, the official break came in 1054. The Eastern church accused the Western church of inserting the *Filioque* clause into the Nicene Creed, which was true, thus being untrue to tradition and the councils. That the pope called on Anselm to defend this idea some four decades later shows both the prominence of the issue and the stature of Anselm.

In all, Anselm authored seventeen treatises and numerous shorter writings, filling six hefty volumes in his collected writings. The piece that stands out among the rest, however, is a dialogue on the nature of the Redeemer and the atonement, his classic theological work *Why the God-Man* (1098).

Anselm's *Why the God-Man*

In the fall months of 1097, Anselm left England in what would be a three-year exile. His journey took him to Cluny, and he spent Christmas at its monastery in the company of Eadmer, who would come to be his first biographer. Then it was on to Lyons and then to Rome for a few months' conference with the pope. By June, he had traveled to Liberi and settled in for a few months' retreat. Dogged by ecclesiastical and political cares, Anselm welcomed the time to turn his thoughts to writing theology. Before he left England, he had started an ambitious project: an attempt to account for the Redeemer and to explain the atonement. Such work was not unique or original to Anselm. So crucial a piece of theology had certainly been the object of attention long before Anselm ever took up the subject. In fact, the atonement, widely written on by the early church fathers, already had a long-established tradition in the history of doctrine. But in the hands of Anselm, with his penchant for exploring new expressions, this doctrine would be forever impacted by that few-month retreat at Liberi.

Prior to Anselm, the ransom theory reigned as the way to understand Christ's work of atonement on the cross. The New Testament authors use the language of ransom when referring to the atonement, and the word picture resonates both with the culture of the first century and with the import of what Christ accomplished. Due to Adam's sin, humanity fell prey to Satan, the prince of the power of the air. Christ's death then paid a costly ransom to win back sinful humanity. Theologians since the time of Augustine had worked this out in rather intricate ways. Augustine spoke of the cross as the "Devil's mousetrap," an image that has a rich history in Christian doctrine. The cross looked as if it would be the defeat of Christ, and so he was tricked by it, led to it as bait in a trap leads a beguiled mouse. In the end, the cross turned out to be Satan's demise and not Christ's.

Theologians in the Eastern church tended to view the atonement differently, preferring to express Christ's work on the cross in terms of *Christus Victor*, "Christ the Victor." Again, hearkening back to Adam, Christ accomplished what the first human could not—victory over sin and death. Through his accomplishment, a sinful humanity could also become victor over sin and death. Both of these reigning views, the ransom view and the *Christus Victor* approach, in fact represent the biblical teaching on the atonement. They, however, perhaps stop short of capturing both the fullness and the essence of what Christ was doing on the cross. For the strict terms of the history of the doctrine, we have Anselm to thank. As he worked away on what would become his classic theological work, he offered the church an entirely different way of thinking about the crucial and central question of what Christ was doing on the cross. His contribution has come to be called the substitutionary view of the atonement—although, if we are seeking to be precise, it might be better to refer to his view as the satisfaction view, which in turn laid the groundwork for an easy next step to the fully developed substitutionary view.

The substitutionary view of the atonement holds that humanity, while responsible for sin, is unable to overcome it or answer for it. Consequently, there is a need for a redeemer who is a substitute, one who would and is qualified to take the penalty of sin. As the angel asks the elders through his tears in Revelation 5:2, "who is worthy to open the scroll and to break its seal?" While this view represents a wide swath of biblical teaching, Anselm did not arrive at it through Scripture. Instead, he arrived at it through cleverly constructed and tightly argued logic, written in the form of a dialogue. In the first chapter, Anselm reiterates his view on the limitations of reason. We should not, he begins, "expect to come to faith through reason, but," he continues, we should be "gladdened by the understanding and contemplation of the things [we] believe, and as far as possible to be 'ready always to satisfy everyone that asketh . . . a reason for the hope that is within,'" quoting 1 Peter 3:15. This initial perspective is important, for it shows that Anselm is not substituting a reasoned argument for faith. As he did in *Proslogion*, he views reason as a meaningful and fruitful way to support an already established belief taken by faith.

He then turns to the question that he will answer in his logical argument: What was it that compelled God to become man and through his death on the cross to restore a sinful, fallen humanity? Why, as the title states, did God become man? Anselm frames the answer, which takes up the entire book, in the form of a dialogue with a figure named Boso. Anselm first met Boso at Bec. Boso was the quintessential seeker and, hearing of Anselm's reputation as a formidable thinker, traveled to Bec in order to have his doubts assuaged. So taken with Anselm, Boso stayed on, becoming a monk in service at Bec. When Anselm began writing *Why the God-Man* in 1095, he sent word to the monastery requesting Boso's presence at Canterbury to help in thinking through and writing the book. Boso, then, is not just a mouthpiece for Anselm; he actually speaks on his own and likely made significant contributions to sharpening Anselm's thesis and expression. Boso's conversation also makes for some helpful flattery along the way: "The way by which you are leading me," Boso tells Anselm, "is so thoroughly guarded by reason that I do not see how I can turn aside from it either to right or to left." At the end of his life, Anselm would once again send word to Bec requesting Boso's presence during his later years, testimony to a friendship forged in the mutual pursuit of ideas and service to God.

As the dialogue progresses, Anselm leads Boso to realize that there is a rather simple answer to the question of why God became man: it is the only means by which humanity could be saved from sin. Of course, one would counter that God is infinitely resourceful, so why couldn't he have devised some other plan for redemption? Anselm shows why only the God-man and his death on the cross will suffice. He first helps us see the great weight of sin. God cannot simply dismiss sin, sweep it under some cosmic rug somewhere else; he would no longer be a just God and, consequently, no longer be God. That is precisely, however, the dilemma. For, as sin is so grave that it must be atoned for or paid for, humanity is simply unable to make the payment. Even given an infinite number of chances, he reasons, the gulf remains inseparable. "This," he has Boso say, "is a very painful conclusion." The God-man, however, speaks directly to this dilemma.

A popular expression runs that we owed a debt we could not pay, while Christ paid a debt he did not owe. Though not stating it in those precise words, this idea was first given expression by Anselm. He writes, "Sinful man owes God a debt for sin which he cannot repay, and at the same time he cannot be saved without repaying." He made the clear point that humanity stood under a great weight of sin, that this sin had to be paid for, and that humanity was unable to provide the payment. Conversely, God could pay for the sin, but he had not committed the offense. What's more, the very nature of God demands that he be separated from sin. The God-man solves the dilemma. As perfect (or complete) man, he fully identifies with humanity and bears the burden of sin. As perfect (or complete) God, his death is of infinite value and a satisfaction for the wrath of God. The theological term is *propitiation*, which means "satisfaction of wrath." In this case, God's wrath, due to sin, is fully satisfied by what Christ has done on the cross as the God-man. Not only does Anselm offer reasons for the nature of Christ's atoning work, he also offers an explanation for the incarnation and even for the Trinity. He shows how God both pays for the penalty of sin, in the person of Christ the Son, and remains separated from sin simultaneously. Boso offers the following summary of the conclusion to the long argument of *Why the God-Man*:

> The heart of the question was this: why did God become man to save man by his death, when it seems that he could have done this in some other way? You have answered this by showing, by many necessary reasons, how it would not have been right for the restoration of human nature to be left undone, and how it could not have been done unless man paid what was owing to God for sin. But the debt was so great that, while man alone owed it, only God could pay it, so that the same person must be both man and God.

Thus it was necessary for God to take manhood into the unity of his person, so that he who in his own nature ought to pay and could not should be in a person who could.

In the final chapters, Anselm demonstrates how this work of Christ on the cross is consequently applied to humanity. Christ's work did not go unrewarded, yet he himself was not in need of the reward, as he is in need of nothing and is not in need of forgiveness. He gives the reward, Anselm concludes, to those with whom he identified, to those for whom he died. Sinful humanity is "bound by so many great debts, languishing in poverty and deepest misery," in dire need of what Christ freely gives. So his death, as the God-man, is applied to humanity. And this causes Boso to exclaim, "The world can hear nothing more reasonable, nothing more delightful, nothing more desirable. Indeed, I gain such great confidence from this, that already I cannot say how great the joy is that makes my heart leap."

Why the God-Man is not easy reading. The tightly reasoned dialogue and logical development may have been par for the course in the medieval era, but such writing is not commonplace in the present day. Ours is not a world where we typically speak of reasonable things as delightful and delightful *because* they are reasonable. This does not detract, however, from the ongoing value and impact of the work. Anselm demonstrates that theology is sometimes challenging work, but necessary and fruitful—and, at the end of the day, a great cause for rejoicing in what God has done.

Anselm's Legacy

Anselm is one of the truly bright spots in the Middle Ages, especially from the Protestant perspective. He made significant contributions to both philosophy and theology.

Truly he is a towering figure in the history of ideas. But to think of Anselm as the consummate ivory-tower theologian does a disservice to his legacy. His is a theology deeply imbued with devotion to God. It is not uncommon for Anselm to break from his tight logic and argument in his theological treatises to insert a prayer to God. In *Proslogion*, once he makes the argument for the existence of the perfect being, he then addresses God directly and prayerfully: "And You, Lord our God, are this being. You exist so truly, Lord my God, that you cannot even be thought not to exist. And this is as it should be." Later he can't help but offer praise to God, exclaiming, "I give thanks, good Lord, I give thanks to You, since what I have believed before through Your free gift, I now so understand through Your illumination." By the time he concludes the book, he has extolled the great joy that comes to one who knows and loves God, a love of one's whole heart, whole mind, and whole soul. Like a medieval tapestry, Anselm's work weaves together piety and intellect, rigorous thought and deep devotion. In his writings, he points to and models a holistic commitment to God—whole heart, soul, and mind.

He also intended his philosophical and theological labors to serve the church. His works have an apologetic angle, as well as an intention to bolster the faith of believers. Boso concludes *Why The God-Man* by declaring that what he has set forth in the book would satisfy "even pagans" as to the merits of faith, to which Anselm adds the final word: "If what we think we have discovered by reason is confirmed by the testimony of truth," referring to Scripture, "we should ascribe this, not to ourselves, but to God, who is blessed forever." He saw his own contribution as merely pointing to the compelling and persuasive nature of the testimony of God's Word. In the process, he made significant contributions. He developed the ontological argument for

God and set theologians in the direction of the substitutionary view of the atonement. He argued for the double procession of the Holy Spirit, at a time in the church when that issue deeply mattered. And he modeled the apologetic approach of faith seeking understanding, an approach that places the premium on faith but recognizes the necessary and subordinate role of reason and argument.

Among Roman Catholics, Anselm is regarded as a saint and was declared an official doctor of the church, an honor that lends a great deal of authority to his writings. Eadmer, his pupil and first biographer, wrote his *Life of Anselm* with the intention of gaining Anselm's canonization. Ever since, that tradition has revered him. It is hard to assess what Anselm would think of this. He was clearly a product of the church of the medieval era. Protestantism is nowhere on the horizon, leaving Anselm and his medieval contemporaries with only two options: the Roman Catholic Church or paganism. Yet it also seems that Anselm understood that the system of merits and saints etched deep into the face of Catholicism was lacking. It wasn't the saints' merits that mattered; it was solely the merits of Christ and his work on the cross. That much can be said about Anselm with certainty. While he should not be revered, perhaps he should be remembered. Even more, perhaps he should be read. This monk-turned-archbishop has left a legacy for the church worthy of attention. His writings remind us that the Battle of Hastings was not the only significant event to come from the eleventh century, and that the Bayeaux Tapestry was not the century's only legacy.

A Note on the Sources

For a brief biography of Anselm, see G. R. Evans, *Anselm* (1989). For a scholarly biography, see R. W. Southern, *Saint*

Anselm: A Portrait in a Landscape (1990). A Latin edition with parallel English translation of *Proslogion* is available in M. J. Charlesworth, *St. Anselm's Proslogion* (1979). For *Why the God-Man*, see Eugene R. Fairweather, ed., *A Scholastic Miscellany: Anselm to Ockham* (1961). For an overview of the medieval church, see G. R. Evans, ed., *The Medieval Theologians* (2001), and Jaroslav Pelikan, *The Growth of Medieval Theology (600–1300)* (1978).

5

Thomas Aquinas
Summa Theologica

> The things that we love tell us what we are.
>
> Thomas Aquinas

Nothing more than a dumb ox. That was the estimate of the early associates of Thomas Aquinas. That premature estimate, however, could not be further from the mark. The so-called dumb ox ("dumb" referring more to his silence than a pejorative remark on his intellectual capacity) went on to be one of the most significant figures in the history of the world. Within the Christian tradition, Aquinas ranks a very close second only to Augustine. His writings were immense, filling shelves. Not the least is his magnum opus, the multivolume *Summa Theologica*, an unprecedented encyclopedic theology that served as a benchmark for centuries. His thought dominated theological discussions in the latter Middle Ages, casting its shadow over the Reformation and extending to the present day. Not only was Aquinas made a saint, but a later papal decree declared his thought eternally valid. As has been widely stated, the bellowing of this dumb ox could be heard the world over.

Aquinas's position in the history of Christian thought is beyond debate. Whether you are a philosopher or theologian, you simply cannot ignore Aquinas and his thought: *Thomism*, the term used to refer to his thought and contribution, must be reckoned with. Yet while his position in the history of the Christian tradition is secure, the assessment of his contribution is a bit more complex and ambiguous— for Protestants, that is. Ever since the days of Martin Luther and the Reformation, Aquinas has been viewed ambivalently at best within the Protestant tradition. Some extol his virtues; others are suspicious of him, while still others reject him outright. Much of this has to do with some of the same issues that Anselm wrestled with, as seen in the last chapter. Two specific areas come into play. The first concerns Aquinas's view of the relationship between faith and reason. Second is his understanding of the fall, sin, and grace—what theologians have summarized as his discussion of nature and grace. There are other issues as well, which are endemic to his time and place in history in the medieval church. These two areas, however, not only tend to be the center of discussion concerning his work, they also get at the heart of the legacy of Thomas Aquinas.

Like Anselm, Aquinas belongs to that sometimes-foggy era of the Middle Ages, an era quite unlike our own. In the pages that follow, we'll explore Aquinas's life within the context of the medieval world. By the 1200s, significant changes had occurred, making the world of Thomas Aquinas slightly different than Anselm's.

Aquinas's Life and Times

Thomas, born in 1225, came from Aquino, Italy, situated between Rome and Naples. His father was of a certain nobility, affording Thomas the opportunity to study at the

University of Naples with Benedictine monks. His bookish nature suited him well to the task and it was clear that a life of scholarly service as a monk was in order for Thomas. After his study, however, Thomas felt inclined to join the Dominican order instead of the Benedictines. This caused some consternation among his family members. The Benedictines were seen as a much more respectable order. In fact, it was quite commonplace for a family with a number of children to send the youngest to a monastery or convent. The famous mystic Hildegard of Bingen viewed herself as a tithe to the

FIG. 5.1

Timeline of Thomas Aquinas's Life

1224/25	Born in Aquino, Italy
1230-1239	Studies at Abbey of Monte Cassino
1239-1244	Studies at University of Naples
1244	Joins Dominican order
1245-1248	Studies in Paris with Albert the Great
1248-1252	Studies at Cologne
c. 1250	Receives ordination as priest
1252-59	Teaches at Paris and at Sorbonne; begins writing
1259-1265	Various stays throughout Italy
1265	Publishes *Summa Contra Gentiles*
1265-1268	Teaches at Rome; begins work on *Summa Theologica*
1268-1272	Teaches at Paris
1273	Falls into "trance"; never writes again
1274	Dies at Fossanova, March 7

church as she was the youngest of ten. But when Aquinas expressed his desire to join the Dominicans, who not only took a vow of poverty but actually enforced it and were known to take to begging to meet their needs, this did not sit well with his family's concern not to have their status tarnished. His siblings took quite extreme measures to forestall his plans, including kidnapping him in the family estate. At one point during his kidnapping, they hired a prostitute and sent her into his room in order to cause him to break the other vow required of a monk. Undeterred, Aquinas drew a log from the fire and chased her from the room. Eventually the news of his family's attempts to keep him from the monastery even reached the Vatican. Words of not-so-subtle exhortation were sent back to the family, and Aquinas was freed to enter the Dominican order.

As mentioned in the last chapter, the monasteries represented one side of the great structure of the church in the Middle Ages. Some looked to the monasteries as a means of reforming from within. Their vows of celibacy, poverty, and service often stood as a rebuke of the excesses and abuses in the clergy and the hierarchy of bishops. In fact, most times the different monastic orders started specifically with the intention of being a force of reform. Some woodcuts in the later Middle Ages depicted this as the perception of the laity. A popular form consisted of a two-paneled early version of a cartoon, technically referred to as a diptych. The one side had a picture of the pope or of a bishop dressed in courtly fashion, jeweled and lavish. The other depicted a monk in simple garb accompanied by words from the gospels remembering that Christ had nowhere to lay his head. As the case often happens, however, over time the orders grew in numbers and resources, and some of the early commitment that had so driven them ebbed. Consequently, new orders were formed. This was the case with the

Dominicans, established by Saint Dominic (c. 1170–1221) in 1216. Dominican convents and monasteries quickly sprang up throughout Italy, France, and Spain, many established by Dominic himself in his last few years.

Aquinas further offers a window on the Middle Ages by his schooling at the University of Naples and then through his association with the University of Paris. As mentioned in chapter 4, the monasteries were a significant factor in the history of education and the preservation of knowledge. Not only did they preserve the great literary works of the ancient world through the scribal duties, they also established the early universities that remain the centers of learning to this day. Aquinas spent a number of years lecturing at the University of Paris, the notes of which form the substance of the *Summa Theologica*. University life in those days was quite on par with life in the monastery. In keeping with the rigors of discipline, lectures began in the early morning—Aquinas's lectures, delivered to a packed room, began at 6:00 AM. The main subject was theology, followed by philosophy. Education was far from democratic, as only a select few enjoyed a university education. For that matter, only a select portion of the populace could claim literacy. Prior to the invention of the printing press, books were scarce and highly valued, having to be painstakingly hand-copied.

Shortly after Aquinas took the Dominican habit, after the aforementioned reluctant family consent, he began his studies at the University of Paris under Albertus Magnus, or Albert the Great. Albert brought with him the commentaries on Aristotle by the Muslim scholar Averrhoes. This amounted to a double guilty-by-association charge in the eyes of the church in the thirteenth century. First, ever since the early centuries of the church, Plato was to be preferred to Aristotle, the latter being too far out of synch with Christian theology. The second guilty association came in the form of Averrhoes, a Muslim. Certainly, that alone meant that his work could not be trusted. Paris was, however, a young university, and without a centuries-rich tradition to contend with, new ideas could flourish there. Albert found a place, in other words, and he found no more willing reception than in his star pupil, Aquinas.

After his study at Paris from 1245 to 1248, Aquinas went to Cologne for four years. In 1252, he returned to Paris as a lecturer in theology. He stayed for the next seven years, increasing in his influence and writing widely. He then spent a few years at the University of Naples, before making his way to Rome, where he played a significant role in the University of Rome from 1265 to 1268. Next, he returned to the University of Paris for another four-year term of lecturing, during which he wrote his *Summa Theologica*. In 1273, an event of singular importance occurred in his life. By his own account, he claims to have had a vision in which God spoke to him directly and that drastically changed the direction of his life. Others contend that he had some physical setback, perhaps even a stroke. Regardless, Aquinas swore off his *Summa Theologica* project, referring to it as amounting to nothing more than straw.

He had what might be called a mystical turn, eschewing the life and rigors of the scholar in favor of a more direct and experiential route to the knowledge of God. This transition in his life represents in miniature two significant competing schools of thought in the Middle Ages, referred to under the broad categories of scholasticism and mysticism.

Aquinas's Thought and Writings

If Thomas Aquinas had produced only the *Summa Theologica*, then that would qualify him as one of the most significant figures in both philosophy and theology. Yet, amazingly, the massive *Summa Theologica* constitutes only part of his literary legacy. In addition, he also wrote one of the first missiological texts, the *Summa Contra Gentiles*, a book arguing against Judaism and Islam, with the latter receiving the lion's share of his attention. Today, Islam's rapid expansion gains notice, and so it was in the medieval era as well. By the time of the sixteenth century, Islam would be encroaching on Europe's western border, a phenomenon memorialized in Shakespeare's *Othello*. Islam's challenge called for an answer, and Aquinas offered one in his *Summa Contra Gentiles*. He also authored numerous commentaries on the works of Aristotle, which raised the suspicions of his colleagues and hounded his legacy in certain quarters in the church. Further, he authored commentaries on various biblical books. And he wrote many minor works and sermons that could literally fill volumes. Consequently, one of the few things that Aquinas held in common with Luther was that they both ran through secretaries and scribes with frequency.

One of Aquinas's major works, which some see as surpassing the *Summa Theologica*, is the *Disputed Questions* (*Quaestiones disputatae*). By Aquinas's day, the disputation had prevailed over the method of merely offering commentary—Latin *lectio*—on the past masters of any given subject. The disputation was a lively give-and-take of making arguments and counterarguments for and against different propositions. Aquinas's *Disputed Questions* ranges from the topics of truth to the soul. It reflects his ad hoc interaction with his students more than a systematic treatise.

Aquinas's commentaries on Aristotle, as mentioned above, grew out of his fascination with the ancient philosopher first fueled by Albert the Great at Paris. Prior to the thirteenth century, Plato had received all of the attention. Aquinas changed that. He found in Aristotle an entirely new and fresh way of reasoning, and, what may have excited him the most, a new way of arguing for God's existence. Though the cosmological argument had first been given expression in Plato's *Timaeus*, the argument was developed most in the writings of Aristotle. And it was this argument that intrigued Aquinas. Named for the Greek word for "world," *cosmos*, the cosmological argument is built on the law of cause and effect. The world is an effect, and it must therefore have an equal or greater cause. Aristotle had framed all of this in terms of motion and spoke of an unmoved mover, or a principal that started motion, and hence started everything that exists. Aquinas framed it in terms of causality, speaking instead of an uncaused cause, or of a "first cause."

Rather than start with the idea of God, as Anselm had, Aquinas started with the world around him. Seeing the creation, he asked a simple question: What (or who) caused it? It would not suffice to say, "Nothing," for the law of cause and effect prohibits that answer. There must be a cause. This cause, however, cannot be like that which followed after it. Aquinas refers to the creation and created beings as contingent beings, which means they depend on, or are contingent on, something else for their existence. The first cause is different. The first cause is what Aquinas refers to as a necessary being, that is to say that this being is independent, or not contingent on another for its existence. He then drew the conclusion to the argument, stating that this necessary being is God. This, briefly stated, is the cosmological argument, an argument that has a rich history in philosophy and theology. Today the argument tends to be coupled with the teleological argument—from the Greek word *teleos*, which means "design"—which looks not only to a cause for the effect of the world but argues that this cause must be an intelligent being, and is often referred to under the broad category of intelligent design. Aquinas gave the argument its philosophical and theological base. Over the centuries, and especially recently, it has been injected with a great deal of science.

It is quite instructive to see how the argument worked in Aquinas's own context. This brings in his contribution to the relationship of faith and reason, that all-consuming medieval quest. Aquinas may not have nuanced the relationship between faith and reason exactly the same way as Anselm and Augustine. They were careful to give priority to faith, granting it first place in inquiry, all the while arguing for the necessity of reason. Others in the medieval era sometimes split the two asunder. The mystics tended toward downplaying reason entirely: Christianity was a matter of faith and could not be a matter of reason. Others, though they were in the minority in the medieval era, tended to put reason over faith or even, though quite rarely, excluded faith. Aquinas sought to see them in tandem, but he moved reason up to a higher position than in the thought of Augustine or Anselm.

The medieval debate over faith and reason is quite instructive for today. As Christians think about their faith and apologetics, invariably the relationship between the two comes up. Perhaps not using the same terminology, speaking instead of the relationship between the head and the heart or of the merits to making arguments for Christianity versus simply recounting one's testimony, the root issue remains the same. The medieval debate and the various positions it spawned provide helpful models. In fact, differing approaches to apologetics today largely stem from these various camps of the medieval era. Those who follow the classical approach to apologetics emphasize the role that the classic philosophical arguments for God's existence, largely developed by Aquinas, play in apologetics. Those who prefer the presuppositional approach tend to side with Anselm.

The other positions on the issue of faith and reason in the Middle Ages may also be found today. For instance, the approach that some refer to as *fideism*, from the Latin for faith, holds that reason or argument plays no role in evangelism or apologetics. Fideism finds its roots in the Middle Ages. The debate between faith and reason in the thought of Thomas Aquinas comes into sharper focus as we look at his magnum opus, the *Summa Theologica*.

Aquinas's *Summa Theologica*

Isaac Newton is said to have read everything. That is, he read every single book that was available at that time. That might very well have been the case. As for Aquinas, he didn't have to say that he read everything; all you have to do is read his *Summa Theologica*, and you very quickly come to see that he had. Clearly, any reader of the *Summa* is struck by the magnitude and scope of the work. Encyclopedic. Monumental. Unprecedented. In the case of the *Summa*, these all do not go far enough. No stone is left unturned as Aquinas makes his pilgrimage through the theology of the early church, the philosophy of ancient Greece and Rome, and the pages of Holy Writ in his quest for the truth, not just on one subject, but on them all. Of course, as a medievalist, he begins his pilgrimage with God. By the time he finishes his course, though he left the work unfinished, he has touched on just about all things related to God and creation and other beings and the self. The *Summa* entails ethics and law, philosophy and theology, and hermeneutics and commentary on the biblical text.

The structure of the text consists of three parts. Each of these parts consists of a series of questions, grouped under what Aquinas terms "treatises," broken down into questions. The questions are then fleshed out in a series of articles, numbering anywhere from four up to ten or more for each question. These individual articles are further broken down into a series of objections, where Aquinas typically quotes the opinions and views of past thinkers and follows them with a series of corresponding replies and summary statements. Here are the staggering statistics: 38 treatises, 3,120 articles, and over 10,000 objections. What's more, Aquinas considered his *Summa* to be well "suited to the instruction of beginners."

The *Summa* is slightly different from Aquinas's other significant works mentioned above that are grouped under the title *Disputed Questions.* In that work, we are given a fairly accurate picture of what transpired in the lectures of Aquinas at Paris, Naples, and elsewhere. The *Summa* reflects his years of teaching, but puts the material in a much more unified and systematic format. In fact, in a very short prologue, Aquinas points to the merits of the *Summa* over other works as they are more disjointed and may bring "weariness and confusion." The *Summa* is certainly not disjointed.

Each line of thought in the articles is carried out thoroughly and minutely. Aquinas, however, rarely digresses or pursues objections just for their own sake. Instead, he has injected his work with the same discipline, rigor, and structure that dominates his mind. It is exhaustive, but very little in it may be classified as what so many readers of term papers politely call "filler." This is not to say that contemporary readers will find all of Aquinas's articles and their corollary objections and replies welcome and satisfying. Some may even call to mind a typical take on medieval theologians that has them arguing over how many angels can fit on the head of a pin. From our perspective, in other words, it might be easy to peg Aquinas as the consummate ivory-tower theologian. Before one renders such a judgment, however, Aquinas deserves a deeper look.

When understood within his historical context, the seemingly endless series of objections and replies take on a purposefulness, even urgency. Does God, and what we know of him through Scripture, stand scrutiny, or does it all collapse? In many ways, this drives the *Summa*, which is to say that the *Summa* is primarily driven by apologetic concerns. Both Augustine and Anselm concluded that Christianity is a reasonable faith, and both went to great lengths to demonstrate it. Aquinas went further. In fact, perhaps he went too far. There are different camps on interpreting Aquinas and the value of his work. While all agree that in sheer volume and scope the *Summa* is virtually unsurpassed, not all are willing to line up with its views and conclusions. Much of the debate centers on Aquinas's connection to Augustine and, more pressing, to Paul. Aquinas revered both. In fact, throughout the *Summa*, he does not even need to refer to them by name. Paul becomes *The Apostle*, while Augustine is *The Theologian*. Showing his respect for and debt to Aristotle, Aquinas refers to him as *The Philosopher*. All reverence aside, the question remains as to how much Aquinas actually follows Augustine and Paul. For this, we will look at one of the most turned-to sections of the *Summa*: Aquinas's discussion of nature and grace. The *Summa* is simply too large for a meaningful survey in a mere few pages. Hopefully this look at a key piece of it will serve well to reflect the whole.

The question of nature and grace factors prominently in both theology and philosophy. As for the latter, it has a great deal to do with the competing schools of thought known as determinism and libertarianism. Are creatures controlled or free? Of course, significant ethical implications ensue from the answer. On the theology side, the question of how Adam's sin relates to his posterity comes into focus through this question, as does the issue of divine sovereignty and human freedom or, as some prefer, human responsibility. This question, it may be recalled, came into sharp focus through the debate between Augustine and Pelagius, a debate that never really was settled by the church and continued to Aquinas's day. Interestingly enough, the debate, especially as it gets worked out in Aquinas's thought, raises the issue of merit in terms of salvation. And it is this latter piece that moves front and center at the Reformation.

Aquinas begins his understanding of the relationship between nature and grace by turning to the fall. He divides human nature into two categories: supernatural virtues and natural virtues. The supernatural virtues were lost in the fall by Adam and, as a direct consequence of humanity's connection to him, for all of his posterity. These supernatural virtues are regained by grace at salvation. Adam and his posterity, however, retain what Aquinas refers to as natural virtues after Adam's fall. Aquinas then puts the intellect in the realm of natural virtues. In other words, the human intellect escapes the fall. Theologians since the time of Augustine speak of the *noetic* effects of the fall, using the Greek word for "mind," *nous*, and indicating that the intellect indeed is marred by sin.

Aquinas takes a different position. He sees the problem brought about by sin as lying more with the will (the desire to do the good) than the intellect (the knowledge of the good). Aquinas puts it this way in the *Summa*: "Now [humanity's] nature is impaired by sin more in the desire for good than in the knowledge of truth." Consequently, Aquinas lays great stress on the arguments for the existence of God. These arguments can be understood and even affirmed by one without grace because of the abilities of the intellect. In fact, as seen below, God moves in a person who has first, through his intellect and knowledge of God, made himself ready to receive God's grace. As Aquinas scholar A. M. Fairweather puts it, when compared to Augustine, Aquinas has a "kindlier" view of humanity and nature.

The implications of Aquinas's view are strongly felt when he discusses grace and merit in questions 109–114 in the section of the *Summa* he entitles *Treatise on Grace*. Throughout this section, he refers to grace as a "help," like the type of help that medicine provides for one who is sick. So he writes, "A man can in no wise rise from sin by himself, without the help of grace." He further observes, "One who is infirm, similarly, can make some movements by himself, but cannot move himself naturally like a man in health, unless cured by the help of medicine." The metaphor is telling, especially when contrasted with the biblical metaphor. The biblical metaphor for the results of sin is not spiritual sickness, but spiritual death. This requires that God work in bringing those dead in sin to new life in Christ. Grace is more than "a help." In Aquinas's model, humanity is simply sick, and can limp about toward God, who offers full healing through his grace.

Aquinas's subtlety on this point cannot be overlooked. All through this section, he emphasizes grace, given to us because of Christ's work on the cross. He stresses that it is necessary, that it is what ultimately brings one into relationship with God. What is telling, however, is the way in which that grace relates to nature and merit. He uses the term *merit* to summarize what we contribute to salvation, while grace summarizes God's contribution. He expresses the relationship this way in question 114 on merit: "For it seems congruous that if a man works according to his own power, God should reward him according to the excellence of his power." A little later within question 114, he adds, building on his view that the will is free even after Adam's fall, "This merit is congruous, since when a man makes good use of his own power, it is congruous that God should perform works that are more excellent, according to the surpassing excellence of his power." In other words, Aquinas is not putting merit (humanity's contribution) and grace (God's contribution) on equal footing. Nevertheless, merit contributes to the equation. "Grace does not destroy nature," Aquinas observed, "but perfects it." In other words, it's not grace overcoming nature that brings us to salvation. Instead, it's both grace and nature working together.

Aquinas takes it one step further by claiming, "One man can merit the first grace for another by congruous merit." This line provides the basis for the notion of sainthood in Roman Catholicism, the notion that the merits of the saints can effect salvation in others. The technical term is *supererogation*, which refers to works that are above or beyond that which is necessary. The saints have more merit than they need, which allows for the ordinary or common folks to tap into the excess. Aquinas also adds the following in a discussion of giving alms, or doing good deeds for the poor: "One deserves to be received into everlasting habitations for the sake of one's deeds of pity towards the poor." Aquinas, in this particular discussion, is not nuancing works or merit as an evidence of grace in one's life, nor is he appealing to works or merit as a result of grace in one's life. Instead, he is seeing the works or merit as bringing about grace.

While these selections point to significant shortcomings in Aquinas's theology, there are many parts of the *Summa* worth paying attention to. At one point, he says that to love God is the highest thing we can strive for, adding that to love him is to enjoy him. At another point he offers a brilliant definition of *theology*, noting that it is "taught by God, teaches about God, and leads to God." The first two points stress that God is both source and subject of theology, while the last reminds theologians that God is also the end of theology. In fact, in the context, "leads to God" speaks of worship. For Aquinas, the task of theology should naturally lead one to worship God. The *Summa Theologica* takes its rightful place among the classic texts of the Christian tradition.

Aquinas's Legacy

As mentioned, Aquinas's legacy is checkered; it truly depends on whom you ask. A typical Renaissance portrait finds him flanked by Peter and Paul, with Mary holding the Christ child and looking down from heaven. The apostles are offering direct insight into the Bible as Aquinas holds it before him, and the Virgin sends direct illumination. Thomas Aquinas and his thought are indeed revered within the Roman Catholic tradition. Outside of that tradition, there is a bit of difference. First, while all admire his logic and his literary output, as well as his significant impact on the history of Christianity, not all see that impact for the good. Some see his work as having a negative impact, as the passages above from the *Summa Theologica* demonstrate. At the very least, one should see that Aquinas was not entirely faithful to the Augustinian tradition, as he might have thought he was. His lack of agreement with Augustine bears notice. This precisely led him down the path of wavering on the true impact and consequences of sin, and it eventually led to his emphasizing merit and the human contribution to salvation.

Aquinas's thought dominated the latter centuries of the Middle Ages—what historians sometimes refer to as the high Middle Ages. During this time, the church drifted further and further away from grace alone, poured out through Christ and his work on the cross, and closer and closer to mingling grace with merit. By the time of Luther and the early decades of the sixteenth century, the grace of Christ alone as the means by which one moves from sinner to saint was all but eclipsed. In no small way did Aquinas set the stage for that misstep along the timeline of Christian history.

But not all of Aquinas's legacy may be so bleak. He, after all, wrote on a number of subjects and cast his contribution fairly far afield. As we will see in the next chapter, Aquinas represents one of the significant schools or movements in the Middle Ages: scholasticism. This movement stands counter to mysticism, a movement represented well in Thomas à Kempis and his classic work, *The Imitation of Christ*. As a firm scholastic, Aquinas advocated a rigorous approach to theology, leaving no stone unturned in his quest for truth. While very few theological students (especially Protestant ones) may actually be reading the *Summa* these days, Aquinas's method and style have impacted the systematic theologies they are reading. For centuries, he influenced the method of studying religion or theology in the universities. And his methodology has also had lasting impact on philosophy.

Historians are not sure what to make of that curious event in the last months of Aquinas's life. As mentioned earlier, on December 6, 1273, just months before he was to die, he had some type of experience that shook his world. He claimed to have had a direct vision of God during morning Mass. This vision caused him to abandon his work on the *Summa*, explaining why it remains incomplete. And it caused him to condemn his own lifelong pursuit—"All I have written seems as straw," he said. He then declared, "I now await the end of my life." At the Cistercian Monastery at Fossanova, Italy, he died on March 7, 1274. A certain ambiguity surrounds this event, leaving it open for interpretation. Some think Aquinas suffered a stroke. Regardless, Aquinas was wrong about his judgment of his work, as it has had much more staying power than mere straw. His work and his legacy have stood through the centuries.

A Note on the Sources

The massive *Summa Theologica* will run fifty large volumes when completed in its authoritative, scholarly edition. For summaries and selections in English, see Thomas Aquinas, *Selected Writings*, ed. Ralph McInerney (1999). Selections from the *Summa* dealing with the doctrines of humanity, sin, and salvation have been helpfully drawn together in A. M. Fairweather, ed., *Aquinas on Nature and Grace* (1954). Timothy M. Renick offers a brief and entertaining biography in *Aquinas for Armchair Theologians* (2002). Aidan Nichols, *Discovering Aquinas: An Introduction to His Life, Work and Influence* (2002), offers a lucid and concise treatment. For a larger discussion of Aquinas's role in the medieval church, see the books mentioned at the end of chapter 4.

6

THOMAS À KEMPIS
THE IMITATION OF CHRIST

Whoever desires to understand and take delight in the words of
Christ must strive to conform his whole life to him.

Thomas à Kempis

A Tale of Two Thomases. Perhaps that could be
one way to understand the church in the later
Middle Ages. The first Thomas is the one of the
last chapter, Thomas Aquinas. The second is the subject
of this chapter, Thomas à Kempis. Their difference jumps
to the surface when you contrast their two works, the
Summa Theologica and *The Imitation of Christ.* The first is
logical and exact, subpoint upon subpoint. The second
work does have a structure and organization, but it flows
more like a meditation, like a prayer, than a textbook.
The *Summa* as an intellectual tour de force demonstrates
the cogency of Christianity. *The Imitation* concerns itself
more with experience—one's own experience of God.
Both are manuals for beginners—a beginner might ap-
preciate *The Imitation* much more readily—on the road

to Christian truth. But their respective authors lead the beginner down rather different paths to that destination.

As Aquinas and his *Summa* represent the movement referred to as scholasticism, à Kempis and his *Imitation of Christ* represent a competing movement in the medieval era: mysticism. À Kempis's work actually stands at the culmination of this long stream of medieval mystics and has retained a place within the history of the Christian tradition as one of mysticism's most enduring and appealing texts. In the pages below we'll explore this life and this text, as well as the mystical stream in Christian thought.

À Kempis's Life and Times

Much of Thomas à Kempis's life remains a mystery. Some even question if he in fact authored the anonymous *Imitation of Christ*, though it is generally accepted that he did. Historians conjecture that he was born around 1380. He died either at the end of July or early August of 1471. Consequently, we find him at the period known as the high or later Middle Ages, a time of unrest on many fronts. Politically, the great Holy Roman Empire was beginning to feel the pressure. The pope in Rome was beginning to lose his grip on the nation-states to the north, such as Great Britain and Palatinate Germany. Theologically, the heretic John Wycliffe (1329–1384), who died just as à Kempis was in his early years, launched a challenge to long and deeply held positions of the Roman Catholic Church. In his books *On Divine Dominion* (1375) and *On Civil Dominion* (1376), he questioned papal authority and the church's hierarchy. He rejected the doctrine of transubstantiation (that the communion wafer and wine literally become the body and blood of Christ upon the priest's pronouncement) and proffered an early version of the view of the priesthood of all true believers.

Most importantly, and the primary reason the church condemned him as a heretic, he believed in the sole authority of Scripture in the life of the church, preaching from Scripture and serving as a principal force behind the first English translation of the Bible, the Wycliffe Bible (1384). Wycliffe was joined by Jan Hus (1372–1415), a contemporary of à Kempis. Hus mounted his challenge from Prague in Bohemia, the modern-day Czech Republic. He pushed for many of the same reforms that Wycliffe did. He, too, challenged the pope's civil authority, restricting him to matters ecclesiastical instead. He also argued for the authority of the Bible and committed such heretical practices as introducing congregational singing and doing away with priestly garments or vestments. Wycliffe died of

FIG. 6.1

Timeline of Thomas à Kempis's Life

1380	Born near Kempen, Cologne
c. 1393	After attending local school, sets out to find his brother, John
1393–1400	Studies at Deventer with Brothers of the Common Life
1400–1406	Takes residence at Mt. St. Agnes; receives ordination as priest; writes *The Imitation of Christ*
1406	Gains admission into Augustinian order
1432	Returns to Mt. St. Agnes; reenters Brothers of the Common Life; writes numerous biographies, histories, sermons
1471	Dies at Mt. St. Agnes, c. July

natural causes, but his bones were later exhumed and burned. Hus met his death as a martyr at the stake.

The fourteenth and fifteenth centuries were a time of tremors, signaling the upheaval that would come in the six-teenth-century Reformation. The tremors, however, were not limited to the political and theological realms. These centuries leading up to the Reformation were also a time of spiritual challenges. The church had grown quite large and wealthy and quite lethargic spiritually, causing even a casual observer to notice that something had gone amiss. A signif-icant representative of this spiritual challenge is Gerard Groote (1340–1384) and the new movement that he founded, the Brethren of the Common Life. Functioning much like a monastic order, the Brethren sought to recap-ture the early ideals of the monastic orders, summed up in the charge to be true disciples, imitators of Christ. A similar movement was founded for women.

Groote came from wealth and was well established in an academic career at the University of Paris and elsewhere when he broke away from it all to begin a new order devoted to poverty and service. He and his followers were to live sim-ply, devoted to Christ and following his example, literally, as unfolded in the gospels. A few centuries earlier, Francis of Assisi (1181–1226) had started a similar movement, known later as the Franciscan order, which stressed helping the needy and destitute—a legacy lasting to this day, as evi-denced in the Franciscan health care system and hospitals. Groote's attempts to reform the church largely revolved around what he saw as a misplaced devotion: that the church had more than one foot in this world. Consequently, he sought to return spirituality to the center of the Christian life. His movement is also referred to as the *Devotio Mod-erna*, or "New Devotion," emphasizing the critique on the institutional church on a spiritual front.

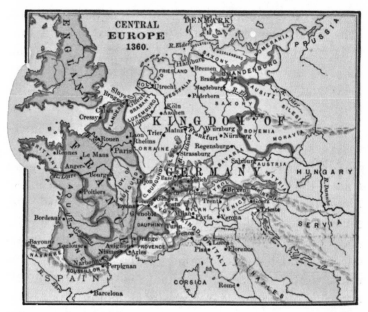

6.2 Fourteenth Century Europe

À Kempis found the life and legacy of Groote, who had died the year he was born, to be a most worthy example. À Kempis was born in Kempen in the Rhineland. He had an older brother, and both sons were dedicated to the Lord, a sign of deep piety in the à Kempis household. Medieval families could afford to give one child to the church, but rarely two. His older brother, John, had already joined the Brothers of the Common Life. After his early schooling, Thomas set out to find him and join him, traveling to Deventer, where Groote had founded the Brothers of the Common Life just a few decades earlier. John had already moved on from there, so Thomas set out again. When he did meet up with his brother, John counseled him to return to Deventer. Thomas spent seven years studying with the Brothers of the Common Life, enabling him to spend a brief time with Florentius (1350–1400), who had succeeded Groote as leader of the movement before his death. After this, he finally joined his brother, who was now prior of the Augustinian monastery at Mount St. Agnes. Thomas spent another seven years here, during which he was ordained as a priest and wrote a number of works, including *The Imitation of Christ*.

The monastery at Mount St. Agnes focused great attention on scribal duties, efforts that over the centuries of the Middle Ages preserved for the church and culture the great texts of the Greco-Roman world and the early church. And these efforts also resulted in a plethora of manuscripts of the biblical text. Thomas's work as a scribe was well known, and his duties of copying the Bible over the years had clearly left their impression. The monastery, however, was not immune to the politics that plagued the medieval era. The pope had placed the country under an interdict, that powerful tool that nullified ecclesiastical activity and the sacraments. The monks were forced to leave Mount St. Agnes. While in exile, Thomas's brother John took gravely ill for a number of months and was attended to by Thomas until his death. The interdict was lifted, and Thomas and the others returned. He remained there for nearly forty years until his death. At one point, he was elected Procurator, a post requiring him to handle civil affairs in the region. One of his biographers, L. A. Wheatley expresses how such a task did not suit him well, "as it required knowledge of temporal affairs, and with these he was not very conversant." So à Kempis went back to the life of a simple monk, the life he knew best. He died at the age of 91 or 92 sometime in the summer months of 1471.

In merely a few decades, Martin Luther would be at the center of the reform movement that prevailed. Luther and the Protestant Reformation, however, owe a great deal to these early, pre-Reformation attempts at reform. Luther and others built on the legacies of Wycliffe and Hus, and they also took advantage of the political mood that was quickly swaying from central power in Rome to regional and national power in the Rhineland and in England. On a popular level, Luther and the other Reformers were further able to gain great ground and to gain it quite quickly because of the efforts of Groote, à Kempis, and others. The *Devotio Moderna* had touched on a nerve from the perspective of the laity. It revealed a widespread dissatisfaction with the lackluster spirituality of the church, leaving the masses looking for something more than what the institutional church had to offer. À Kempis's *Imitation of Christ*, as well as many other similar texts, gained wide readership precisely because they so well met a need in the church at the time.

There was another reason that the mystics and their texts flourished in the later Middle Ages. Thomas Aquinas, as mentioned earlier, represents well the movement referred to as scholasticism. More often than not, the scholastics tend to be misunderstood and criticized. They are seen as reducing Christianity to mere intellectual propositions debated in the academic corridors and classrooms. They are often depicted as thriving on the splitting of theological hairs. The problem is that for some of the scholastics, the description is not too far off the mark. Unfortunately, the select few unjustly impugn the entire group and movement. At its best, scholasticism reminds us that Christianity is a rigorous faith, capable of withstanding intellectual scrutiny and offering a coherent worldview. At its worst, it reduces Christianity to a bunch of Spocks, ruled by the rational.

It was the worst side of scholasticism that fostered the counter-response of mysticism. From the days of the early church, a mystical strain may be traced through the history of the Christian tradition. This strain, however, reaches a zenith in the later Middle Ages. Among the many texts, two stand out: à Kempis's *Imitation* and an anonymous text, *The Cloud of Unknowing*, written sometime in the late fourteenth century. We have two faculties, *The Cloud* tells us—the power of knowledge and the power of love. Because God is so incomprehensible, the power of knowledge or the intellectual faculty fails to reach him. This is a not-so-subtle critique of Thomas Aquinas. The power of love, however, comprehends God perfectly and totally. What's more, *The Cloud* continues, "Every single creature, moreover, will know him differently. Thus each loving soul on its own can, through love, know him, who is wholly and incomparably more than sufficient to fulfill human souls or angels that could possibly exist." This brief glimpse at *The Cloud* reveals a great deal about mysticism and knowing God. For the mystic, the knowledge of God is personal, is experiential, and defies description. The favorite words of the mystic include *beyond* and *above*, *deep* and *immeasurable*, *more than* and *incomprehensible*, *inner* and *inmost*, *experience* and *devotion*. *The Cloud* counsels one not to use the intellect. You should be careful, it warns, "not to put any great strain on your mind" as you seek to know God. Instead, experience him.

À Kempis's manual for devotion, *The Imitation of Christ*, is a bit more concrete but shares much in common with *The Cloud*. But these are only two among many texts of mysticism. There were various strains in addition to Thomas à Kempis's Brothers of the Common Life and the community out of which came *The Cloud*. St. Francis represents another, as does Meister Eckhart (1260–1327), who eventually established a following in Strasbourg and in Germany at places like Erfurt, where Luther would study law. Mysticism also gave voice to many women in the church, such as Hildegard of Bingen (1098–1179), Julian of Norwich (1342–1413), Catherine of Sienna (1347–1380), and Marjory Kempe (1373–1433)—all of whom wrote widely read texts, mostly consisting of visions, and wielded great influence on the church. Other significant figures include Bonaventure (1221–1274), a Franciscan monk whose *The Mind's Journey to God* enjoyed a wide audience; Nicholas of Cusa (1401–1464), who wrote in his famous book, *On Learned Ignorance*, that we know by not knowing; and the so-called Victorines, Hugh (1096–1141) and Richard (1123–1173), who served at the abbey of St. Victor.

These mystical texts tended to overlook this world, pointing to the realities that lie beyond. Being lost in a heavenly vision had far more to offer than the grind of daily life. The mystics would look to nature, but tended to see it as primarily a revelation of things invisible. This approach's chief adherent is Francis of Assisi. One of his poems has come down to us, with significant modifications, as the hymn "All Creatures of Our God and King," which sees among the wind and breezes and clouds and rivers voices of praise to God. It wasn't nature in the grit and grime that the mystics were after; it was nature as a vehicle to express spiritual realities. In fact, Francis often retreated to the seclusion of forests, preaching to the animals and hearing God audibly communicate to him through them. The other element that defines mysticism, as mentioned above, is experience. God is not known in books, but in experience. Unfortunately, this supplanting of books sometimes included the Bible itself. God was seen as the living word still speaking, and speaking in a much livelier way than the written word in the pages of Scripture.

Not all of the mystics, or those who get categorized as mystics, followed suit. Bernard of Clairvaux (1090–1153) is a prime example. Often considered a mystic, Bernard does evidence a deep and vital piety in his work. But he anchored his devotion firmly in the Word of God and in the person of Christ. Next to Augustine, Bernard is the one whom Luther quotes the most, with one of his favorite texts being Bernard's poem-turned-hymn "O Sacred Head, Now Wounded." Bernard first acknowledges, "Mine, mine was the transgression, but thine the deadly pain," before crying out, "Lord, let me never, never outlive my love for thee." Bernard's other classic text is *On Loving God*. Here he offers reasons why we should love God and commends both what he terms a *rational* and a *spiritual* love of God. Contemporary language might render this as loving God with mind *and* heart.

It also must be pointed out that while the mystics tended to overlook this world for the next, some of them emphasized service and work in this world as the means of honoring God as his disciple. This recaptured one of the early emphases of the monastic orders. Finally, the mystical tradition also emphasized prayer. Reaching back to the beginnings of monasticism, prayer, alongside of service, was another central activity. The monasteries offered opportunity for significant, uninterrupted times of prayer throughout the day. As the different monastic institutions flagged in this area over time, prayer became less an essential and more a perfunctory activity. By the time of the later Middle Ages, the mystics were seeking to regain the role of prayer in the life of the church, and some of their texts, consequently, amounted to prayer manuals. This, as well as many of the other elements of mysticism, finds expression in à Kempis's *Imitation of Christ*. It was not, however, the only book he wrote. Following is a brief look at his other contributions before a discussion of his classic text.

À Kempis's Thought and Writings

While many of his works are not well known, besides *The Imitation of Christ*, à Kempis wrote nearly thirty volumes.

These include his *Speeches and Meditations on the Life of Christ* and his *Soliloquy of the Soul*, practical works originally written for his own edification that were then used to aid his fellow monks in their devotion to God. In these he extols the virtue of utter abandonment of the self before God. He also wrote a work entitled *Sermons to Novices*, a precursor to *The Imitation*. Here is a most memorable line addressed to the novices, the ones taking the first probationary step to becoming a monk: "It's not the hood that makes the monk, for that can be worn by an ass." À Kempis was after the inner life and not the outward appearance or motions. He also wrote a history of the *Devotio Moderna* movement, *A Chronicle of Mount St. Agnes*, as well as no fewer than eleven biographies of the movement's founders and significant figures such as Gerhard Groote and Florentius. À Kempis's historical writings offer more than chronicles; he used them to commend Groote and the *Devotio Moderna*. In his *Life of Florentius*, he not only describes cloister life, but also uses Florentius as a platform to instruct novices in the proper ways of monastic life. Consequently, even his historical writings may be classified as devotional texts.

"Never be altogether idle, but to be either reading or writing, or praying or meditating, or laboring on something for the good of the community," à Kempis once advised the novices—advice he himself took fully to heart. For in addition to his work as biographer and historian, he also wrote a number of meditations and devotional texts. Among them is *Life of a Good Monk*, where he writes, "Every day, every hour, resign thyself without delay," sentiments repeated in *The Imitation*. In his *Valley of the Lilies*, à Kempis criticizes the anti-intellectual tendencies of his fellow mystics as he writes, "Woe to the priest who is unlearned and without the sacred books; he is often a cause of error to himself and to others. A priest without holy books is like a soldier without arms, a horse without a bridle, a ship without a rudder, a writer without pens, or a bird without wings." Obviously, books were not looked down upon by à Kempis; instead, he extolled the virtues of learning. One of the things he enjoyed most about the monastery at Mount St. Agnes was the library, and he cherished his own scribal duties in adding to its collection. He even transcribed copies of his own books—a task that gives new meaning to the concept of being self-published.

Much of à Kempis's thought in his various writings comes into crystallized expression in *The Imitation*. By far his most well-known work, this book not only represents the best of his thinking but, according to most historians, serves as the best representative of the teachings and thought of the Brothers of the Common Life. It is a landmark book that not only took its place in its own time, but continues to hold sway. In the pages to follow, we will take an in-depth look at this classic work.

À Kempis's *Imitation of Christ*

While *The Imitation of Christ* is a meditation, it certainly has structure and organization. À Kempis constructed his work in four books or sections. The first is "Counsels on the Spiritual Life," followed by "Counsels on the Inner Life" and "Counsels on Inward Consolation," and concluding with "On the Blessed Sacrament." The first three books all point to mysticism's emphasis, discussed above, on the personal, inner, and spiritual life. À Kempis quickly takes one's eyes off this world and off material things and realities, turning them to spiritual matters and the world to come. Each of these four books consists of a number of short sections he calls chapters, most of which contain five to ten paragraphs. Throughout each book, à Kempis quotes or refers to Scripture quite heavily—over one thousand times (if one includes the apocryphal books) by some counts. The books form a logical progression and read a bit differently from each other.

Like a composer of a prelude to a grand symphony, Thomas à Kempis packs as much as he can into the very first chapter (which shares the title of the book, "On the Imitation of Christ") of the very first book, "Counsels on the Spiritual Life." Particularly, three things stand out. First, after starting with a biblical quotation, he cuts right to the chase: we are to follow Christ's "life and way if we desire true enlightenment and freedom from all blindness of heart." It's not merely Christ's teachings that are to be followed; we are to pattern our lives after his. À Kempis, to put the matter another way, was asking, "What Would Jesus Do?" long before those four words became a popular saying. This leads him then to mention the second crucial point, that it's not a matter of words or right thinking, but of life and right living. As he writes, "Of what use is it to discourse learnedly on the Trinity, if you lack humility and therefore displease the Trinity? Lofty words do not make a man just or holy; but a good life makes him dear to God." Unpacking these sentences, we find à Kempis taking aim at the scholastics and those who emphasize getting theology right. À Kempis makes Christianity a matter of lifestyle, not doctrine. Finally, he ends this brief chapter with the appeal to resign this life for the next, commanding, "Strive to withdraw your heart from the love of visible things, and direct your affections to things invisible." This is, as he titles this first book, a discussion on the spiritual life.

The best way to achieve this spiritual life becomes the exclusive domain of the monastery. Consequently, most chapters in book 1 deal with monastic life either explicitly or implicitly. À Kempis commends the monastic practices of

Bible study, prayer, and prolonged times of solitude and silence; of a life of contrition, asceticism, and self-denial; and of resignation from the world. He is careful to point out that the spiritual life does not necessarily come automatically in the monastery. "The habit and tonsure," he observes, "are of small significance; it is the transformation of one's way of life." It is in imitating Christ that one achieves the spiritual life. Yet it becomes obvious that à Kempis offers little help as to how that is accomplished outside the monastery walls. Here we see the great medieval divide between this world and the one to come or between the spiritual labors of those in the monastery or the church and those merely temporal and material labors of everyone else.

Book 2, "Counsels on the Inner Life," is the shortest of the four books with only twelve brief chapters. Here à Kempis interprets Christ's teaching in Luke 17:21 that "The Kingdom of God is within you," as a call to forsake the world and seek Christ within our own hearts. He then calls upon his own soul, his own inner life, "Prepare your heart for your Divine Spouse, that he may deign to come to you." Consequently, book 2 offers a battle cry against anything that may compete with the heart's devotion to Christ. Following chapters preach submission and purity of mind and unstinting devotion to and love of Christ.

The third book, "Counsels on Inward Consolation," is a dialogue between Christ and the "Disciple" and constitutes the largest of the four books at fifty-nine chapters. Here the reader listens in as the Disciple seeks God in prayer and listens to his answers. In the process, he offers a dynamic view of revelation, as chapter 3 in this section bears out. After the Disciple demonstrates that he is ready to hear Christ's instructions, à Kempis has Christ saying, "I have taught the Prophets from the beginning of the world, and I do not cease to speak to all men today." But, Christ acknowledges, many are hardened to the voice by being more entranced by the world than by God, following "the desires of the body, than the good pleasure of God." As this chapter progresses, it becomes clear that the words of Scripture are not to be known on the surface, but experienced in life, through Christ's "visits in life," which come in the two ways of trial and consolation. The one corrects faults, while the other encourages "progress in virtue." The ultimate virtue, as the dialogue brings us to see, is love. In typical mystical language, à Kempis has the Disciple pray, "Deepen your love in me, O Lord, that I may learn in my inmost heart how sweet it is to love, to be dissolved, and to plunge myself into your love. Let your love possess and raise me above myself, with a fervour and wonder beyond imagination." The key mystical terms are all present: *deep*, *above*, *beyond*, and *inmost*.

As à Kempis moves through book 3, he adds more virtues to love, including humility, joy, patience, obedience, dependence upon God, gratitude, and resignation of the self and of the world. Many of the ways he expresses these virtues have direct bearing on the close-knit community of the monastery. À Kempis speaks with a pastoral heart. After running through these virtues, he acknowledges that he has set the bar quite high, and consequently he counsels, through the words of Christ, not to despair. So he encourages that patience is necessary with our own selves, advising that when we do fall, "Let it pass. It is not your first mistake, or anything new; nor, if you live long, will it be your last." There's plenty of realism mixed in with his spiritual platitudes, plenty of grace and forgiveness accompanying law and duty.

Book 4, "On the Blessed Sacrament," seems to take a different course from the previous three as à Kempis moves from matters inward and personal to matters public and corporate in taking the sacrament. Yet here, too, he

continues his focus on the personal. The dialogue is continued between Christ and the Disciple, and this book, like
the third book, is a prayer and response. The book begins
by cobbling together some gospel texts culminating in
Christ's words at the Last Supper (Luke 22:19) and Christ's
proclamation as the bread of life in John 6. In this book, the
medieval context of *The Imitation* comes into clear view. Utilizing typology, the Disciple contrasts the ark of the covenant
with the body of Christ. Then he turns to the relics: "Many
make pilgrimages to various places to visit the relics of the
Saints, wondering at the story of their lives and the splen-
dour of their shrines; they view and venerate their bones,
covered with silks and gold." While this may be a meaningful experience for such pilgrims, it does not compare in the
least to the sacrament of the Lord's Supper. "Here on the
altar are You Yourself, my God," à Kempis declares, reflecting the doctrine of transubstantiation, which holds that the
wafer and the wine literally become the body and blood of
Christ. Further expressing medieval Roman Catholic
thought on the sacraments, à Kempis looks to the sacrament
as the indispensable means of grace, as the means of salvation. Theologians refer to this stance as sacramentalism or
sacerdotalism. À Kempis puts it this way: "For as often as
you consider this Mystery and receive the Body of Christ,
you set forward the work of your redemption, and become a
sharer in all the merits of Christ."

The sacrament is the ultimate step in discipleship. There,
à Kempis argues, the outer self is left behind and the inner
self is joined in mystic communion with Christ. There, as à
Kempis exclaims throughout book 4, the heart is united
with Christ. It is on this spiritual plane that true discipleship occurs and life really matters. Consequently, he cannot
keep himself from ending *The Imitation* with one final swipe
against an intellectual faith, writing in the very last sentence

of the book, "For were the works of God readily understandable by human reason, they would be neither wonderful nor unspeakable."

Earlier in *The Imitation*, à Kempis writes, "Let the love of
pure truth draw you to read." He has the Bible in mind as
he offers this counsel. That the pages of *The Imitation* over-
flow with biblical quotations demonstrates that his own love
of the truth led him to read again and again. In fact, in the
course of his scribal duties à Kempis not only read the Bible
but more than likely wrote it out multiple times. He feels
compelled, however, to take his readers beyond the words
of the Bible as he aims to take them into communion with
its author, with Christ. À Kempis wrote originally to his literal disciples, those under his care at the monastery.
Through the centuries and numerous reprints—one seminary library I visited has two entire shelves filled exclusively
with nineteenth-century editions of *The Imitation*—à Kempis has picked up a great many more disciples along the way.

À Kempis's Legacy

The mystics enjoyed wide readership during the Middle
Ages, and they (as well as more contemporary mystics) continue finding a mass market now, which is certainly true of
The Imitation of Christ. The contemplative life has always had
its appeal. As our own age becomes increasingly technolog-
ical, fast-paced, and materialistic, the appeal grows all the
more strong. The challenge presented by the medieval mystics and mysticism, however, is the relationship of faith to
reason and especially to the Bible and its propositions. By
lodging everything in subjective experience, one loses the
checks and balances offered in a faith firmly anchored in
the Bible. The contemporary mystic Thomas Merton
(1915–1968) illustrates the problem well. He finds as much

insight into spirituality in Buddhism as he does in Christianity, especially in his later writings. He might speak well, even to the point of persuasion, of the soul's devotion to God, but he undercuts his own advice by his inability to ground it in sound doctrine.

We should be careful, however, not to paint the medieval mystics with a broad brush. There was much diversity among the movement. Bernard of Clairvaux was not quite the same as Thomas à Kempis, who was not quite the same as the anonymous author of *The Cloud of Unknowing*, and so on. They shared similarities, to be sure, but there were also differences. In its finest hour, mysticism reminds us of the importance of devotion to God, that he is indeed the living word. It reminds us that at most times we are rather full of ourselves and fixated on this world and that we would be far better off to take the eternal perspective. Mysticism wasn't always, however, at its finest. More often than not, the mystics grounded their devotion in personal experience rather than on Scripture. Further, they tended not to offer much help for living out one's Christianity in the world. They commended escapism instead, fostering a withdrawal from the world in order to get in touch with the true reality. Consequently, one might experience God in the moment of the vision or in times of spiritual ecstasy, but translating that experience into the daily grind did not always come easily, if it came at all.

Speaking of its more immediate legacy, mysticism and à Kempis clearly impacted the Reformation. As mentioned above, the fourteenth and fifteenth centuries witnessed the tremors that would eventuate in the cataclysmic change brought about in the sixteenth century. One of the reasons that the Reformation was able to spread so quickly among the laity was the widespread dissatisfaction with the spiritual life of the institutional church. Gerard Groote, Thomas à Kempis, and others gave voice to that dissatisfaction that was felt by so many of the laity. In response, à Kempis and his book offered a moral or spiritual reform. Instead of following in the trappings of wealth and power that had come to stain the church, he pointed to a different way of life. He pointed to the model of the Suffering Servant, the one who had not a pillow upon which to lay his head.

The Brothers of the Common Life had won many adherents and sympathetic followers at a distance, and à Kempis had found many eager readers of his classic text. But he and his book were unable to bring about the significant, substantive, and lasting reform that would come only in the next century. Perhaps it was because his attempted reform of the church's spirituality lacked a theological foundation. In other words, the problem with Roman Catholicism in the later Middle Ages was more than a problem of a lackluster spirituality; it was at base a misguided theology that had sent the church astray. Thomas à Kempis had correctly diagnosed the problem by only half, and his prescription followed accordingly.

Others would offer a more charitable view. *The Imitation of Christ* has had a long and rich history and is in fact widely reprinted today. Many may use it devotionally, and not a few have found it to be a challenging and even life-changing book. Whether one takes a more or less charitable view of à Kempis and his book, he and it take a rightful place in making a significant contribution to the history of the Christian tradition. It offers great insight not only into the mysticism of the later Middle Ages, but also into those perennial desires embodied by that particular movement. In one of à Kempis's shorter writings, entitled *Opera Minora*—Latin for "Minor Works"—he advises, "He who knows and reads many things, and does not act up to what he has known and learned, departs hungry and empty from a good table." The one Thomas, Aquinas, spent a great deal of time teaching what we should know; the other Thomas, à Kempis, reminded us to live according to what we know.

A Note on the Sources

From the many English editions of à Kempis's classic work, see Leo Sherley-Price, *Thomas à Kempis: The Imitation of Christ* (1972). For a study of mysticism, see Bernard McGinn, *The Flowering of Mysticism: Men and Women in the New Mysticism (1200–1350)* (1998). For a source of primary readings, see Ray C. Percy, ed., *Late Medieval Mysticism*, in the Library of Christian Classics: Ichthus ed. (1995). See also the sources mentioned at the end of chapter 4.

PART THREE

THE REFORMATION

7

MARTIN LUTHER
THE SMALL CATECHISM

Martin Luther the Reformer is one of the most extraordinary persons in history and has left a deeper impression of his presence in the modern world than any other except Columbus.

Ralph Waldo Emerson

I haven't yet progressed beyond the instruction of children in the Ten Commandments, the Creed, and the Lord's Prayer. I still learn and pray these every day with my Hans and little Lena.

Martin Luther, 1531

Just about everyone in and out of the church knows something about Martin Luther. He nailed, although some historians are wondering if that is indeed the case, the Ninety-Five Theses to the church door at Wittenberg, igniting the Protestant Reformation that swept across Europe and profoundly changed life in the modern world. At the time, of course, the earth-shattering impact of that singular event was not fully felt. As Pope Leo X, from the de' Medici family of Florence whose patronage of the arts led to commissioning Michelangelo to paint the Sistine

Chapel ceiling, declared upon reading a copy of the Ninety-Five Theses, "Ah, the ramblings of a drunken German—he will think differently once he sobers up." Luther never sobered up.

Luther's Life and Times

From the posting of the Ninety-Five Theses, Luther moved to debating the spirit behind his protest, namely, that the church at the beginnings of the sixteenth century had drifted far from its scriptural moorings. These debates set him at odds with his own church. Luther hoped to be a catalyst for reform from within. He truly thought that,

FIG. 7.1

Timeline of Martin Luther's Life

1483	Born in Eisleben, November 10
1501–1505	Attends University of Erfurt; receives B.A. and M.A.
1505	Makes vow during thunderstorm, July 2; enters monastery
1507	Receives ordination
1509	Receives B.A. in Bible
1510	Makes pilgrimage to Rome
1511	Enters Black Cloister, monastery at Wittenberg
1512	Receives doctorate in theology; lectures at Wittenberg
1517	Posts Ninety-Five Theses on church door, October 31

given the rightness and weight of his arguments, he could convince the church of its error and lead it home, back to its biblical roots. Instead, Leo X issued a papal bull, declaring Luther a heretic and demanding he recant or be excommunicated. "Arise, O Lord," the decree began, calling Luther a wild boar loose in God's vineyard of the church and trampling the precious gospel underfoot. Such irony. Luther responded in typical fashion. With the expiration of the sixty-day time limit for Luther to recant, he burned it, along with an effigy of Leo X. Subtlety was never Luther's weakness.

Leo X demanded that Luther be delivered to Rome. Had he been sent there, following a mock trial, he certainly

1520	Writes Three Treatises
1521	Condemned as a heretic following Diet of Worms, April 16–18
1522–1546	Preaches and teaches at Wittenberg; engages in extensive writing
1524	Publishes first hymnal
1525	Marries Katharina von Bora, June 13
1525	Writes *The Bondage of the Will*
1529	Writes *The Small Catechism*
1534	Publishes complete German Bible (New Testament in 1522)
1545	Publishes complete edition of Latin writings
1546	Dies while traveling in Eisleben, February 18; buried at Wittenberg

would have been put to death. But Frederick the Wise, the ruler of Saxony (where Luther lived and worked), intervened, simply refusing to send him to Rome and instead arranging for him to appear before the Imperial Diet, scheduled at Worms in the spring of 1521. Here, before Charles V, dukes and politicos, and a host of church officials, Luther was given a singular choice: recant all of his writings or be condemned a heretic and be executed. And, here, he delivered his famous "Here I stand" speech. He could not recant, he told the imperial audience, because his conscience was held captive to the Word of God. In just a short time, from October 31, 1517 to April 18, 1521, Luther gave the entire Western world a new religious option. Between paganism and the Roman Catholic Church, one could now be a Protestant. A whole new world was discovered.

Yet Luther's life did not come to a halt at Worms. Through the craftiness of Frederick the Wise, who arranged to have Luther "kidnapped" and squirreled away in his castle at Wartburg, Luther survived his death sentence, living a very full and eventful life until 1546. He did not simply pass off the scene after 1521. In fact, precisely during these later years Luther accomplished some of his greatest work. In 1525, he wrote the theological classic *The Bondage of the Will*. One year earlier, he had published his first hymnal, but it would not be until 1527 that he would write "A Mighty Fortress Is Our God," arguably the greatest hymn of the Christian church. He taught literally hundreds of students at the University of Wittenberg, students who went on to fill pulpits across Germany and throughout Europe. He fought and toiled and built a new church, centered on the Bible and devoted to the gospel. It is estimated that Luther published about two works a month from the late 1510s on, an almost unfathomable amount of literature. These include a number of timely tracts, mostly aimed at criticizing the papists, but they also include some timeless works, such as his *Three Treatises*, published in 1520, and *The Small Catechism*, 1529.

Luther has been memorialized in two films. First, there was the classic black and white, followed by a more recent blockbuster simply titled *Luther*. Both poignantly depict the inner and outer struggles of Luther with the church. Both interpret Luther *theologically*. That is, as far as Hollywood movies go, they get Luther rather well. Yet both movies have a significant shortcoming. They both stop abruptly at 1529 with the triumph of the Augsburg Confession. To be sure, that event signaled the victory of Luther and the gospel, as well as it served politically to solidify the German lands in their anti–Roman Catholic stance. But Luther's life did not end abruptly in 1529. He lived another sixteen years, during which he continued to face trials and challenges. His health declined. He constantly had to defend himself from misinterpretation and overzealous followers. He wrote prodigiously. He watched his beloved thirteen-year-old daughter take ill. He was at her side when she died. And through it all, he remained faithful. He persevered. These last years of Luther's life should not be overlooked.

It is further worth noting that Luther did not appear in a vacuum. He built on the reform efforts of figures like John Wycliffe and Jan Hus who had preceded him. His ideas also came at a time when there was a widespread dissatisfaction with the spirituality of the church. Further, there was a breakdown of the hold of the Holy Roman Empire and of the pope on Europe. Luther's time was of the rise of the nation-state and the emergence of modern national identities, not to mention that the invention of the printing press and the dawn of the Renaissance were all conspiring to bring about a new world. Luther's reforms and thought are best seen against this backdrop of

7.2 Wittenberg, 1546

the sea change occurring in the Western world, a change that he himself had no small part in bringing about.

Luther's Thought

The so-called Reformation *sola*s, a series of Latin expressions, well summarize Luther's thought. The first of these, *sola Scriptura*, or "Scripture alone," speaks to the authority of the Bible. Luther uses this term to counter the claim that the church's authority lies in its councils or in the teachings of its bishops or popes. He did not mean, as some wrongly interpret him, that the church does not need tradition or creeds. Further, he did not mean that individual Christians simply need their Bibles and can do quite well without teachers and preachers. For Luther, *sola Scriptura* concerns the church's authority, which rests only on the Word of God. In looking at Scripture, especially in the teachings of Paul, Luther finds the central teaching that salvation is by faith alone through grace alone, which he summarized as *sola fide* and *sola gratia*. Luther once said, "The one doctrine that I have supremely at heart is that of faith in Christ, from whom, through whom, and unto whom all my theological thinking flows back and forth day and night." This reflects the crucial doctrine of justification by faith alone.

This doctrine rests on the next *sola*, *solus Christus*, which means "Christ alone." This idea counters the prevailing doctrine and practice in medieval times of looking to the sacraments for righteousness and salvation. Instead, *solus Christus* captures the biblical teaching that there is only one mediator between God and humanity, the God-man Jesus Christ (1 Tim. 2:5). The last *sola* relates to one of Luther's most profound teachings, what may be called the doctrine of vocation. In Luther's day, the Latin word *vocatio*, meaning

FIG. 7.3

The Reformation *Solas*

Sola Scriptura	Scripture Alone
Sola Fide	Faith Alone
Sola Gratia	Grace Alone
Solus Christus	Christ Alone
Soli Deo Gloria	For the Glory of God Alone

"calling," was applied only to those who took up churchly professions. Outside the convent, monastery, church, and cathedral, people merely worked. Inside those walls, however, they served God. Luther did something revolutionary when he applied the term *vocatio* to all the spheres of life, to the professions, and to all nature of work. This means that being a spouse, parent, or child can be viewed as a calling, and so can being a peasant farmer or a merchant. The final *sola* expresses this as *soli Deo gloria*, "for the glory of God alone." These words conveyed for Luther the idea that all of life and all in life could be done for the glory of God; it was not only church work that mattered.

One significant area of Luther's thought that often garners attention, but can be confusing, is his theology of the cross. To understand this, we first need to see Luther's thought on sin. Two Latin words describe his view. First, there is the word *radix*, which means "root." We are not sinners because we sin. Instead, we are sinners because of who we are; we are sinners at the root. Luther learned this truth from Augustine, who had learned it from Paul in such texts as Romans 5:12–21. If our problem were sins, we could overcome them by heaping up merits to tip the balance in our favor. But if our problem is in being a sinner, then we need a grace that transforms us.

The second Latin word to describe Luther's view of sin is *incurvitas*. This refers to our tendency to be inward, to look to ourselves, to trust in ourselves. We are "curved in." Now we can understand Luther's theology of the cross. The cross, Luther said, was God's NO to our *incurvitas*, God's NO to our attempt to merit salvation, to earn grace. The theology of the cross takes our attention off of ourselves and puts our attention, and our hope, squarely on Christ and his work on the cross. Luther's theology of the cross points us away from any feeble attempts to merit God's favor, attempts that ran rampant in Luther's day. Instead, his theology of the cross teaches us to rest in Christ.

Luther also made significant theological contributions in his teaching on the priesthood of believers, the church, and worship. All of these teachings are worthy of further

FIG. 7.4

Reformation Catechisms

Lutheranism	*The Small Catechism*	1529
	The Large Catechism	
Reformed	[John Calvin's] *Catechism of the Church of Geneva*	1541
	The Heidelberg Catechism	1563
Presbyterian	*Westminster Shorter Catechism*	1648
	Westminster Larger Catechism	

exploration. The Reformation *sola*s and Luther's theology of the cross, however, well summarize a great deal of his teaching, as well as that of the Reformation in general. They continue to be helpful teaching tools for today's generation of the church and serve well as a foundation of sound doctrine. Luther viewed doctrine as crucial for the church's survival, and precisely this conviction led to *The Small Catechism*.

Luther's *Small Catechism*

Though *The Small Catechism* might not be the first choice of Luther's texts for our survey of theological classics—that place would easily be afforded to *The Bondage of the Will*—it certainly merits attention. One reason is that the catechism reveals a side to Luther that many simply do not know, but one that they should. In addition to his work as theologian and church reformer, Luther was one of the first Christian educators. He regularly, practically daily, taught his own children and those of Wittenberg in his home. The catechism represents the sum and substance of that teaching. But it was not the only thing he taught. He so enjoyed Aesop's Fables that he published his own translation of them.

Another reason is that this work represents a significant genre of Reformation literature: the catechism. The word *catechism* literally means "to sound out" and connotes learning by speaking. The teacher would ask a question and the pupil would sound back the question with a prescribed answer. This technique relies on repetition and memorization. Frequently used in medieval times, it was not an innovation with Luther. He and the other Reformers made some significant and unique contributions by aiming their catechisms at children. And of course, their catechisms had a radically different content from that of the medieval counterparts.

Further, Luther's catechism merits our attention for its ability to challenge its readers of all ages. Luther himself once remarked, "I haven't yet progressed beyond the instruction of children in the Ten Commandments, the Creed, and the Lord's Prayer"—the three texts that form the hub of his catechism. We need to remember a little about Luther for the full impact of his words to take effect.

Dr. Martin Luthers kleiner Katechismus
(1529)

Das erste Hauptstück
Die zehn Gebote

Das erste Gebot
Ich bin der Herr, dein Gott;
du sollst keine anderen Götter neben mir haben.

> Was ist das?
> Wir sollen Gott über alle Dinge fürchten, lieben und vertrauen.

Das zweite Gebot
Du sollst den Namen deines Gottes nicht mißbrauchen.

> Was ist das?
> Wir sollen Gott fürchten und lieben,
> daß wir bei seinem Namen nicht fluchen,
> schwören, zaubern, lügen oder trügen,
> sondern denselbigen in allen Nöten anrufen,
> beten, loben und danken.

7.5 Luther's *Small Catechism*

His was an admirable intellect. He translated the New Testament from the Greek into the German in merely two months—and it was a good translation. He wrote prodigiously, filling over one hundred hefty volumes in his collected writings. If the catechism had the ability to challenge Luther, especially given his résumé, then there just might be something for others.

Finally, the catechism merits attention as it embodies some of Luther's finest writing. His other works reflect the heat of battle as polemical treatises largely aimed at academics and church leaders. In *The Small Catechism*, Luther speaks with clarity, simplicity, and grace.

"We cannot perpetuate [doctrine]," Luther once remarked in a sermon, "unless we train the people who come after us and succeed us in our office and work, so that they in turn may bring up their children successfully." He saw firsthand the disaster that waited down the road for generations that were pointed in the wrong direction. He belonged to a church that, at the beginning of the sixteenth century, was reaping an unfortunate harvest sown over the previous centuries. When he formed the new church, he was determined to see it pointed in the right direction. So he continued in his sermon, "Therefore let every head of a household remember that it is his duty, by God's injunction and command, to teach or have taught to his children the things they ought to know." "The youth," he said on another occasion, "is the church's nursery and fountainhead." He knew that if the Reformation were to have any lasting impact, then the church must programmatically, purposefully, and explicitly teach the next generation.

Of course, the next generation needs to be taught the right things. In the late 1520s, Luther did a great deal of touring the *Evangelische*, or gospel churches (soon to be named Lutheran), in Germany. What he found discouraged him. Describing conditions as deplorable and wretched, he noted that the laity knew very little of sound Christian doctrine and that the clergy were not much better off. Upon returning to Wittenberg, he tasked his lieutenants with developing a curriculum to remedy the situation. Unhappy with their efforts, he undertook the work himself, producing *The Large Catechism*, sometimes called *The German Catechism*, and *The Small* (or *Child's*) *Catechism* in 1529. The first was a manual for pastors, containing extensive discussions of Christian ethics, doctrine, and practice. The latter was a much smaller version for children, an aid for the heads of households to teach their children what they ought to know. Both texts revolve around the Ten Commandments, the Apostles' Creed, and the Lord's Prayer. In his treatment of these, Luther offers a summary of Christian ethics, doctrine, and practice.

Luther once remarked that "whoever knows well how to distinguish the gospel from the law should give thanks to God and know that he is a real theologian." The relationship between law and gospel receives extensive treatment in his thought. The law, according to Luther, is to convict and to show our sin. Further, the law accuses us, even torments and horrifies us. Yet in the midst of the law, grace abounds. Consequently, Luther begins with the law, the Decalogue, as offering a clear portrayal of both sin and grace.

A definite pattern emerges from this section of the catechism that follows through the entire text. He cites the commandment, then asks simply, "What does this mean?" ("*Was ist das?*"). Admittedly, the repeating question lacks originality and variety. Whatever qualities may be lacking in the question, however, he supplies in the answer. Concerning the first commandment, "You shall have no other gods," Luther asks his trademark question, "What does this mean?" and then follows by answering, "We should fear, love, and trust God above all things." This tendency to pull a positive teaching from the negative command reverberates throughout his discussion of the Ten Commandments. In fact, he adapts the first part of the answer to the question concerning the first commandment, "We should fear and love God," to begin the rest of the answers. Luther is keeping those children and us from simply viewing the Ten Commandments as an external law code. He also keeps us from moralism, by grounding the basis and motive for keeping the Ten Commandments in nothing other than an expression of grateful obedience to God. According to Luther, one's relationship to God centers on an obedient Christian life.

His treatment of the fifth commandment (the Lutheran numbering scheme differs from that of the rest of Protestantism), "You shall not kill," represents this part well. Luther informs us, "We should love and fear God, and we should not endanger our neighbor's life, nor cause him any harm, but help and befriend him in every necessity of life." In keeping with his teaching on social ethics, he appeals to Christ's summary of the law as loving God and loving one's neighbor as the orienting principle for one's treatment of others. Keeping the commandment not to take the life of another probably does not present the large majority of us with much of a challenge. But it is quite a challenge to keep the spirit of this law, and, as Luther expressed, to help and befriend our neighbor in every necessity of life. Turning to the fourth commandment, we should not only keep from despising our parents, but "honor, love, serve, obey, and esteem them." We should not only refrain from bearing false witness about another, as the eighth commandment requires, but also "apologize for him, speak well of him, and interpret charitably all that he does." And so Luther walks through the Ten Commandments.

Using the familiar words of the Apostles' Creed, Luther explains basic doctrines of the persons and work of the Trinity in the second part of the catechism. In unfolding the words of the creed, Luther groups its separate phrases around the three articles of creation, redemption, and sanctification. These three works reflect the particular involvement of the members of the Godhead: God the Father, the Son, and the Holy Spirit. Beginning with God as Creator, Luther makes the broad and general opening statement of the creed, "I believe in God, the Father almighty, maker of heaven and earth," rather concrete and personal for his young auditors. To be sure, this means that God created the entire, vast universe and everything in it merely by his word. But what impresses Luther here is not so much this fact, but that, in the words of his answer to the question, "What does this mean?" "God created me and all that exists." He continues to exclaim that he believes that God "has given me and still sustains my body and soul, all my limbs and senses, my reason and all the faculties of my mind, together with food and clothing, house and home, family and property." God also "provides me daily and abundantly with all the necessities of life, protects me from all danger, and preserves me from all evil." All of this attests to God's "pure, fatherly, and divine goodness and mercy, without any merit or worthiness on my part." Consequently, according to Luther, only one response is adequate: "to thank, praise, serve, and obey him."

In the second article, concerning redemption, Luther supplements the words of the Apostles' Creed in his answer by using phrases from the Nicene Creed. While the Apostles' Creed does mention the deity of Christ by referring to him as "our Lord," it does not emphatically do so. One can also infer Christ's humanity from the various phrases of the creed, but again it lacks an emphatic statement concerning his humanity. Luther, borrowing from the Nicene Creed, makes these implicit teachings explicit in his answer by referring to Christ as both "true God" and "true man." The bulk of Luther's answer, however, expounds Christ's work of redemption on our behalf. This work, which "delivered me from all my sins, from death, and from the power of the devil," enables me "to live under him in his kingdom," and also challenges me "to serve him."

Luther turns his attention to the work of the Holy Spirit and the believer's sanctification in the last article. His answer concerning the meaning of the final phrases of the Apostles' Creed reveals that the Holy Spirit enables me to come to Christ. Not only has the Spirit "called me through the gospel," but he also "enlightened me with his gifts, and sanctified and preserved me in the true faith." This gift of the Spirit extends beyond me to the entire church, which he also sanctifies and preserves. Luther ends each of these three sections with the words, "This is most certainly true." Familiar words, like those of the Apostles' Creed, sometimes risk the danger of glib expression. Luther's parting words in explaining what the creed means remind us of the absolute importance of these doctrines to the Christian's life.

Luther next turns to address the spiritual discipline of prayer by looking to the model words of Christ. He viewed prayer as an essential part of the Christian life in part simply because it was commanded by God. But also, he recognized it as a necessary means to living the Christian life. In *The Large Catechism*, he explains how this is so: "Nothing is so necessary as to call upon God incessantly and drum into his ears our prayer that he may give, preserve, and increase in us faith and obedience." Prayer further causes us to reflect on our needs. "Each of us," Luther exhorts, "should form the habit from his youth up to pray daily for all his needs."

We do this not because God needs to be made aware of our needs, but to impress upon us our dependence upon him.

Luther also recognized prayer as a discipline with a promise. As Luther expresses at the end of the section on the Lord's Prayer in *The Small Catechism*, God "himself commanded us to pray like this and promised to hear us." Luther derives the basis for this statement from the first petition, "Our Father, who art in heaven." When asked what this means, the answer given is: "Here God would encourage us to believe that he is truly our Father and we are truly his children in order that we may approach him boldly and confidently in prayer, even as beloved children approach their dear father." Consequently, we pray because God commanded us to, because we need to, and because we can be confident that our prayers are heard. As Luther works through each of the phrases of this prayer, he sometimes asks an additional question ("How is this done?") after the familiar "What does this mean?" In the process, Luther finds the Lord's Prayer to be a perfect model of prayer, as its various petitions provide an ample reminder of "all the needs that continually beset us, each one so great that it should impel us to keep praying for it all our lives."

After the Lord's Prayer, Luther continues his teaching on Christian practice by addressing the sacraments. In later editions of the catechism, Luther attached sections addressing morning and evening prayers and prayer at the dinner table. Interestingly, Luther advises not only a prayer of blessing before the meal, but also a prayer of thanksgiving after the meal. He further attached sections on the "Table of Duties." These final points consist "of certain passages of the Scriptures, selected for various estates and conditions of men, by which they may be admonished to do their duties." In each of these entries for the table of duties, Luther offers not one word of his own advice. He simply collects various Scripture passages, letting the Bible inform us of our duty in our various roles in life. *The Small Catechism*, though a short text, consequently comes fairly close to a comprehensive statement on Christian ethics, doctrine, and practice.

Luther's Legacy

While Luther wrote the first catechism of the Reformation, he did not write the only one. Zacharias Ursinus and Kaspar Olevianus produced the *Heidelberg Catechism* for the Reformed churches in Switzerland, and in addition to writing the *Westminster Confession of Faith*, the Westminster Assembly also composed both the *Shorter* and *Larger Catechisms*. These texts were intended to accomplish what Luther's did—summarize and present doctrine for the next generation. While retaining some of the elements of Luther's catechism, they also do some things differently. Before tackling the Ten Commandments, the creed, and the Lord's Prayer, the *Heidelberg Catechism* offers a thorough discussion of doctrine under three heads: "The Misery of Man," "The Redemption of Man," and "Thankfulness." In these three sections, the catechism is first teaching that we need the gospel; second, declaring the gospel; and third, instructing how to live in light of the gospel, to live a life of obedience in gratitude for the work that Christ has done. The first question and answer, famously called "Heidelberg One," vies as the most eloquent and profound writing in all of theological literature:

Question: What is your only comfort in life and in death?

Answer: That I with body and soul, both in life and death, am not my own, but belong unto my faithful Savior Jesus

Christ; who, with his precious blood, hath fully satisfied for
all my sins, and delivered me from all the power of the devil;
and so preserves me that without the will of my heavenly Father, not a hair can fall from my head; yea, that all things
must be subservient to my salvation, and therefore, by his
Holy Spirit, he also assures me of eternal life, and makes me
sincerely willing and ready, henceforth to live unto him.

What Heidelberg One accomplishes in its eloquence, the
first question and answer of the *Westminster Shorter Catechism* accomplishes in its concision. "What is the chief end
of man?" it asks before responding, "Man's chief end is to
glorify God and enjoy him forever." The last very carefully
chosen seven words waste not a single letter in answering
the ultimate question of life. The catechism proceeds to lay
out in brief the doctrinal content of the *Westminster Confession of Faith*, discusses the requirements of the Ten Commandments—the summary of the moral law—treats the
Lord's Supper, and ends with the petitions of the Lord's
Prayer. For centuries, these catechisms and confessions of
the Reformation era defined the church's theology, practice,
and worship—even to the present day, though not as preva-
lently. They became guides, not just for the learned theologians, but also for the faithful in the pews. They show that at
the end of the day the Reformation entailed a serious return
to the Bible, a thoroughly constructed theology, and a
deeply felt pastoral concern for the worship and piety of the
saints. And this legacy may be traced back to Martin Luther
and his bold move on October 31, 1517.

Luther's impact on the church today goes deep and wide.
In fact, it is so pervasive that, ironically, it more than likely
goes largely unnoticed and is in some cases sadly unappre-
ciated. When members of congregations sing hymns of
praise to God in their common language, Luther should be

7.6 Martin Luther

thanked for his innovation. Prior to his day, the singing was done by a select few and the words were Latin, which, except for a few words here and there, were unintelligible to the audience of worshipers. Of course, Luther would not have viewed his reform as an innovation, but merely as a return. Others prior to Luther had attempted this reform of the church's practice. For instituting the same practice in Prague, Jan Hus was condemned and martyred, and his followers were not able to bring about any widespread reform.

Following Luther, however, congregational singing in the people's own language became the norm for the Protestant congregations, although it would be another two centuries before the English-speaking church would develop its own rich tradition of hymnody.

Luther also oversaw the return of and the centrality of the sermon to the church service. Prior to his day, the Mass was the service. Luther pioneered the modern church service, although he preferred to have the preaching first, followed by hymns, prayers, and the Lord's Supper. He also failed to see the virtue in long-winded sermons. Half an hour at most he thought to be a good length for a sermon, once remarking on his own preaching that "when I have nothing more to say, I stop talking."

Luther further left a lasting impact on missions. Although historians rightly attribute the beginnings of the modern missions movement to William Carey at the turn of the eighteenth century, Luther's legacy here, though little known, is worth retelling. Wittenberg attracted hundreds of students from all over Europe who had come to be trained by Luther. They heard him preach and lecture, and they sat with him around his breakfast and dinner table. And then they returned to their homes, many coming from Catholic lands and not enjoying the protection of a Frederick the Wise. In fact, Luther's first hymn commemorated the martyrdoms of some of his former students who had boldly and sacrificially taken the Reformation to their homelands.

Luther also laid the foundation for the pastor's home. The Roman Catholic Church held to a celibate clergy. Luther found the practice to be unbiblical and began performing marriages for clergy before 1520. He would help nuns escape convents, sometimes play matchmaker, and then perform weddings. One particular group that Luther aided in escaping made their getaway in a fish merchant's wagon of barrels that had contained herring. One particular nun from that group proved especially elusive when it came to Luther's matchmaking efforts: she would settle only for Luther himself. Eventually the confirmed bachelor succumbed and was wed on June 13, 1525. Martin Luther, former monk, and Katharina von Bora, former nun, established one of the first parsonages in modern history. Their mutual love and dependence (Luther referred to her as "Katie my rib") became and remains a model for the all-important marriage and family life of those in ministry.

Leo X could not have underestimated Luther more when he dismissed the German monk in the winter months of 1517. Becoming a household name and one of the most significant figures in Western history, Luther has left a lasting impact on the world. He inspired John Calvin in Geneva, who in turn inspired John Knox in Scotland, who in turn inspired others, and everywhere reform of the church followed. Obviously, Lutheran denominations owe their existence to their namesake. In reality, all Protestant denominations should be saying a grateful thanks for him. He led the church in a return to Scripture and the formation of the doctrines and practices that define Protestantism. His writings, including *The Small Catechism*, continue to impact the church. Luther was undoubtedly right: in order for the Reformation to have a lasting impact, it must reach the next generation. Now, five centuries later, the various Protestant traditions thrive and the various *sola*s of the Reformation continue to define the evangelical church.

A Note on the Sources

For an overview of Luther, see Stephen J. Nichols, *Martin Luther: A Guided Tour of His Life and Thought* (2002). Among the many biographies, see Martin Marty, *Martin*

Luther (2004). For a brief, fascinating recent treatment of the Reformation, see Patrick Collinson, *Reformation* (2004). For the writings of Luther, see Timothy Lull, *Martin Luther's Basic Theological Writings* (1989). *Luther's Small Catechism and Explanation* is available through Concordia Publishing House (1991).

8

John Calvin
Institutes of the
Christian Religion

> What help is it, in short, to know a God with whom we have nothing to do? Rather, our knowledge should teach us fear and reverence; secondly, with it as our guide and teacher, we should learn to seek every good from him and, having received it, to credit it to his account.
>
> John Calvin, *Institutes*, I, ii, 2

> What Thucydides is among Greeks, or Gibbon among eighteenth-century English historians, what Plato is among philosophers, or the *Iliad* among epics, or Shakespeare among dramatists, that Calvin's Institutes is among theological treatises.
>
> Benjamin B. Warfield, *Works*, V, 374

Mention John Calvin and you're sure to get a reaction. He is at once loved and vilified—or, in the words of historian Lewis Spitz, adored or abhorred. In his own day, his detractors composed a little jingle (an anti-commercial, if you will) for him that ran,

"Better with Beza in hell than with Calvin in heaven," a reference to his understudy Theodore Beza. This antagonistic trajectory has a rich and long history, viewing Calvin as intolerant and narrow-minded, even cruel and vindictive. A quite recent treatment of the Reformation, in expressing this view of Calvin, labels him the "quintessential control freak." To be sure, there are those inside and outside the church who think the world and theology would be better off if Calvin had gone the way of law or humanist studies, his original plan, and not the way of theology.

On the other hand, there are many who love him, finding great insight within his teachings. Charles Haddon Spurgeon, belonging to this group, once remarked, "The longer I live the clearer does it appear that John Calvin's system is the nearest to perfection." J. I. Packer once remarked, "Calvin sent me claiming, and reclaiming, all life for God in Jesus Christ, and valuing all goodness and beauty as his gift." Benjamin Breckinridge Warfield adds that he is the apex of theology, and that Calvin's *Institutes of the Christian Religion*, his major theological treatise, stands unparalleled in scope and influence. What makes the work more marvelous still, as Warfield points out, is that when Calvin wrote the first edition in 1535, he was only twenty-five years old and, further still, he had been a Christian just over a year. Reason to marvel, indeed.

Unlike fellow Reformer Martin Luther, no formal denomination takes his name. Yet many would be quick to identify themselves as Calvinists and adherents to Calvinism, indicating an affinity with his teachings, specifically regarding the doctrines of grace. He certainly has been the source of much controversy and debate. Unfortunately, however, many times the debate generates much more heat than light, and Calvinism and Calvin himself are tossed around with little or no reference to his actual writings and teachings. And, more often than not, when Calvin the person is spoken of, it is often as caricature or selectively, even by those who befriend him.

One of Calvin's many accomplishments included the founding of an academy in Geneva, the city of his ministry. As testimony to the perennial nature of students, we have some drawings of a lecturing Calvin, sketched by one of his many students. His signature cap graces his head, his pointed nose and scrawny pointed beard filling in the rest, as a somber and even emaciated-looking Calvin lectures on. This student's drawings in the margins of his notebook resemble the formal portraits to a certain extent, but certainly there is a bit of exaggeration. At the very least, they are, by their nature as amateur drawings, lacking the full dimension of the person. These drawings provide an outline or a glimpse, but they go only that far, as the real and true Calvin eludes them. And so it is with most treatments of Calvin, by both friends and foes alike. It would be impossible in a single chapter to challenge the stereotypes and merely surface portraits of Calvin and of Calvinism that tend to dominate the current discussions. In this chapter, however, some of the portrait can be better filled in; some of the life of Calvin, as it were, can be injected into the discussion of his teachings. If Warfield is right, that Calvin's *Institutes* occupies an unrivaled place in the history of theology, then taking a deeper look into both it and its author may very well be called for.

Calvin's Life and Times

Though Calvin spent most of his adult life in Geneva, Switzerland, his home, and more than likely his heart, was in France. Jean Cauvin was born at Noyon, northeast of Paris, on July 10, 1509, the same year that Luther was lecturing

Fig. 8.1

Timeline of John Calvin's Life

1509	Born in Noyon, France, July 10
1523–1528	Studies at University of Paris; takes B.A. and M.A.
1529–1531	Studies at University of Orleans
1531–1534	Receives appointment to College of Royal Lecturers
1532	Publishes first book, *On Seneca's De Clementia*
1534	Conversion sometime in May
1535	Publishes first edition of *Institutes of the Christian Religion*
1536	Arrives in Geneva on July 15
1538–1541	Expelled to Strasbourg
1539	Publishes *Commentary on Romans*—beginning of publishing numerous commentaries and sermons
1540	Marries Idelette de Bure
1541–1564	Ministry at Geneva
1542	Only child born and dies
1549	Wife, Idelette, dies
1559	Establishes Academy of Geneva; publishes last edition of the *Institutes*
1564	Dies at Geneva, May 27; buried in unmarked grave per his wishes

at Erfurt and growing more and more disillusioned with the Roman Catholic Church. In France, however, no such tremors of reform could be felt as of yet. Calvin was baptized in the local Catholic church and apparently destined, if his father's intentions are any indicator, for the priesthood. His mother, rather devout as she faithfully took her children by the relics in the cathedral, died when he was three. Some parallels to Luther may be found here. Both fathers were beginning to bring some respectability to the family name, though Calvin's father was much more connected, and both fathers wished for their sons to take the family name to further heights—even sacrificing for their educations to help them do so. Both sons could be compared as well. Bright beyond their years and classmates, both sons excelled, and both sons did indeed take the family name to new heights— just not in the way that either father could have conceived or even wished. Luther, however, was to take the path of law and veered into the priesthood; Calvin was to take the path of the priesthood and nearly veered into law.

His name was entered as a cathedral chaplain at Noyon, a position that both provided funding for his education and secured him a future position among the French clergy. Calvin went off to Paris. Historians differ as to the very first stage of his schooling, but all acknowledge that in his teens he made his way to the University of Paris, specifically at the College de Montaigu. Here he was introduced to the writings of the church fathers, notably Augustine. He also gained exposure to the writings and thought of Luther. The university's theology faculty was tasked by the King of France with refuting the German heretic, which made for much discussion in and out of the lecture halls. Apparently little interested in the discussion, Calvin became intrigued by the study of law and what was then being termed the new learning, or the humanism of Renaissance scholarship over against the scholastic methodology of the medieval era. Calvin, consequently, headed south to the University of Orleans, but not before he had taken his master of arts degree from the University of Paris in 1528. Eventually, Calvin returned to Paris, taking a position at the recently established College of Royal Lecturers.

One of the cries of this humanism that so attracted Calvin was the Renaissance slogan *ad fontes*, Latin for "to the fount" or "source." For the humanists, the fount was the great literary sources of ancient Greece and Rome. The quintessential humanist scholar, Desiderius Erasmus (1469–1536), exemplified this approach when he produced his Greek New Testament in 1516—it should not go without notice that in the following year, Luther sparked the Reformation with the publication of the Ninety-Five Theses. (Curiously enough, 1516 was also the year that coffee was introduced to Europe from the Arab world, leading one to argue that coffee and the Greek New Testament combined brought about the Reformation.) Rather than advocating the reading of the Latin translation of the New Testament, or Latin commentaries on the New Testament, the cry of *ad fontes* led to the reading of the New Testament in the original Greek.

In Calvin's case, he was led back to one of the Roman sources of law and political philosophy, the writings of Seneca (4 B.C.–A.D. 65). Calvin, with his doctorate in jurisprudence, published his first book in 1532, a commentary on Seneca's *De Clementia*. He was signaling his presence to the intellectual world of Europe. But as he walked by the bookstalls of Paris, he didn't exactly see the book fly off the shelves. Other things would be in store for Calvin.

While in Paris, Calvin befriended William Cop and William Bude; both came under the influence of Luther, and both had a hand in pointing Calvin in a different direction from law and academic life in Paris. Due to a Lutheresque sermon preached by Cop in Paris, which many scholars think also bears the imprint of Calvin, both Cop and Calvin were prompted to flee Paris and an enraged clerical authority. Sometime in early 1534, Calvin's interest in the ideas that captivated Luther took a much more decisive turn as he, in his own words, threw over his "stubborn addiction" to Roman Catholicism and the "superstitions of Popery," one of his favorite expressions. "God by a sudden conversion," Calvin recalls in the preface to his Psalms commentary, "subdued and brought my mind to a teachable frame." Calvin was brought to Christ sometime in May. On May 21, 1534, he made it official, striking his name from the cathedral registry in Noyon. Adherents of the reform movement in France did not enjoy the protection of a Frederick the Wise that Luther and his cohorts did in Germany. Calvin tried to stay in France for a time and did, remaining under the radar by moving about frequently. As Francis I turned up the heat on the reform movement, however, Calvin thought it best to head for Switzerland, eventually settling in Basel in January 1535. There he took an assumed name, Martinus Lucanius, the first being in honor of Luther and the second a rearrangement of his own name in Latin. It was also during this tumultuous time that he wrote and published the first edition of the *Institutes of the Christian Religion* in August of 1535. Editions, including ones in French, continued coming off the printing press until 1559.

A short time of religious amnesty allowed Calvin to return briefly to Noyon, where he settled his family's estate. He then intended to travel to Strasbourg, Germany, to join with Martin Bucer (1491–1551), who had established the Reformation there. The highway, however, was closed due to wars between Charles V, the Holy Roman Emperor, and Francis I of France. Calvin, consequently, took quite a circuitous route, heading far south and eventually east to the city of Geneva, Switzerland. He stopped at the home of William Farel (1489–1565), intending only to spend the night and to leave the next day for his trip north to Strasbourg. Farel had other plans. He implored Calvin to stay, and when he did not prevail he pulled the trump card, informing Calvin that by leaving he would bring down God's judgment upon himself. The "overnight stay" lasted from 1536 until Calvin's death in 1564, with the exception of a three-year exile to the city of his intentions, Strasbourg.

Calvin and Farel set out to establish Geneva as a city thoroughly committed to the Reformation. In fact, more than likely, they pushed too fast and too hard. Calvin was, after all, a Frenchman and not a native, not to mention that he was still in his twenties. Consequently, both Farel and Calvin found themselves out of favor with the city council and were exiled to Strasbourg. Ironically, this disfavor finally allowed Calvin his wish to join forces with Martin Bucer. They certainly enjoyed working and thinking together. Years later, Bucer made his way to Cambridge, becoming a leading figure in that city and in the university's pivotal role in the British Reformation. While at Strasbourg, Calvin wrote and taught, publishing his commentary on Romans (1539), among other works. He also pastored a congregation of about five hundred French exiles. By 1541, however, the pressures were on Geneva to capitulate to Roman Catholicism, and no one seemed capable of keeping the city moving ahead in the direction of reform. Calvin was called back under the condition that he would be given free rein in ordering the church. He returned and stayed in his adopted city until his death in 1564.

He left Geneva a bachelor and returned from Strasbourg a married man. She was Idelette de Bure Storduer, the former wife of Jean Storduer, an Anabaptist leader who at one time had debated Calvin in Geneva. The family, including two sons, eventually moved from their Anabaptist views, joining Calvin's refugee church in Strasbourg. In the spring of 1540 Jean Storduer died of the plague. Marrying had not been very high on Calvin's agenda. He once wrote, "I shall not belong to those who are accused of attacking Rome, like the Greeks fought Troy, only to be able to take a wife." Circumstances had a way of changing his bachelor predilections, and he married the widow Idellete. They had one child, a son, who died shortly after birth. Nine years into the marriage, Idellete herself died in 1549. Their marriage was filled with much sorrow, for Idellete never really enjoyed good health as the aftereffects from her own suffering of the plague that had taken her first husband. But it was also filled with much joy as Calvin reveled in her love. At the time of her death, Calvin wrote to Farel, "I do what I can to keep myself from being overwhelmed by grief."

After returning to Geneva in 1541, Calvin stepped up his already rigorous schedule. He was preaching five times a week, writing, debating, and organizing the church. Once Mary ascended the throne in 1553 in England, she returned the church to Rome, undoing the reforms of Henry VIII and Edward VI and instigating an intense time of persecution. Those who could fled. Many of these "Marian Exiles," as they came to be called, arrived in Geneva, eager to sit at the feet of John Calvin and ready to learn as much as they could about the reform of the city in the hopes of someday returning to England and putting the same principles into practice. Chief among this group was John Knox (1514–1572), who spoke of Geneva as a perfect little school of Christ. After Mary's death, the exiles made their way back to Great Britain. As for Knox, he attempted to do for Scotland what Calvin was doing in Geneva. Eventually, Knox would be instrumental in founding Presbyterianism.

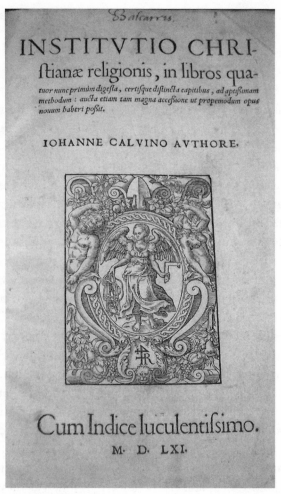

8.2 1561 Latin edition of Calvin's *Institutes*. Courtesy of Montgomery Library, Westminster Theological Seminary.

Not all of Calvin's reforms were religious. During the medieval era, literacy had plummeted. Calvin did much to nearly eradicate illiteracy in Geneva. Women and wives enjoyed little protection under law. Largely through Calvin's efforts, laws against wife-beating and laws to protect the financial estates of wives and widows were enacted and became model legislation for the modern world. Even to this day, Geneva is seen as a model humanitarian city and culture, if not the very symbol of it—a legacy owing in no small part to the decades of Calvin's influence. In 1559, Geneva's Academy, or university, was established, and Calvin again was at the fore. Calvin's legacy in Geneva and beyond, however, is strongest as a theologian, exegete, and churchman.

Not always in the best of health, there is a reason his portraits reveal an emaciated-looking figure. Calvin eventually succumbed to his own frailties in 1564 at the age of fifty-four. He suffered through what he called "diverse maladies," including gout and intestinal parasites, as well as tuberculosis. He was so weakened by the end of his life that often he had to be carried to the classroom lectern or into the pulpit. He preached his last sermon in February 1564, but continued to work mostly from his bed as he persevered through the winter and spring. He died on May 27, 1564. On May 2, he wrote his last letter to Farel, his longtime friend who had conspired to keep him in Geneva. "I draw my breath with difficulty," he wrote, "and every moment I am in expectation of breathing my last. It is enough that I live and die for Christ, who is to all his followers a gain both in life and in death."

Calvin's Thought and Writings

One of the little-known facts about Calvin is his intense missionary zeal. Recently scholars, with Peter Wilcox and Frank A. James III leading the way, have drawn attention to this element in Calvin. By the mid-1550s a mere handful of underground churches were known to be in existence in France. Estimates place that number at over 2,000 by 1652. The home base for this activity was Geneva, and at the center of the enterprise was Calvin. Given Francis I's hatred toward the Reformed church, all of these records had to be kept secret and squirreled away, but now they are coming to light. Calvin trained missionaries and kept tabs on them through reams of correspondence as they were in the field, and the city of Geneva funded the whole project. Calvin lived in Geneva, but his heart was turned to France. Some of these churches, especially in regions where some freedoms could be enjoyed, saw their membership grow into the thousands and multiplied in making daughter churches. Calvin and Geneva also sent missionaries as far away as Brazil. Calvin often spoke of the gospel being for all peoples. He put those words into action.

This missionary zeal is worth mentioning because when the subject of Calvin's thought comes up, the topics of predestination, election, and limited atonement all invariably come into play. And almost as invariably, critics point to how Calvin and Calvinism's particular take on these doctrines squashes evangelistic and missionary zeal. At least as far as Calvin himself is concerned, such a caricature could not be further from the truth. His missionary endeavors and fervent preaching all attest to his commitment to proclaiming the gospel. While the caricature needs to go, it is true that Calvin gives great prominence to the doctrines of grace, and chief among them is the doctrine of election and predestination.

Calvin's thought on these doctrines has been popularized in the acrostic TULIP, standing for the five points of Calvinism. Two caveats are in order. First, it is important to realize that the five points were derived after Calvin's death and further that the acrostic came about much later still. Second, the five points are nevertheless in fact rooted in and reflect Calvin's teaching. The five points are a way of summarizing the Canons, or authoritative teachings, of the Synod of Dort (1618), a meeting of the Reformed churches held in that

FIG. 8.3

TULIP

T	Total Depravity
U	Unconditional Election
L	Limited Atonement
I	Irresistible Grace
P	Perseverance of the Saints

city in the Netherlands. The teaching of Jacobus Arminius (1560–1609), the namesake of Arminianism, prompted the Synod of Dort. Arminius, originally committed to the Calvinist position, began to question Calvin's understanding of election and related doctrines. His followers drew up what they called *The Remonstrance* in 1610, just after Arminius's death. Consisting of five points, *The Remonstrance* challenged the teachings of Calvin and reflected an emphasis on human freedom and choice in matters of salvation. This caused a stir in the churches in the Netherlands, resulting in the council in 1618. There a group of theologians responded to *The Remonstrance,* in an extensive document called *The Canons of Dort.* Running over thirty pages in all, this lengthy document has been summarized in the few phrases that fill out the acrostic TULIP. In fact, the acrostic doesn't quite capture the true flow of Dort. ULTIP is the true order; U, which stands for "unconditional election," was the starting point of the discussion.

A great debate revolves around whether or not Calvin held to TULIP or if it was a later development by his followers. Paul Helm has decisively shown not only did Calvin hold it, but that this summary of the doctrines of grace ran fairly deep for him. The trouble for those who would like to see Calvinism as a later development contrary to the founder's teachings is that they're looking for the wrong language. They do not see Calvin talk a great deal about limited atonement (which is true) and then conclude that Calvin did not and would not hold to it (which is not true). Calvin's starting point for the whole discussion was election. Consequently, Dort starts there as well, in laying out the doctrine of unconditional election. This understanding of election and predestination holds that nothing within human beings warrants God's election or choosing of them for salvation. It is, instead, unconditional, based merely on the mysterious good pleasure of God. Calvin admits that this is a tricky doctrine; in fact, he refers to it at one point as "strange and hard." It is, nevertheless, central to his theology.

This election is procured through the work of Christ on the cross in his atonement. Calvin was quick to emphasize the work of the Trinity in salvation. God the Father decrees salvation (election), Christ the Son provides salvation (redemption and atonement), and the Holy Spirit applies salvation (regeneration and faith). Election, consequently, raises the question of the nature of the atonement. Following Augustine, Calvin viewed it as sufficient for all and as undergirding the universal call of the gospel. In fact, the language of Dort on this point insists that because of the universal sufficiency of Christ's death, the gospel is to be preached promiscuously—not a word often used in theological discussions—to all peoples. But, also following Augustine, Calvin raises the question of Christ's intent when he went to the cross. He died, Calvin concludes, not only to make humanity savable, but to save; he intended to secure salvation, not just make it available.

This work of Christ is necessary because fallen humanity is unable to overcome sinfulness, which leads to the T, "total depravity." It is curious to note that when Calvin's doctrine of humanity is discussed, total depravity is typically the only element that gets mentioned. Calvin's thought, however, is much more complex. He indeed taught total depravity, but he also stressed humanity's dignity, derived from being created in the image of God. Dignity and depravity almost seem contradictory, but they are not. Seeing both together reveals the true complexity of Calvin's understanding of humanity. These twin doctrines also provide for the rich social engagement that one finds in the Calvinist tradition.

The I of TULIP speaks to what theologians refer to as efficacious grace (or "irresistible grace"). Those whom God calls will be saved. Again, Dort holds that this is done in such a way that humans are not mere "stocks and blocks," not mere unthinking automatons. Lastly, the P stands for "perseverance of the saints" or, as J. I. Packer prefers, "preservation of the saints." This latter point became a crucial piece dividing the Calvinist tradition from that of Arminianism and of later Wesleyanism, representing the thought of John and Charles Wesley. In this tradition, one can lose his salvation; in Calvinism, one cannot. As Calvin writes in the *Institutes*, reflecting on John 10:28–29, "As Christ teaches, here is our only ground for firmness and confidence: in order to free us of all fear and render us victorious amid so many dangers, snares, and mortal struggles, he promises that whatever the Father has entrusted into his keeping will be safe" (III, xxi, 1).

One other point concerning the doctrines of grace in Calvin's thought is in order. Luther focused heavily on the doctrine of justification by faith. Calvin wholeheartedly agreed with him and gave a great deal of attention to the doctrine. Revealing his skills as a logician, Calvin spoke of the fourfold cause of justification. The *efficient cause* of justification is the mercy and free love of God. The *material cause* is the reconciling work of Christ on the cross. The *formal* or *instrumental cause* is faith, a work produced in us by the regenerating power of the Holy Spirit. The *final cause* is God's glory. Ultimately, salvation demonstrates God's justice and holiness and elicits the praise of his goodness. Salvation is entirely the work of God, which theologians refer to as *monergism*, referring to salvation as the work of one being, namely, God.

Calvin, however, liked to think of salvation in broader terms than justification. His broader conception may be termed union with Christ, which has been heralded as one of Calvin's great achievements. His notion of union with Christ offers a unified perspective on the Christian life, viewing justification as only the beginning, which results in a changed life and in a life of grateful obedience. Life after justification is referred to by theologians as *sanctification*. Calvin, however, tends not to make a sharp distinction between justification and sanctification. Instead, he views entering and living the Christian life as one continuous whole, with the operative factor in both being grace (*Institutes*, III, xi, 2).

The doctrines of grace constitute only one of the many dimensions to Calvin's thought. The Reformers devoted a great deal of energy to the discussion of the true marks of the church. Luther's list kept growing as he got older. When Calvin weighed in on the discussion, he mentioned three: the two sacraments of the Lord's Supper and baptism, preaching, and church discipline. Each of them represents a crucial component of Calvin's thought.

Calvin did not attend the Marburg Colloquy in 1529, where Martin Luther and Ulrich Zwingli, the Reformer in the Swiss city of Zurich, disagreed over the nature of the Lord's Supper. But he did have much to say on the subject. Calvin held to what might be called the "spiritual presence" view. When we partake of communion, it is as if Christ were present in the elements in a spiritual sense. Or, perhaps expressing it better, we at communion are transported to heaven to the presence of Christ. Much later after Marburg, Luther read Calvin's view on the Lord's Supper and commented, "I might have entrusted the whole affair of this controversy to him from the beginning. If my opponents had done the like, we should have soon been reconciled." When one considers the implications of the break between Luther and Zwingli, among them the Thirty Years' War, that statement is monumental.

As for preaching, Calvin saw nothing more necessary for Christian growth and nothing more central to the life of the church than preaching. He himself had plenty of practice. His first task as a preacher was to exposit the Bible. He, well schooled in the languages and in interpreting literature, gave great attention to exegeting the text. He produced commentaries on nearly every book of the Bible, and his sermons, on such books as Ephesians and Job, are still reprinted today. His commentaries marked a new path for biblical interpreters. Prior to Calvin, much commentary work tended toward spiritualizing or allegorizing the text, or simply offering devotional and mystical reflection. Calvin started us on the path of what today is called the grammatico-historical literary approach. This approach looks at the historical and cultural context, the mechanics of grammatical structures and meanings of words, and the genre of the text. Because of Calvin's attention to these legitimate textual questions that we should be asking as we read the Bible, his commentaries are amazingly helpful in getting the meaning of the text, even nearly five hundred years later.

Among other aspects of his thought, church discipline ranked high for Calvin. This was one of the reasons that he was first exiled from Geneva. He returned on the condition that the city officials take church discipline seriously. Thus the Consistory was established, a body of church and community leaders that reviewed cases of church and civil discipline. Calvin's three marks of the church—the sacraments, preaching, and church discipline—burrowed deep into the British wing of the Reformation, especially among John Knox and among the Puritans.

Calvin also spoke much of the law of God or the Ten Commandments, articulating what has been called the threefold use of the law. The first role of the law is to convict of sin, while the second is to supply normative laws for a civil society. So far Calvin agreed with Luther. But Calvin went one step further, adding his third use, that the law is a guide for life, especially the Christian life.

Had it been up to Calvin, he would have been quite content in the life of the cloistered academic. He once said, "The object of [my] desire . . . [would be] to seek some secluded corner where I might be withdrawn." Providence, as Calvin would like to say it, had something different in mind. Instead of his quiet corner, Calvin lived in the maelstrom of the Reformation. He brought the capabilities of his incisive mind and devoted heart to the life of the church. And nowhere is his impact on the church more felt than in his classic work, the *Institutes of the Christian Religion*.

Calvin's *Institutes*

The *Institutes of the Christian Religion*, first published in 1535, was originally intended as a primer for new Christians. Not incidentally, its author also happened to be a new Christian himself. In six chapters, he offers the basics of doctrine and Christian practice. As his thought matured and he moved into the role of a significant theologian of the Reformation and trainer and educator of pastors, he saw the need to expand his primer. After repeated editions, both in Latin and in French, with the last one coming in 1559, the *Institutes of the Christian Religion* encompassed four books, eighty chapters, and, in its scholarly English edition, 1,521 pages. No longer merely a primer on the Christian life, the *Institutes* ranks as one of the most significant theological treatises in the Christian tradition.

The final edition is structured around four books, or four major sections. These sections follow the formula of the Apostles' Creed. Book 1 treats the doctrine of God, book 2 discusses the doctrine of Christ, book 3 deals with the Holy Spirit, and book 4 concludes by looking at life in the church, what Calvin calls "The Society of Christ." In reflecting the structure of the Apostles' Creed, the *Institutes* also takes on a Trinitarian structure. Further, it relates all doctrine to redemption and grace, or Calvin's notion of union with Christ. We could break down the massive *Institutes* even further, by seeing the whole work as addressing, according to Calvin, two essential questions: the knowledge of God and the knowledge of ourselves. Calvin's way of structuring his theology marks a break from the scholastic method that Thomas Aquinas employed in the *Summa Theologica*. In fact, Calvin differs from Aquinas and most other medieval theologians in many ways beyond structure. Like the medievalists, Calvin, too, quotes Augustine often; he even approvingly quotes some of the medieval authors—Bernard of Clairvaux for one. Unlike them, however, Calvin tends to root his theology deep not only in biblical texts, but also in the arguments and themes of Scripture. As his commentaries serve as pacesetters for contemporary evangelical biblical scholars, so his theology sets the standard and provides the model for theologians.

Calvin begins his *Institutes* with his two essential questions: "Nearly all the wisdom we possess, that is to say, true and sound wisdom, consists of two parts: the knowledge of God and of ourselves." As for the first, he once said that pursuing the knowledge of God would be enough to fill over a hundred lives. It is interesting to note that he starts with the knowledge of God—not, as Aquinas does, with the existence of God. Calvin scholar Ford Lewis Battles points out that this reveals the centrality of revelation in Calvin's thought. Rather than emphasize reason and philosophy and the classical arguments for God's existence, Calvin starts with and focuses on the revelation that God gives to humanity. Calvin takes a top-down approach, not a bottom-up. In other words, true wisdom originates in God as he discloses himself to humanity, not as humanity reasons up to arrive at God.

Calvin looks at these questions—the knowledge of God and of ourselves—in an interrelated manner: looking at one reveals the other. We know God first as Creator, through general revelation in nature and the conscience, and second as Redeemer, through Scripture and Christ. Consequently, then, we know or understand ourselves only in this light, as created and, for God's elect, as redeemed. To know ourselves as created is to know ourselves as dependent upon God, as in the image of God, and, through the fall of Adam, as sinners. The image of God gives us our dignity, the fall our depravity. We should have given God gratitude and responded in obedience to his law. Instead, our first parents disobeyed and the relationship with God was severed. Nevertheless, Calvin maintains that we still have the witness of God as Creator, palpably felt through what he termed the "sense of the divine" (*Divinitatis sensus*), "that some conception of God is ever alive in men's souls" (I, iii, 2). And so continues book 1.

Calvin then transitions from the knowledge of God as Creator to the knowledge of God as Redeemer as he begins book 2. This concept was revealed in the law. In fact, it was revealed from the very beginning, in what theologians refer to as the *protoevangelium*, or first proclamation of the gospel in Genesis 3:15. It came to fruition in the incarnation and the work of Christ on the cross as taught in the gospel. Book 2 is devoted to the person and work of Christ, God the Redeemer, and his work in accomplishing redemption. Book 3 looks at how this accomplished redemption is applied. Here Calvin takes an extensive look at faith and justification, all the while underscoring the work of the Holy Spirit.

It was John Donne who put it so well: "No man is an island." Calvin agrees. For him, it is not so much the issue of redeemed individuals as it is the new redeemed community of the church or, in Calvin's terms, the new society. We do not become, at conversion, unconnected islands. Rather, we become members of the new community, of the body of Christ; Christianity is social, not individual. Book 4, consequently, treats the church and our new life in it. Calvin could not stress the church enough. He once said that whoever wishes to call God his Father must have the church as his Mother—strong words for a Protestant. Calvin had a great deal to say about the church, not the least of which concerns the pure church in light of the corruption of the church in Roman Catholicism. In this final section, he also speaks of church discipline and the sacraments, before ending the *Institutes* with a look at civil government and the church's role in society and culture.

By no means has Calvin exhausted the essential questions of the knowledge of God and of ourselves. He has, however, given the church, both of his day and down through the ages, much to think about as we pursue the answers.

Calvin's Legacy

The five-century celebration of Calvin's birth looms on the horizon: no doubt 2009 will see conferences and publications commemorating the event. Like so many of the other figures we have explored so far, it is difficult to overestimate the legacy of John Calvin. And as mentioned at the beginning of the chapter, that legacy is looked on both favorably and not so favorably.

One aspect of Calvin's legacy that should not go unnoticed is his role as churchman. Though there is no formal denomination that takes his name, Calvin clearly is the father of the many Reformed denominations and, especially through his influence on John Knox, the various denominations of Presbyterianism. His thought significantly influenced many of the confessions and catechisms of the Reformation era, and his *Institutes of the Christian Religion* remains standard fare for college and seminary reading to the present day. He influenced not just the theology of these groups, but also their practice. His discussion of the three marks of the church as the sacraments, preaching, and church discipline holds wide sway within these denominations and is a healthy reminder in our contemporary age when a great deal of thought (and ink) is given to the discussion of church growth and church health.

His influence can also be seen on the practical level of Christian living. One of the things Calvin insisted on at Geneva was locking the church doors in between worship services. For one thing, he was weaning church members off of certain medieval superstitions that only prayers uttered in churches would be heard. But locking the doors meant far more. Calvin was challenging the medieval view that spirituality was a matter for the church and that practicing Christianity belonged only within its walls. He didn't want his parishioners in the church building in between church services; he wanted them in the world and in the marketplace and in their homes. The locked church signified that Christianity extends beyond the walls of the church and that Christian living extends beyond hearing sermons. As Calvin said in his farewell letter to William Farel, all aspects of living are for Christ.

This idea of an all-encompassing Christianity makes for the robust foundation of an engaging worldview. Calvin's principle is that theology and Christianity speak to all of life and all of creation. His was not a Christianity to be interpreted and applied narrowly. For Calvin, it could and should be applied as broadly as possible. Calvin ends his final edition of the *Institutes* with a discussion of the civil government. He acknowledges that this subject might seem "alien," out of place in a systematic theology. It is most fitting, however, because it is in the world that Christianity is to be lived and displayed. We could also add here the extensive attention Calvin devotes to general revelation in the early chapters of the *Institutes*.

Is Calvin, however, merely a model, or do his ideas have something of substance to contribute to the current day? Richard Mouw, himself a part of the long stream that stretches back to Calvin, recently posed this question in his book *Calvinism in the Las Vegas Airport*. Playing off of a scene in a Paul Schrader movie, Mouw raises the question of the relevance of Calvin not only for Christians but also for secular society, answering it in the affirmative rather persuasively. I suspect Calvin would like the title.

Calvin and the other Reformers not only turned the world around in the 1500s, they continue to do so. They were not addressing issues bound by time and culture and place. They were addressing issues of the human condition, the issues of humanity's sinfulness and frailty, of humanity's beauty and complexity as being creatures in the image of God. Calvin identified the longings of the human soul for fulfillment and wholeness when he spoke of the *sensus divinitatis*, the sense of the divine. And he eloquently expressed how redemption and Christ's work on the cross and grace abundantly meet that need when he spoke of the *sensus sauvitatis*, the sense of sweetness, and also of the beauty of Christ. These ideas applied in sixteenth-century Geneva, and they also apply in such twenty-first-century places as the Las Vegas airport.

A Note on the Sources

The standard edition of Calvin's *Institutes of the Christian Religion* is that edited by John T. McNeill and translated by Ford Lewis Battles, published by Westminster John Knox Press (1960). For a biography, see Alister E. McGrath, *A Life of John Calvin* (1990). Two scholarly but quite accessible summaries of his thought are T. H. L. Parker, *Calvin: An Introduction to His Thought* (1995), and David Steinmetz, *Calvin in Context* (1995). For a very accessible treatment, see Christopher Elwood, *Calvin for Armchair Theologians* (2002). For the issue of Calvin versus Calvinism, see Paul Helm, *Calvin and the Calvinists* (1982). For a lucid discussion of Calvinism, see Richard Mouw, *Calvinism in the Las Vegas Airport* (2004).

9

JOHN BUNYAN
THE PILGRIM'S PROGRESS

> I dreamed, and behold I saw a man clothed in rags, standing in
> a certain place, with his face from his own house, a book in his
> hand, and a great burden on his back.
>
> John Bunyan, *The Pilgrim's Progress*

Perhaps no stronger contrast in literature exists than that of John Bunyan's *The Pilgrim's Progress* and Oscar Wilde's *The Picture of Dorian Gray*. Both authors—Wilde is Irish-born, Bunyan is British—wrote their works in Britain; and that's where the similarities end. Arguably the sharpest contrast lies between the two main characters. Bunyan's Christian meets his antithesis in Wilde's Dorian Gray. Both are seeking, pilgrims of sorts. Gray takes a quite different path from Christian and arrives at a far different destination. It might be recalled from Wilde's classic novel, first serialized in *Lippincott's Magazine* before its publication in 1890, that early on Gray, after viewing his own portrait by his friend Basil Hallward, was at once struck by its youth and vigor and beauty and saddened by the realization that this portrait would only mock

his frailty and humanity as he aged, and would forever remind him of what had been and of what had been lost. So
Gray made a deal to have it the other way around: the portrait would age and he himself would remain fixed, sus-
pended in his youth. And then he sealed it, exclaiming,
"Yes, there is nothing in the whole world I would not give!
I would give my soul for that!"

Eventually, Gray realized that his deal with the devil had
come true, but only too quickly did he also realize that it
had become his curse. With every sin, with every display of
the true ugliness of his heart, lines and age cut into the can-
vas and extracted their toll from Gray's portrait, long since
removed to an upper attic room that only he would enter.
But Gray the person remained as youthful and as stunning
as he had been on the day his portrait was finished. His end,
however, came through his own devices. His treachery and
shallow life eventually caught up with him; racked with guilt,
he committed a double suicide, first killing the portrait and
then killing himself—or perhaps, the reader may be led to
believe, the portrait killed him. In the process, Gray the portrait exchanged places with the person. When his servants
entered the private attic chamber after the horrific scream,
they discovered a body that, while having the appearance of
the master of the house, looked nothing like the one they
were accustomed to seeing. And there, on the wall, hung the
portrait of the youthful and beautiful Dorian Gray.

Dorian Gray sought salvation. To put the matter in
more contemporary terms, he sought self-fulfillment and
self-realization. But he sought it within his own self and
on his own terms. At the end of the day, he destroyed himself. In his character of Dorian Gray, Wilde has portrayed
for us a palpable account of the irony voiced in merely a
few words by Christ: that by seeking one's own soul, one
loses it. And then there is Bunyan's Christian. He could

not better illustrate the opposite. He sought to move beyond his selfishness, to escape the self-consumption that plagued Gray. He also met quite a different end as he found his soul, found himself, realized fully in his relationship to God. Christian captures the opposite of Christ's ironic statement: by losing his soul, he gained it.

It is singularly remarkable that Bunyan tells his tale in such a way that it continues to find readers, and many of them, almost four centuries later. His modest past and low station throughout most of his life does not portend the fame of his work. But this poor tinker from Bedford who was the son of a poor tinker, as he is often called, has written the most widely read and influential book next only to the Bible.

Bunyan's Life and Times

The Pilgrim's Progress, though by far Bunyan's most popular work, was not his only book. His published works include about forty works of various lengths. These include *Grace Abounding to the Chief of Sinners* (1666), an autobiography and treatise on conversion; *The Holy War* (1682), another allegory that some see as a better work than *The Pilgrim's Progress*; and *Mr. Badman* (1680), much in the spirit of *The Pilgrim's Progress* and perhaps intended by Bunyan as a bit of a sequel. In addition, he published a number of sermons and doctrinal treatises, poems, and a catechism, which he titled *Instruction for the Ignorant*. Bunyan's works were consumed, both figuratively and literally. The preface to the 1854 edition of his collected writings notes that only one copy of the first edition of *The Pilgrim's Progress* remains and that only a handful of copies remain from the 100,000 copies of the different editions printed during Bunyan's lifetime. An amazing literary legacy, considering that Bunyan never enjoyed formal education and that he came from the poor class at a time when class mattered a great deal.

Bunyan was born in Bedford, England, in 1628. Charles I was the monarch, and by that time it was almost a century since Henry VIII had broken with Rome and established the Anglican Church when he declared the Act of Supremacy in 1534. But that century and the decades that would come to fill Bunyan's life were anything but smooth. The story of Britain and its Reformation is closely linked with the story of its monarchs. Henry VIII did establish the Anglican

FIG. 9.1

Timeline of the British Reformation and John Bunyan's Life

Monarchs	Important Dates
Henry VIII (1509–1547)	1534 Act of Supremacy
Edward VI (1547–1553)	1549 First Act of Uniformity 1549, 1552 *Book of Common Prayer*
Jane Grey (1553)	
Mary I (1553–1558)	1556 Martyrdom of Cranmer, martyrdoms, and "Marian Exiles"
Elizabeth I (1558–1603)	1559 (Second) Act of Supremacy
	1563 *Thirty-Nine Articles*
	1563 Foxe's *Book of Martyrs*
James I (1603–1625)	1611 Authorized Version of the Bible (KJV)
	1620 Plymouth Colony, Massachusetts Bay

Church and he did break with Rome, but his reforms did not run all that deep, especially on the theological level.

Following Henry's death in 1547, Edward VI ascended the throne. At nine years of age, Edward VI relied heavily upon his advisers, and fortunately, he was surrounded by politically wise and, on the ecclesiastical side of the kingdom, theologically minded ones. Consequently, theological and ecclesiastical reform made great strides under his reign. *The Book of Common Prayer* was produced and became the liturgical standard for the church. In the same year, 1549,

Monarchs	Important Dates
Charles I (1625–1649)	1628 Birth of John Bunyan
	1640s British Civil War
	1647 Westminster Standards
Oliver Cromwell, Lord Protector (1649–1658)	
Charles II (1660–1685)	1661–1672 Bunyan's imprisonment
	1672 Declaration of Indulgence
	1678 *The Pilgrim's Progress* published
James II (1685–1688)	1688 August 31, Bunyan's death
William (1689–1702) and Mary (1689–1694)	1689 Act of Toleration

Parliament passed the First Act of Uniformity, which would later haunt the Puritans. All of this came about by the efforts of Thomas Cranmer, Archbishop of Canterbury. Edward VI, however, suffered from syphilis, contracted at birth, and from tuberculosis, and his reign did not last long.

In order to sustain the Protestant momentum, an attempt was made to put Lady Jane Grey on the throne. Though of royalty, she was not in the line of succession. The attempt failed, with Jane Grey managing to eke out only a nine-day reign. Though her place on the stage of history was brief, she remains an impressive figure, and quite the theologian. In the course of her trial, after which she was beheaded, Jane Grey was examined by John Freckenham, Mary I's chaplain. The interview became a theological debate, in which Freckenham tried to trip up Jane Grey on the issues of salvation by faith and the sacraments. He thought he had caught her on the role of works, the Achilles' heel for the Protestant position. She held her ground. In reply to his challenge that "It is not sufficient only to believe," she responded:

> I deny that, and I affirm that faith only saveth; but it is meet for a Christian to do good works, in token that he follows the steps of his Master, Christ, yet may we not say that they profit to our salvation; for when we have done all, we are unprofitable servants, and faith only in Christ's blood saves us.

She wasn't coached, and she was under tremendous pressure—her life was at stake. Yet she was articulate and graceful.

Following the nine-day reign of Jane Grey, Mary I came to the throne. The product of the first of Henry VIII's six marriages (Mary's mother was Catherine of Aragon), Mary was a devout Catholic like her mother. As she came to the throne in 1553, a great reversal of all the reforms occurred. Catholicism was restored and the Tower of London bulged with religious prisoners, earning Mary I her infamous title "Bloody Mary." Cranmer was martyred, as were Nicholas Ridley and Hugh Latimer, and many others who eventually would be memorialized in Foxe's *Book of Martyrs*, first published in 1563 as *Actes and Monuments.* Others, such as John Knox, fled England for the safe haven of Geneva. There they studied under John Calvin and produced the first English Bible with study notes, *The Geneva Bible* (1599).

Mary I's reign came to an end with her death in 1558 and was followed by the reign of her half-sister Elizabeth I, daughter of Henry VIII and Anne Boleyn. Elizabeth I's long reign witnessed England's ascendancy over Spain with the defeat of the Spanish Armada in 1588, and the supremacy of England in the Western world. On the theological front, Elizabeth I brought about the second Act of Supremacy in 1559, taking England back to Anglicanism. In 1563, the *Thirty-Nine Articles* became the doctrinal standard of the Anglican Church. Yet Elizabeth I was more concerned with placating the various religious constituencies within England than with theological orthodoxy or precision: hers was a reign of tolerance. This approach was at odds with those who desired a church composed of serious disciples of Christ who took their religious commitment seriously. Cambridge University served as the hub of this movement and, over the next century, would extend its shadow of influence not only over England, but also over New England. Bunyan himself would come under this shadow, though he was never trained formally. This group often spoke of a pure church, over and against a national church. They argued that church membership should be contingent upon the sincere profession of faith and not simply on one's national identity and baptism as an infant. Their quest for a pure church eventually earned them the title of "Puritan," originally a term of derision.

The Puritans were also called "Nonconformists" due to their violation of the Act of Uniformity and "Dissenters" due to their dissenting from the state church of Anglicanism. It might be best to view both of these terms, *Puritan* and *Nonconformist*, as umbrella terms encompassing a diverse group with some beliefs and practices in common and some in distinction. These different groups consisted of the Baptists, the Presbyterians, and the Independents or Congregationalists. They were in agreement against Anglicanism and tended away from high-church tendencies. They also took church membership and church discipline quite seriously, holding to the church as the significant component of life. They believed that the Bible was central to all of life and especially to the church service. In other words, Sunday was the apex of the week, the church service the focus of the day, and the Bible and the sermon the center of everyone's attention.

Theologically, they held to the doctrine of the covenant, seeing it as governing all of life. There was first the covenant relationship of God with humanity. Next came the covenant relationship of the family: husband and wife and parents and children were in a covenant relationship. Then followed the covenant relationships of Christians within the church. Finally, individuals were in covenant relationship to the state, this latter idea especially coming to the fore with Puritans in New England. The Puritans held to the thought of the Augustinian-Calvinistic view of the doctrines of grace. They especially stressed that salvation is *monergistic*, which means literally "of or relating to the work of one." From start to finish, salvation is a work of God. The Puritans disagreed over forms of church government and the issue of believer's versus infant baptism. Bunyan held to all of the Puritan distinctives of the centrality of the church, the supremacy of the Bible, the doctrine of the covenant, and Calvinism. He allied himself with the Baptists on church government and baptism, though on the latter point he was ambivalent.

Returning to the monarchy and the ups and downs of the Reformation in Britain, James I, a Stuart, followed Elizabeth I, the last of the Tudor monarchs, on the throne in 1603. As an Anglican, he followed Elizabeth I's trajectory. During his reign, a number of Puritans sought to leave England for the New World, where they intended to establish a colony where they could freely practice their faith in 1620. James I was followed by Charles I in 1625, and with his reign the Reformation took a few steps back. His wife was Roman Catholic and influenced Charles I in that direction. He was also, by most accounts, inept as a ruler and could be doggedly inflexible. All of these traits conspired to set him at odds with Parliament, resulting in the English Civil War in the 1640s. In this same decade, a very distinguished group of scholars and churchmen, called by Parliament, met in the Jerusalem Chamber and other rooms at Westminster Abbey. In 1647 they produced the Westminster Standards, consisting of the *Westminster Confession of Faith*, the *Larger* and *Shorter Catechisms*, and *A Directory for the Public Worship of God*.

The parliamentary forces in the Civil War were under the leadership of Oliver Cromwell. They eventually defeated the king's army, tried Charles I for treason, convicted him, and beheaded him. Cromwell became Lord Protector for the decade of the 1650s, the first time in centuries that Britain was without a monarch. As a Puritan with a largely Puritan Parliament and the Westminster Assembly still convened, Cromwell along with Britain saw the Reformation take many steps forward. But it did not last long. At Cromwell's death the protectorate fell apart, and Charles II came to the throne in 1660, instituting the era of Restoration. The king was restored, Anglicanism was restored, and the Puritan decade was reversed. Suspected to have Roman Catholic affinities, Charles II officially converted to Catholicism on his deathbed in 1685. He was followed by James II, who failed miserably in his attempt to take England back to the Roman Church. With his forced exile in 1688, William and Mary came to the throne. At this point, Anglicanism became firmly established, but the Act of Toleration, signed in 1689, meant that finally the Nonconformists could preach and practice their religion without threat of censure or jail. The reign of William and Mary also witnessed a significant shift in power from the monarchy to Parliament.

Bunyan's life story now can be set against this backdrop. Bunyan was born an Anglican, though not with any deeply religious proclivities, in 1628. We do not know much about his childhood, other than his family was of the poorer class. In 1643, he began a three-year service with the parliamentary forces during the Civil War, though there is not much indicating that his particular regiment saw much action. In 1647, he married his first wife. We do not know her name, though some conjecture it was Mary, for it was customary to name the first daughter, who we do know was named Mary, after the mother. Both Bunyan and his new wife were poor. She had the rather simple dowry of two books, *The Plain Man's Pathway to Heaven* by Arthur Dent (1601) and Lewis Bayly's *The Practice of Piety* (1612). In the evenings after his day's work as a tinker (a mender of metal wares), they would read these two books together. Through their influence, as well as simply overhearing two women discuss spiritual matters as he happened by on the street one day, Bunyan

Charles CHARLES II.

9.2 Charles II

came to Christ in the early 1650s, most likely 1653. Much like his character Christian in *The Pilgrim's Progress*, Bunyan came to Christ after an intense and extended time of struggle.

Once converted, he came under the discipleship of John Gifford, pastor of the Baptist or Separatist Congregation in Bedford. Bunyan even began preaching by the end of the 1650s. And in 1656, he published his first work, *Some Gospel Truths Opened*, a disputation against the Quakers. In 1658, his first wife died, leaving him with four children; the oldest, Mary, was blind from birth. He married Elizabeth in 1659, and together they had two children. The next year was crucial. As Charles II came to the throne, the freedoms that Bunyan and his other Puritan colleagues in ministry enjoyed came under attack. In November 1660, Bunyan became one of the first Puritans to be arrested for holding an illegal religious service, the old legislation was reenacted, and Bunyan was sentenced to a three-month jail term beginning in January 1661. He was to be released at the end of the three months on the condition that he promise not to preach. Bunyan could not meet the condition, and so the three months turned into twelve long years. He feared most for his family as they would be without support, and he absolutely dreaded what might await his beloved blind daughter, Mary.

The church in Bedford rose to the occasion and supported the family throughout his imprisonment. Bunyan also contributed to his family's support by making shoelaces. So his fears for his family were never realized. In fact, Mary eventually memorized the route from her home to the prison, and the highlight of Bunyan's day came every evening as Mary arrived with a bowl of soup for her father. While she brought soup, Elizabeth made daily treks to the courthouse to plead for her husband's release. During his imprisonment, he was occasionally allowed to attend church services at Bedford, and he could have guests, as he frequently did, in his cell. Always a lover of music, he fashioned a flute from one of the legs of his formerly four-legged stool. But he found writing the best way to pass the time. He wrote *Grace Abounding*, his spiritual autobiography that was published in 1666, and a number of other books. Toward the end of his term he started work on another book about a man who was walking in the woods, came across a den, and lay down to sleep. As this man slept, he dreamed a dream of a journey.

While in prison, Bunyan was called to be pastor of the Baptist church at Bedford, and he took up his call upon his release in 1672. That year, Charles II, revealing his ties to Roman Catholicism, issued the Declaration of Indulgence, which extended a degree of religious freedom "to all his loving subjects," including Roman Catholics and Nonconformists alike. Bunyan would spend the rest of his years preaching and writing, interrupted by a second six-month jail term in 1677, released largely through the efforts of John Owen (1616–1683). He died on August 31, 1688, having contracted a fever on a horseback ride to London to preach. Though Bunyan has left a significant literary legacy, none of his works surpasses his story about a man who dreamed a dream, the story of *The Pilgrim's Progress*.

Bunyan's *The Pilgrim's Progress*

It is hard to think of aspects of Christian life that *The Pilgrim's Progress* does not touch upon. As Christian makes his journey from the City of Destruction to the Celestial City, he encounters every obstacle and every challenge that faces Christians in every age and in every culture. Bunyan has a remarkable ability to frame Christian's journey in such a way as to capture the universal elements of the Christian life. The story and its characters and scenes capture the imagination, making it a delight to readers both young and old. Yet the simplicity of *The Pilgrim's Progress* belies the theological depth and substance that it offers.

Once our narrator begins to dream his dream, we find that he sees a man, Christian, "clothed in rags and standing in a certain place, with his face from his own house, a Book in his hand, and a great burden on his back." He's

9.3 Christian reading his book

reading the book and he's weeping. He alone, amidst his family and his friends and his neighbors, feels the great weight of the burden on his back. So troubled, he can't sleep, and the daylight of morning brings no relief. And almost as immediately, he comes across Evangelist, the first of many aptly named characters he will face on his journey.

Christian shares his plight with Evangelist, who points him
to the light beyond the Wicket Gate, away from his home
and his city. Christian sets out running for the gate, but his
family calls after him. He "put[s] his fingers in his ears, and
[runs] on crying, Life, Life, Eternal Life." And so Christian
begins his journey.

The Pilgrim's Progress is an allegory, but Bunyan's intent
is not opaque. The characters and the scenes and setting
readily reveal Bunyan's aim. Obstinate and Pliable, Mr.
Worldly Wiseman, Timorous and Mistrust, Faithful and
Hopeful, Mr. By-Ends and Mr. Money-Love and Mr. Facing Both Ways, Ignorance and Atheist, and many others all
help and hinder Christian in various ways as he makes his
journey. He goes through the Slough of Despond, passes by
Mount Sinai and Interpreter's House, before coming under
the shadow of the cross on Mount Calvary. Next comes the
Hill of Difficulty, the Palace Beautiful, the Valleys of Hu-
miliation and of the Shadow of Death, Vanity Fair, Doubting Castle, the Delectable Mountains—all before Christian
crosses the River of Death, reaches the shore, and has the
gates opened before him as he enters the Celestial City. All
the while, Bunyan's text overflows with biblical quotes and
allusions, a testimony to the centrality of the Bible to the
Puritans and Bunyan. These characters and these scenes, all
arising from Scripture and from life, tell the tale of the journey from the kingdom of darkness to the glorious kingdom
of light.

It is striking that Bunyan does not start at the cross. Before the cross, Christian must be made aware of his burden,
and what's more, he must be made aware of his utter inability to do anything about it. This is all the more apparent as he trudges through the Slough of Despond and
stands underneath the cragged edges of Mount Sinai. In
vain, he thinks he can find relief from his burden through

morality and legalism. He then realizes the futility of it all. Evangelist comes along and once again sets Christian on the right path. He then comes to Mount Calvary and the cross and the grace of God made available through the death and resurrection of Christ, all symbolized in the empty cross on the hill. At the bottom of the hill there is an open sepulcher or tomb. When Christian comes up to the cross, the burden falls off his back, rolls into the sepulcher and is gone forevermore. He is "glad and lightsome, and [says] with a merry heart, *He hath given me rest by his sorrow; and life, by his death*" And he bursts out in song:

> Thus far did I come loaded with my sin,
> Nor could aught ease the grief that I was in,
> Till I came hither: What a place is this!
> Must here be the beginning of my bliss?
> Must here the burden fall from my back?
> Must here the strings that bound it to me crack?
> Blest Cross! blest Sepulcher! Blest rather be
> The Man that there was put to shame for me.

Yet Christian is only beginning his journey, for many twists and turns await him—and all, he will soon find out, is not bliss. Right after the cross and his conversion, Christian faces the Hill Difficulty. He then finds rest and nourishment in the Palace Beautiful, which serves in the allegory to represent the church. Bunyan expresses his view of the church well as he describes the Palace: "It was built by the Lord of the Hill, for the relief and security of Pilgrims." Before Christian can enter the Palace Beautiful, he is met at the door by the Porter, who calls in Piety and Prudence and Charity to quiz Christian. He recalls his journey, especially testifying to his experience at Mount Calvary. This scene represents the Puritan view of church membership, as Christian speaks of his conversion and his desire to follow

Christ. He is then let in, just in time for dinner, where "the table was furnished with fat things, and with wine that was well refined; and all their talk at the table was of the Lord of the Hill." This represents the centerpiece of church, the sermon, and the sacrament of the Lord's Supper. The focus is on Christ. It overflows with nourishment for Christian as he makes his pilgrim way. Next, Christian sleeps in the chamber of Peace, another beautiful metaphor of the church. In the morning, he is led into the Armory, where he is equipped and sent on his way to continue his journey.

Much awaits him. There is Vanity Fair, which made for a good title for William Thackeray and a most fitting description of the world. Here this ancient fair runs year-round, a nonstop attempt to ignore that burden that is on everyone's back. And here you can buy everything, see everything, experience everything—and all of it is absolutely hollow, pure vanity. Aldous Huxley made the point in *Brave New World* that we as human beings have a seemingly infinite appetite for distractions, and Bunyan symbolizes this idea in his ancient fair. Christian and his companion, Faithful, do not fit in at Vanity Fair. The residents there notice that the two speak a foreign language, and when they are harangued with the mob's cry to "Buy, Buy, Buy," Christian says, "We buy the truth." They are arrested, and here Faithful meets his end. Christian then is joined by Hopeful, and they continue on their journey of twists and turns and highs and lows.

One such low is Doubting Castle and the confrontation with the Giant of Despair. That Bunyan, writing in a prison cell, would have Christian go through such an experience is understandable. This is no mere bump in the road; so severe is the trial that Christian muses out loud that death would be better, the grave easier. Hopeful, true to his name, inspires Christian to soldier on. And then Christian comes to his senses. "What a fool," he declares himself. He was rotting in a dungeon when he could be free. He remembers that he has a key, called Promise, and with it opens the doors of the dungeon and the doors of the castle yards, and they run to their freedom. Now quite far along on his journey, Christian has yet to make one final hurdle, the River of Death. Through Hopeful's encouragement, the remembering of the promises of God to never forsake his children, and even ministering angels, Christian reaches the shore, easily runs up to the gates, and enters the Celestial City. The bells of the city ring out in joy, and he hears the words, "Enter ye into the joy of your Lord."

Even though it was an allegory, readers of *The Pilgrim's Progress* were quite disappointed that Christian's family were left behind in the City of Destruction. Consequently, Bunyan wrote a second part in 1684. Here Christiana, Christian's wife, and their children make their own journey. Scholars have noted the tone of the second part differs from that of the first. Here, there is much less angst as the pilgrims make their way; the difficulties are still there, but the characters seem to overcome them a bit more easily. Some say the difference in tone is attributable to Bunyan's circumstances in writing. While he wrote the first part, Bunyan was imprisoned and alone and more prone to a despondent outlook. During the writing of the second part, he was free and enjoying the company of his family and the fellowship of his church. Some even take these differences to the level of being contradictory or conflicting views of living the Christian life. While it is certainly right to see the differences, it might be best not to read the two parts against each other, but in a complementary way. As the words of an old blues song indicate, we all have to go through the valley; no one can do it for us. In other words, sometimes we have to go it alone, as it were. But then there is the community of God's people and the wonderful statement from the Apostles' Creed, "the

CHRISTIANA AND HER CHILDREN AT THE
GATE.

9.4 Christiana and her children at the gate

communion of saints." Taken together, the two parts of *The Pilgrim's Progress* reflect the full-orbed and complex nature of living the Christian life—the journey from the City of Destruction to the Celestial City and all that lies between.

Bunyan's Legacy

Bunyan lies buried in Bunhill Fields. At the time, the plot *was* in the fields, but over the centuries the city of London grew and surrounded this cemetery with busy streets and modern high-rises and office buildings. From the sixteenth century and its beginnings until 1854, when the last person was buried there, this place served as the Nonconformist cemetery for those outside the pale of the Church of England. Isaac Watts is buried there, as is John Owen, Susanna Wesley (the mother of Charles and John), author Daniel Defoe, and poet William Blake—and the list goes on. Bunyan's tomb is quite impressive, a concrete monument extending above the ground with a likeness of Bunyan carved on the top. And like the famous character Christian, this statue has a book in his hand. The cemetery has a large sidewalk running through the middle, a convenient and pleasant tree-lined path for many as they cut through the block, saving some steps. People pass by in great numbers, and some pause and sit on the benches within feet of Bunyan's grave, probably entirely unaware of the work and significance of the one buried in the tomb. The buses, cars, and taxis drive by on the street just outside of the gate, and the Londoners carry on their business in the many floors of the buildings that surround and look down on the cemetery.

The modern world meets the old as one sits in Bunhill Fields, and consequently many thoughts come to mind. Chiefly, what might this person and his book have to say to all of these people who pass by his tomb? How does *The Pilgrim's Progress* speak to, as many have called it, a post-Christian and a postmodern world?

Bunyan would be overwhelmed by the change in the world since his death in 1688. Certainly the world has made much progress, but in some ways much remains the same. We are still pilgrims. In that respect, one might well argue that not much progress has been made at all. Vanity Fair has expanded, and many more distractions and obstacles have arisen along the path. But the statue on Bunyan's grave with the book in its hand quietly testifies to a different path and a different way to live. It is perhaps fitting that his grave with its statue is in the midst of the modern world and all of its trappings and not secluded in a churchyard. At first glance, Bunyan's *The Pilgrim's Progress* appears to have nothing to say to the world as it walks by his grave. In reality, his book has never gone out of style and has never ceased to call to pilgrims to consider a different path as they go through life, to put their fingers in their ears and run after life, eternal life.

Many throughout church history since Bunyan's day have read, or first had read to them, *The Pilgrim's Progress*. As but one example, J. Gresham Machen grew up with the Bible, the Westminster Standards, and *The Pilgrim's Progress*. Consequently, Machen's biographer, Ned B. Stonehouse, found an apt title for his mentor and subject: Mr. Valiant-for-Truth. Among the Victorian townhouses of Baltimore, a young Machen learned of the cost of truth, of the unpopularity extracted for being valiant in its defense. Machen found himself alienated from the powers within his denomination. Eventually, he felt forced to leave Princeton Theological Seminary, and then he was kicked out of his church. For him, the character he so readily identified with in Bunyan's allegory, Mr. Valiant-for-Truth, became all too real. But it also became reassuring for Machen as he took his costly stand.

For countless others, *The Pilgrim's Progress* became the singular influence, next to the Bible, as they made their way to the Celestial City. Its memorable characters and vivid scenes put forth a biblical vision for living the Christian life that remains unmatched. Its simplicity draws one in, fascinating the child's mind. Yet it also has much to offer its more seasoned readers as Bunyan captures the full texture and depth of the journey of the Christian life.

The legacy of *The Pilgrim's Progress* may be felt on many levels. First, as a work of allegory it stands with the finest of the world's classic literature. The word *Bunyanesque*, though not appearing often, nevertheless made its way into the dictionary to characterize those who adopt his literary style. Charles Dickens even tips his hat to Bunyan in his clever naming of characters such as Mr. M'Choakumchild, the imperious teacher in *Hard Times*. Second, it is a quintessentially Puritan book and represents well not only the British wing of the Protestant Reformation, but also the crucial group of people who so deeply influenced the church and culture in both the Old World and the New for centuries. Bunyan's teaching on the church, his understanding of the Christian life as a life of discipleship, his constant alarms warning of hypocrisy and self-deception, and above all his focus on the gospel and the cross of Christ, all make *The Pilgrim's Progress* a truly Puritan work. Bunyan was buried in a Nonconformist cemetery for a reason.

For him, one was not a Christian because he or she was born into a Christian society; there was nothing de facto about it. His was a quite different point of view. His character Christian truly became a Christian when he stood at the hill in the shadow of the cross and the burden of sin upon his back rolled off and was swallowed up in the grave. In many ways, this viewpoint stands at the heart of the Reformation as Bunyan beautifully speaks to the triumph of the gospel and the glory of the cross.

Some of Bunyan's fellow Nonconformists did not stay in Old England; instead, they made their way to the New World, where a pure church might be established and thrive. In fact, by the time of Bunyan's death, they were already well into the second generation of their experiment, and in less than two decades one of the last of the Puritan voices, Jonathan Edwards, would be born. Through their voluminous writings, Bunyan and the Puritans continue to wield influence over the church. Not all agree with their views on church and state, or on theology, but the Puritan movement continues to challenge believers on the nature of the church and the church's singular treasure of the gospel. The Puritans understood grace, and they understood that those with grateful hearts, entirely due to and dependent on that grace, should desire to live a holy life of service. J. I. Packer, probably one of the closest examples that contemporary Christians will ever have of the Puritans, once remarked that Puritans are best likened to California's redwoods: towering, stately, the symbol of spiritual wisdom and maturity. They are indeed from another era, but they, and especially Bunyan, cast their shadow into ours.

A Note on the Sources

Editions of *The Pilgrim's Progress* abound. One with a helpful introduction, notes, and Scripture references is by N. H. Keeble for the Oxford World's Classics series (1998). For insightful biographies on the Puritans, see William Barker, *Puritan Profiles: 54 Puritans* (1996). See also Kelly M. Kapic and Randall C. Gleason, *The Devoted Life: An Invitation to the Puritan Classics* (2004). For a scholarly treatment of the British Reformation, see A. G. Dickens, *The English Reformation*, 2nd ed. (1989). See also Paul F. M. Zahl, *Five Women of the English Reformation* (2001).

PART FOUR

THE MODERN AGE

10

JONATHAN EDWARDS
HISTORY OF THE WORK
OF REDEMPTION

And therefore the Work of Redemption being, as it were, the
sum of God's works of providence, this shows the glory of our
Lord Jesus Christ as being above all, and through all, and in all.
Jonathan Edwards, 1739

You were the unconscious instrument of—of—what word have
we moderns for Providence . . . ?
Edith Wharton, *The Age of Innocence*, 1920

I
n 2003, a number of books were published and a number of conferences were held in churches, seminaries,
and such places as the Minneapolis Convention Center and the Library of Congress—all of this to celebrate the
tercentenary of Jonathan Edwards's birth. Edwards made
headlines in papers across America, especially in the religion
section of various Sunday papers as October 5, the date of
his birth, fell on a Sunday in this anniversary year. The *Wash-
ington Post* and the *New York Times*, among many others, took

note. Edwards even made it into the *Wall Street Journal*, with the very clever title running, "Hell,Yes." His alma mater,Yale University, where he took both bachelor's and master's degrees before serving as an instructor, took the time to honor one of its many famous former sons.Yale hosted an exhibit that pulled together various material artifacts surviving Edwards and his immediate family, featuring a writing desk, portraits, a small document chest, a fragment of a wedding dress, and a snuffbox from the nineteenth century—the lid adorned with Edwards clad in his wig and Geneva bands. The exhibit also included a sampling of a literary legacy that virtually overwhelms librarians and still intrigues scholars, pastors, and laity alike. At 300, Edwards was more popular than ever before.

He had not, however, always enjoyed such good press. In 1903, the bicentennial of his birth was also commemorated by a conference atYale Divinity School. One of the speakers made the comment that perhaps it was good that Edwards had died when he did, for if he had lived longer and written more, it would just have been more hellfire and brimstone stuff, more outdated and outmoded and stifling theology. Of course, this refers to the Edwards that most know, the Edwards of the well-worn sermon "Sinners in the Hands of an Angry God." For the half-century before 1903 and for a good bit of the twentieth, this perception of Edwards reigned, especially in the academy. Outside of the academy, Harriet Beecher Stowe could not resist taking a swipe at Edwards and his theological (and literal) grandchildren in *The Minister's Wooing* (1859). Oliver Wendell Holmes Sr. vilified him in an essay.

Edwards, however, was in good company. He and the other American Puritans, all lumped together, were the unfortunate skeletons in America's intellectual closet. The sooner they were cleared out, the better. But then along came H. Richard Niebuhr. He saw in Edwards specifically and the Puritans by extension the precise antidote for the theological malaise that, in the first half of the twentieth century, plagued American mainline Protestants. As Niebuhr so well put it, "A God without wrath brought men without sin into a kingdom without judgment through the ministrations of Christ without a cross." Of such a theology Jonathan Edwards would have nothing to do, and to such a theology Jonathan Edwards had much to say. Curiously, this exact point did not escape the writer of the *Wall Street Journal* piece commemorating Edwards's 300th birthday in pointing out one of his key contributions "to the American experiment: the tempering of Enlightenment rationality with Christian Realism." Edwards should be heard by the modern world, this argument goes, because he raises such a contrary voice to it.

In addition to Niebuhr, Perry Miller also contributed to the turnabout of perceptions of Edwards in the academy and in popular culture. Far from seeing the Puritans as cloistered and intellectually obtuse, not to mention mean-spirited and dour, he portrayed them as they were, culturally and intellectually rich and engaged, underscored by a deep theological foundation and fueled by a vivid spirituality. And in no small way did Perry Miller, and his scholarly heirs Harry Stout and Ken Minkema, contribute to Edwards's revitalization. And as we mentioned above, this revitalization has also been felt within the church.

One question looms over this entire discussion: why all this fuss over Edwards? It's not simply that he's a provocateur. The reason is that Edwards has something meaningful to say. In the pages that follow, we'll explore his life and his ideas, focusing on one of his books that takes a unique place among the other classic texts considered so far. This book, as we will see below, never got written.

Edwards's Life and Times

The leaves had turned their colors and the air was crisp in the town of Stockbridge, Massachusetts, nestled along a bend in the Housatonic River as it snaked through the Berkshire Mountains. Edwards sat in his upstairs room, reading the letter again. Richard Stockton, who would soon be putting his name to the Declaration of Independence, had written on behalf of the board of trustees of Princeton University, inviting Edwards to serve as president. For the last seven years, since 1751, Edwards had grown to love his congregation of Mohawks and Mohicans in the frontier town of Stockbridge. He was writing, producing his major works *Freedom of the Will* (1754) and *Original Sin* (1758), and he had a number of other projects in the works. Ambivalent about the invitation, he entrusted the decision to a council of peers, who decided that he should take the position and move to New Jersey. He preached his farewell sermon in January 1758 and made his way south. Edwards, then a missionary, was now to be a college president. The bulk of his adult life, however, had been spent as a minister, a role for which his childhood home in East Windsor, Connecticut, well prepared him.

Timothy Edwards (1669–1758) came to East Windsor fresh from Harvard, remaining the town's pastor for sixty years. He and his wife, Esther, the daughter of Solomon Stoddard, had eleven children, Jonathan being the only brother to his ten sisters. By the time Edwards was ready for college, at thirteen, Harvard had already become suspicious to a theological conservative like his father, so Jonathan went to Yale. He received his bachelor's degree and master's degree, in between pastoring briefly a Presbyterian church in New York City. After taking his master's, he stayed at Yale as an instructor for two years until he received a call

Fig. 10.1

Timeline of Jonathan Edwards's Life

1703	Born on October 5 in East Windsor, Conn.
1716	Enters Yale
1720	Receives B.A. degree from Yale
1722-23	Serves pastorate in New York City
1723	Writes "Spider Letter" in October Receives M.A. degree from Yale
1724-26	Works as a tutor at Yale
1727-29	Serves as assistant minister, Northampton Church
1727	Marries Sarah Pierrepont on July 28
1729-50	Serves as minister, Northampton Church
1731	Writes "God Glorified in the Work of Redemption"
1735	Writes "The Most High, a Prayer-Hearing God"
1737	*A Faithful Narrative* is published
1738	Preaches series "Charity and Its Fruits" (published in 1851)
1739	Preaches series "History of the Work of Redemption" (published in 1774)
1740-42	Instrumental in the Great Awakening
1741	Preaches "Sinners in the Hands of an Angry God"
1746	*Treatise Concerning Religious Affections* is published
1749	*An Humble Inquiry Concerning Communion* is published
1750	Dismissed by Northampton Church on June 22
1752-57	Serves as minister at Indian missionary outpost in Stockbridge, Mass.
1754	*Freedom of the Will* is published
1758	Becomes president of Princeton College Dies on March 22 in Princeton, N.J.

to serve as assistant minister to his aging maternal grandfather, Solomon Stoddard, in Northampton, Massachusetts. Edwards's name was put down in the church record of 1727 as the assistant minister. The record from that same year also records a marriage between Edwards and Sarah Pierrepont, a minister's daughter from New Haven, who had captured Edwards's heart ever since he first met her while he was a student at Yale.

Shortly into his tenure as assistant minister, Stoddard died, leaving young Edwards, at twenty-five, as the minister of the second-largest church in New England. Through his preaching (although Edwards puts the credit elsewhere), revival came to Northampton and other churches along the Connecticut River Valley. Edwards sent a lengthy record of the revival to be printed in the Boston papers to encourage the churches along the coast. That letter made its way across the Atlantic to Old England and into the hands of the hymn-writer Isaac Watts (1674–1748). Watts wanted more, which Edwards sent along. The result was Edwards's first book, originally published in London, *A Faithful Narrative of the Surprising Work of God* (1737).

In the 1740s, revival came again, only this time it swept beyond the Connecticut River Valley over the entire area of the colonies. Known as the "Great Awakening," the revival saw Edwards serving as its principal theologian and George Whitefield (1714–1770) as its main preacher. Of Whitefield it has been said that he could win over an audience merely by saying "Mesopotamia." And as he traveled the colonies, tens of thousands came to hear him preach. This age of revivalism even extended beyond the colonies, spanning across the Atlantic to England, as Whitefield was joined there by John and Charles Wesley. We will see that side of things in chapter 11. Back in the colonies, not everyone affirmed the Great Awakening. In fact, the event forced a great split between the New Lights (those favorable to the revival) and the Old Lights (those opposed to it). Sarah Edwards expresses part of the tension in her description of Whitefield:

> It is wonderful to see what a spell he casts over his audience by proclaiming the simplest truths of the Bible. I have seen upwards of a thousand people hang on his words with breathless silence . . . A prejudiced person, I know, might say that this is all theatrical artifice and display; but not so will anyone think who has seen and known him.

The Old Lights could not get past the nature of revival preaching, and they thought the itinerant preachers and evangelists like Whitefield undermined the authority and place of the local minister and of the local church. The New Lights rejoiced in all those who were coming to Christ and joining the church.

Edwards's church at Northampton saw its share of this growth—that is, until about the mid-1740s, when things trailed off and the spiritual fervor cooled. At this time, Edwards took a hard look at a practice instituted by his grandfather, one that he had felt quite uncomfortable with. Stoddard practiced open communion, allowing those who had not professed Christ or joined the church to partake. Edwards thought this not only unbiblical, but also symbolic of the spiritual laxity of his congregation. He abolished it, a move that upset his relation to the leadership of the church and led to his dismissal. So the church record for 1750 notes, "Revd. Jonathan Edwards was dismissed."

Edwards had a number of offers when he was dismissed from Northampton. His Scottish friends invited him to Scotland, and colleagues in Boston invited him there. But he went west to Stockbridge, Massachusetts. With a long-time interest in missions to the Native Americans, Edwards had watched intently as the town of Stockbridge was incorporated in 1739 and the church established there. In 1751, he began serving as pastor to the 250 or so Indians and the dozen English families. As mentioned above, his tenure came to an end with the invitation to Princeton.

Edwards arrived in Princeton in January 1758. After a few short weeks in office he took a smallpox inoculation, from which he developed pneumonia, eventually causing his death on March 22, 1758. Edwards had accomplished a great deal by the time of his death. Had he lived longer, he would have completed what he saw as his magnum opus, his treatise that he titled *The Scheme and Progress of the Work of Redemption*. While this particular work was to be unfinished, plenty of others were completed. In the next section, we'll survey Edwards's vast writings and summarize his thought.

Edwards's Thought and Writings

While a student at Yale, a copy of John Locke's *Essay Concerning Human Understanding* (1690) came into his eager hands. John Locke (1623–1704), known as the father of empiricism, fundamentally changed how we think about knowledge, the world around us, ourselves, and God. Edwards said that the reading of that book was to him like counting gold is to a miser; he devoured it. Yet as Edwards continued to wrestle with Locke and Locke's theory of ideas and of knowledge, Edwards came to disagree with Locke. Locke prompted Edwards to devote a great deal of attention to how we come to know things, and how we come to have assurance or certainty concerning what we know.

This question encompassed much more than the work of John Locke. In fact, in many ways it may be seen as the question of the Modern Age. The answer that came from

Locke, as well as from other philosophers of the modern era, resulted in the view that human rationality, or human reason, is the ultimate arbiter and authority in the realm of knowledge. This view lies at the heart of what we call the Enlightenment or the modern period, marking a definite shift in the history of ideas. Questions of faith and knowledge and of God all began to be met with different answers than in the medieval and Reformation eras. The ultimate question that emerged concerned the role of religion in modern life. Edith Wharton's character Madame Olenska in *The Age of Innocence* catches herself before she is able to say reflexively that Newland Archer is an "unconscious instrument of" *providence*. In fact, she stammers. Unable to come up with a substitute, she surrenders: "What word have we moderns for Providence, Mr. Archer?" Wharton's character encapsulates the problem of modernity: Without religious answers, how is a modern to understand the world?

Edwards seems to be an unlikely respondent to the problem of modernity. His was a different world, a colonial and Puritan world and an agrarian culture, whereas the modern world is secular and industrial. He seems so far removed. We should not, however, be so quick to think that Edwards is not unprepared to be a decisive critic of, even a prophet to, the modern world. He stood on the cusp of the Enlightenment and Modernism and, as we will see, became one of its most astute critics, but his criticism was deeply rooted in a theological foundation of perennial integrity. In short, Edwards asserted that contrary to modernity's belief in the autonomy of human reason, God's revelation is absolutely necessary for us to know anything at all. Further, he added that it requires the work of God to have certainty and assurance for that knowledge. Further still, God is intimately engaged and intertwined in the workings of the world. There is no other word for *providence*. There is no other base from which one can make sense of the world or find meaning in life.

Related to modernity's belief in the autonomy of human reason is its twin notion of the self-sufficiency and independence of human beings. Just a few short decades after Edwards's life, Benjamin Franklin expressed this principle in the colloquial expression, "God helps those who help themselves." Edwards could not disagree more. The problem with modernity is not just a problem of knowledge. The problem also has to do with a much-too-high view of humanity and a much-too-low view of God. Edwards answered by talking about sin, and he did so in such a way as to restore humanity and God to their proper places. This much we know from reading "Sinners in the Hands of an Angry God." But for Edwards the key does not lie in being consumed with sin and hell and judgment. As he says in "Sinners," and much more forcefully elsewhere, "Christ has flung the door of mercy wide open." The key lies in Christ.

It might surprise one to learn, especially if the exposure to Edwards runs only as deep as the "Sinners" sermon, that the words Edwards used most were *beauty, joy, delight, pleasure, love, excellency*, and *harmony*. All of these words may be summed up in Christ. And as John Piper, Sam Storms, and many others have persuasively argued, the beauty of Christ may very well be at the center of Edwards's theology. If Edwards were to be asked which sermon he'd rather be known for, it might very well be his final installment in a sermon series on 1 Corinthians 13. He called it "Heaven Is a World of Love," and in it he unveiled a portrait of heaven as the perfect place of love, with Christ as the fountain of love at its center, and all the saints gathered free from, in his words, the "clogs" of sin. This vision of heaven not only applied to the life to come. As Edwards says in that same sermon, "if heaven is a world of love, then the way to heaven is the way of love." This is not the Edwards that readers of only "Sinners" know. He was much more complex than any contemporary stereotype will allow.

In addition to his thoughts on knowledge, sin, Christ, and heaven, Edwards spent a great deal of time thinking about the question of what he termed genuine religious affections. How, in other words, can we know what counts for the genuine work of God in a life, especially in our own life? No mere theoretical question, this stemmed from the trenches of the revivals and their aftermath and the New Light/Old Light controversy. Edwards defended the revivals, to be sure. But as the revival fervor waned, he took a long look at the whole phenomenon that would come to mark, if not identify, much of American evangelicalism (and even evangelicalism as it spread around the world): revivalism. After Edwards and the Great Awakening, nineteenth-century America witnessed the Second Great Awakening and the likes of Charles Grandison Finney (1792–1875). After Finney came Dwight L. Moody (1837–1899), Billy Sunday (1862–1935), and then Billy Graham (1918–).

Edwards's mature thoughts on revivals and revivalism come in his classic work *Religious Affections* (1746). Among the many things Edwards accomplishes in this work (and it well repays reading) is his final answer to the question that arose from the revivals: what constitutes a genuine work of God? He offers, after defining his concept of the *affections*, a list of twelve signs that do not necessarily evidence a genuine work of God and twelve that do. His first list includes things like outward or physical manifestations and zealous talk of religious things. It is important to catch exactly what he is saying here, and exactly what he is not saying as well. These things neither prove nor necessarily disprove a genuine work of God. All too often, they are taken too definitively in either direction; Edwards soberly advises caution. As for the second list, we may summarize his thought this way: true religion consists in holy affections grounded upon the work of the Holy Spirit in conversion, result in assurance of salvation, and evidence themselves throughout one's life in love and holiness. The latter comes from his twelfth and final sign, a life that bears fruit. Christianity is, in his words, to be the "business of life." As we saw in John Bunyan's *The Pilgrim's Progress*, the Christian life is a journey. Unfortunately, revivalism tends toward seeing it as a sprint, run in fits and spurts. Edwards had learned from his own experiences in the revivals that the natural tendency is to see religious zeal waxing and waning. In *Religious Affections*, he offers an alternative model.

In addition to this and other treatises, Edwards also left behind a literary legacy of approximately 1,200 to 1,400 sermons, many of which have never been published. He also wrote a series of notebooks, termed "Miscellanies," addressing a wide range of topics. His was an active and voracious mind, providing fodder for scholars even now into the twenty-first century. These writings reveal the many components of his thought, not the least of which concerns his philosophy of history. In fact, for Edwards, this may very well be the central question, and he addresses it in *History of the Work of Redemption*.

Edwards's *History of the Work of Redemption*

John Milton (1608–1674) begins his epic poem *Paradise Lost* speaking of Adam's "first disobedience" and the "loss of Eden," and quickly adds "till one greater Man restore us." Not merely the poetic rendering of Genesis 1–3, Milton intends a history of the human condition. In the same spirit, though much lesser known, is the epic poem of New

England colonial minister Edward Taylor (1645–1729). *Gods Determinations*, which is nothing short of magisterial as it runs 2,102 lines, begins, "Infinity, when all things it beheld/In Nothing, and of Nothing, all did build." He moves from the creation of the world to the fall, then to redemption, and ends with the new heaven and the new earth. Milton and Taylor were joined by others, such as America's first poet, Anne Bradstreet (1612–1672). In "Weary Pilgrim, Now at Rest," she encapsulates these sweeping stories of human history. She tells the grand story in miniature. All these poets were, in verse, capturing God's plan for the world, seeing at its very center God's plan of redemption. What these Puritan poets were doing in verse, Edwards did in a sermon series.

It should come as no surprise that these Old and New England Puritans would be so concerned with portraying God's scheme of redemption, and seeing his hand in all that transpires, good and bad. The Puritans thought of the twin doctrines of sovereignty and providence as reflexively as they breathed. When they thought of events throughout human history, when they contemplated human affairs in their own time, and when they wrestled with all that was occurring in their own lives and families, they could not help but to interpret all of it in light of God's grand

FIG. 10.2

The Work of Redemption: The Sum of All God's Works

	Period 1	Period 2	Period 3
Begins with	the fall of man	the incarnation of Christ	the resurrection of Christ
Ends with	the incarnation of Christ	the resurrection of Christ	the end of the world

scheme. Edwards himself was deeply rooted in this tradition, and his *History of the Work of Redemption* is his contribution to it.

This text is an unlikely choice for our survey of classics
for two reasons. First, *Religious Affections* clearly eclipses it
in popularity and in what we might call staying power. In

10.3 *History of the Work of Redemption.* Edwards first preached his series on the history of
the work of redemption in 1739. He began his work on revising the sermons for publication
in the 1750s, as evidenced in the title page from his manuscripts, although he was unable
to finish the work.

other words, it's the classic Edwards work that everyone turns to. Second, this book, as briefly mentioned earlier, was never actually written. This needs further explanation.

Edwards's son, Jonathan Edwards Jr., edited a sermon series that his father had preached in 1739, publishing it first in Edinburgh in 1774 and then in America in 1793. Edwards preached this series in 1739, on the eve of the Great Awakening. He chose as his text for the series Isaiah 51:8, and then managed to extricate thirty sermons from it. Of course, Isaiah 51:8 just proved a starting point for him. By the time Edwards was done, he had brought in nearly the entire Bible as he relentlessly turned over every stone in laying out for his congregation God's grand plan for the world, all hinging on Christ's work of redemption. His son dutifully edited the manuscripts—it almost takes a blood relative to decipher his handwriting—and then published the book.

In what would come to be Edwards's final months, however, he turned his attention to what would be his magnum opus. He left behind a title page with some intriguing clues as to how he would go about pulling the book together. He refers to the book in his letter to Richard Stockton concerning the presidency of Princeton. *The Scheme and Progress of the Work of Redemption*, the unfinished book, would have looked at Genesis 3:15, Edwards's thoughts on the millennium and eschatology, and Galatians 3 and its fulfillment of so much of the Old Testament; Edwards would have also brought in his thoughts on the spirit world and Satan. He had been studying a great deal about other cultures, and that would have found a place, as well as his understanding of history since the closing of the New Testament right up to wrangling between the French and British empires of his day. In true Puritan fashion, of course, all of this was interpreted religiously—and the French were, after all, "Romish."

And undoubtedly finding a place among all of these other components of his magnum opus would be the sermon series from 1739. In God's providence, however, this book would remain a mere sketch and outline. Not long after he wrote out the title page, Edwards died.

It would be somewhat fruitless, and not entirely safe, to speculate on what that project might have been. Nevertheless, we do have something to go on when we look back to the sermon series. Perhaps to help us keep all of this straight, we should designate two *History of the Work of Redemption*s: one as the sermon series and one as the unfinished book, acknowledging that there would be both overlap and distinction. The next few pages will be devoted to the sermon series.

In this series, Edwards tackles the most significant questions, including the meaning and purpose of history and the world, as well as the individual's place in this grand scheme. He gives a one-word answer: *Christ.* Seeing this is crucial to understanding not only Edwards, but also much of the Puritans. This approach, labeled *Christocentrism* (which simply means that Christ is the center of all things), becomes for them a hermeneutic, or a way of interpreting Scripture, and a way of understanding God's work in the world. Christ and his work of redemption is the hinge for everything—every event, every biblical text, every aspect of theology. Edwards sees this operative principle in Paul, in such places as Ephesians 1, and throughout the rest of Scripture. And this is what he sees in Isaiah 51:8, "For the moth will eat them up like a garment, and the worm will eat them like wool; but my righteousness will be forever, and my salvation to all generations" (ESV).

This text fits perfectly with Edwards's idea. Against the backdrop of human frailty and temporality—"the way of all flesh," so to speak—stands the permanency and integrity of

God's work of redemption. The stories in the Boston papers that Edwards greedily read were not for him the ultimate story. The tales of foreign cultures and foreign lands masked something greater. And as he looked into his children's and grandchildren's eyes, he might very well have thought of the generations to come. For Edwards, the story of history and the story of an individual life find meaning only in relation to Christ. In fact, he unpacks three epochs of human history in the sermon series. The first stretches from creation and the fall to the incarnation of Christ. All of this lies in seed form in Genesis 3:15. Like Milton, who collapses all time from Adam's fall "till one greater Man restore us," Edwards sees that human history is ultimately about Christ and his work in undoing what Adam did. The second epoch runs only thirty-odd years, the earthly life of Christ ending with his resurrection and ascension. The third epoch then stretches from this pivotal event until the end of the world. The majority of the sermon series traces out these epochs, encompassing both biblical history and extrabiblical history.

The Puritans took sermons gravely seriously, and they nearly perfected the art of preaching. They produced manuals, the classic being William Perkins's *The Art of Prophesying* (1592), a text that Edwards not only read but also from which he memorized large portions. *Prophesying*, the Puritan word for "preaching," was in fact an art and also a science. They developed the plain style and the sermon form, which started with a text, then stated a doctrine, initially in one proposition that would be systematically developed, and then concluded with an application, which they termed "Use" or "Improvement." One can see this structure in all of Edwards's sermons. In this series, however, Edwards does something quite clever. He turns the entire thirty-sermon series into one grand sermon form. The doctrine that he is expounding is the simple

10.4 "Artist's Conception of Main Street, Northampton, 1786," by Maitland de Gorgorza.

proposition: "The work of redemption is a work that God carries on from the fall of man until the end of the world." This he traces through the three epochs. *Redemption,* as he uses the term, however, must not be interpreted narrowly. For Edwards, *redemption* serves as shorthand to encompass all that God does. And this extends beyond humanity to the very creation itself. Isaac Watts, Edwards's contemporary, catches this in the third stanza of the great Christmas carol "Joy to the World":

> No more let sins and sorrows grow,
> Nor thorns infest the ground;
> He comes to make his blessings flow
> Far as the curse is found.

The curse ruptured the relationship between God and Adam and all of his posterity, between Adam and Eve and Cain and Abel, and so on. It even extended to the ground. The cross offers a full and exhaustive reversal. The blessings from the cross flow as "far as the curse is found." Edwards puts it this way: Christ "restores all the ruins of the fall." For Edwards, Christ's work of redemption could not be conceived of too broadly.

Once Edwards expounds the doctrine, he turns to the application in the final sermons in the series. When he gets here, the doctrine of providence rests chiefly on his mind. The various acts of God throughout history appear disparate, even contradictory, yet they all conspire to bring about God's central work of redemption. And so it is with individual lives. If redemption helps make sense of the world, then providence helps make sense of an individual life. Without redemption and providence, events "look like confusion, like the tossing of waves." "Things will look as one confused revolution came to pass after another," he remarks, "merely by blind chance, without any regular or certain end." Redemption makes sense of it all on the grand scale.

On the smaller scale, it's providence that Edwards turns to. In the final sermon, he uses the illustration of a river, his favorite. Imagine, he tells his audience, "a large and long river, having innumerable branches, beginning in different regions, and at a great distance from one another." He continues:

> The different streams of this river are apt to appear like mere confusion to us, because of our limited sight, whereby we cannot see the whole at once. A man who sees but one or two streams at a time, cannot tell what their course tends to. Their course seems very crooked, and different streams seem to run for a while in different and contrary ways: and if we view things at a distance, there seem to be innumerable obstacles and impediments in the way, as rocks and mountains, and the like; to hinder their ever uniting and coming to the ocean; but yet if we trace them, they all unite at last, they all come to the same issue, disgorging themselves in one into the same ocean. Not one of all the streams fails.

Edwards's sermon series takes its place alongside of the grand Puritan epics like *Paradise Lost* in offering a philosophy of history that runs counter to appearances and looks beyond the surface. In the series, he also moved beyond the grand scale, offering a place to stand for the individual and a basis for meaning and purpose in life. Unlike the burgeoning modern world coming into being, Edwards looked for these answers in God. For Edwards—and for the other Puritans, for that matter—there can be no other word, no substitute for *providence*.

Edwards's Legacy

No other American theologian or pastor receives nearly the attention that Edwards does. And the reason is, as mentioned above, that he has something meaningful to say. As a critic of the modern world just as it was dawning, he has much to say to us as we see it in its twilight

10.5 Jonathan Edwards Memorial, First Church, Northampton. Courtesy of First Church, Northampton, Massachusetts.

years, succumbing to the ambiguous postmodern era. A world without religion and without God, the quest of modernity, simply does not make sense and breaks down. In the early decades of the twentieth century, J. Gresham Machen was intrigued by the construction of the Empire State Building in New York City. It had given him pause to consider the great achievements of the modern world. He then compared this skyscraper and all that it represented in its accomplishment with the grand cathedrals of the medieval era. The Empire State Building and its elevators have the power to lift the body, but they do little for the soul, he observed.

Edwards foresaw that the modern world would be marked by advancement and by progress. Some of that he applauded; improvements in science, medicine, and travel caused him to marvel. He also saw that the modern world was bringing along new ideas concerning God and humanity and salvation as well. These he did not see as advancements. Like Machen and H. Richard Niebuhr, referred to earlier, he saw modernity's unhealthy view of the self and of God. He foresaw an emaciated gospel and a feeble Christ, resulting in a vacillating church. In response to the challenges of his own day, Edwards heralded a thoroughly God-centered view of all things, including the grand sweep and the microscopic details of human history. Edwards reminds those of us who live in the modern or postmodern world that the religious view of the world is the only one that we may take.

A Note on the Sources

For the scholarly edition of the sermon series, see John F. Wilson, ed., *A History of the Work of Redemption*, vol. 9 of *The Works of Jonathan Edwards* (1989). See also a reprint of the edition published by Jonathan Edwards Jr., Jonathan Edwards, *History of the Work of Redemption* (2003). For a survey of Edwards's life and thought, see Stephen J. Nichols, *Jonathan Edwards: A Guided Tour of His Life and Thought* (2001). Two recent collections of essays engaging various aspects of his thought and legacy include Darryl Hart, Sean Lucas, and Stephen Nichols, eds., *The Legacy of Jonathan Edwards: American Religion and the Evangelical Tradition* (2003); and John Piper and Justin Taylor, eds., *A God-Entranced Vision of All Things: The Legacy of Jonathan Edwards* (2004).

11

JOHN AND CHARLES WESLEY
JOURNALS, SERMONS, AND HYMNS

> You servants of God, your master proclaim,
> and publish abroad his wonderful name.
>
> Charles Wesley, 1744

They logged well over 300,000 miles on horseback, preached in excess of 50,000 sermons, and wrote about 7,000 hymns. The movement they started now numbers in the tens of millions worldwide. They hailed from a family of nineteen brothers and sisters in all. Impressive statistics all. And, behind these staggering statistics and impressive legacy stand two brothers, John and Charles Wesley. Their impact may be acutely felt in their country and the world over. But they are the most unlikely candidates for such a role that anyone could imagine. They were minister's sons, so the fact that they both followed in their father's vocation is not at all surprising. They both were extremely talented, intellectually and in terms of leadership skills. They could move audiences with the power of their words; they were poets. Even with all of these things in their favor, however, even the casual observer is left marveling at the accomplishments of these two brothers, especially when one considers the early decades of their lives.

Either one of the brothers Wesley is certainly worthy of a chapter all to himself. Yet their lives are so intertwined that separating their stories would fall short of the full picture of their contribution. To be sure, each made his own singular contribution. John Wesley rises to the surface when we think of the sermons, the revivals, and the eventual emergence of the Methodist Church. When we sing hymns such as "And Can It Be," "Hark! The Herald Angels Sing," and "O for a Thousand Tongues to Sing," it's Charles Wesley who deserves our thanks. But Charles was just as involved in the revivals, the preaching, and the organizing of the church. And John wrote his fair share of hymns. They studied together, went to America as missionaries together, and founded a church together. They were even converted within three days of each other; one reading Martin Luther and the other hearing someone read Luther. Consequently, their story may be best told together. Both left a lasting legacy on the Christian tradition. Their names are associated with English hymnody, with the revivals of the eighteenth century, and with the movement of pietism, not to mention Methodism. In the pages to follow, we'll explore their lives and legacy.

The Wesleys' Life and Times

Two men were born in 1703, one in Old England and the other in New England. Although they would come to take divergent paths theologically, each would impact his own nation and leave a lasting legacy palpably felt to this day. In fact, 2003 witnessed a tercentenary celebration of each of them with new biographies published and conferences held devoted to their thought and legacy. The one, Jonathan Edwards, would be forever associated with the revivals in New England, John Wesley forever associated with those in the homeland. Further, both were closely associated with George Whitefield. Theologically, Whitefield had more in common with Edwards, but he spent much more time, both in person and in correspondence, with Wesley. It was not a straight line, however, from Wesley's birth in 1703 to his assuming a prominent role in the revivals in England in the 1740s.

The elder of the two brothers, John was born on June 17, 1703. Four years later, Charles was born on December 18, 1707. Neither one liked to celebrate his birthday, celebrating instead the day of his conversion. Charles would eventually commemorate the anniversary of his conversion, the day "he began to live," by writing a hymn. We know it now by the title drawn from the first line. Charles, however, originally entitled it "For the Anniversary Day of One's Conversion," and originally it contained eighteen stanzas. The original seventh stanza, which commonly serves as the first one today, declares:

> O for a thousand tongues to sing
> My great Redeemer's praise,
> The glories of my God and King,
> The triumphs of his grace.

Many years would come, however, before either Wesley brother was converted, even though they grew up surrounded by the gospel and as objects of their mother's faithful prayers in the bustling home of Susanna and Samuel Wesley Sr. Ordained in the Anglican Church, Samuel served the parish at Epworth, England, situated in Lincolnshire on the east coast about one hundred miles north of London. They were, as mentioned, two of

FIG. 11.1

Timeline of John Wesley's Life

1703	Born at Epworth, Lincolnshire, June 17
1709	Rescued from rectory fire
1720–1726	Studies at Christ Church College, Oxford University
1726	Elected Fellow, Lincoln College, Oxford University
1728	Receives ordination in Anglican Church
1729	Helps found Holiness Club
1735	Begins journal
1735–1738	Serves as missionary to colony of Georgia
1738	Conversion on May 24—"Aldersgate Experience"
1739	Inspired by George Whitefield, begins preaching outdoors
1744	Hosts first annual Methodist Conference
1751	Marries Mary Vazeille in February
1758	Wife dies
1790	Records last entry in journal
1791	Dies at City Road, London, March 2

nineteen children—eight of whom died in infancy and all of whom were threatened on February 9, 1709, as fire raged through the Epworth rectory. Having just reached one year of age, Charles had no firsthand recollection of the event. It had profound significance, however, on John, who was approaching his sixth birthday. Recalling the event numerous times in his later years, John Wesley

FIG. 11.2

Timeline of Charles Wesley's Life

1707	Born at Epworth, Lincolnshire, December 18
1726	Enters Christ Church College, Oxford University
1729	Helps found Holiness Club
1735	Receives ordination in Anglican Church
1735–1736	Serves as missionary to colony of Georgia
1738	Conversion on May 21; composes "And Can It Be That I Should Gain"
1739	Begins preaching outdoors
1742	Publishes *Hymns and Sacred Poems*
1747–1748	Introduces Methodism to Ireland
1749	Marries Sarah Gwynne, April 8
1788	Dies at Marleybone, England, March 29

often referred to himself as "the brand plucked from the fire," his life spared by God for later accomplishments.

As one can imagine, finances were strained in the large family. Even so, Samuel and Susanna saw to it that all were well educated and, when the time came, ready for university studies. Both John and Charles went to Oxford. John studied at Christ Church College, Oxford, before his ordination in the Anglican Church, a credential he retained for the rest of his life. In 1726, he returned to Oxford as a Fellow at Lincoln College. That same year, his younger brother Charles enrolled at Christ Church College as a King's scholar. Charles, by his own account, squandered his first year before returning to the disciplined regime of study drilled into him by his mother. Later on he gathered like-minded students, including his elder brother and fellow Oxford scholar George Whitefield, among others, and formed the Oxford Holy Club. Historians now trace the formation of the Methodist Church to those days at Oxford and Charles's Holy Club. The members of the club adhered to a strict ethic and regimen, earning a derisive label by their not-so-seriously-minded peers: "Methodists," stubborn disciples of their self-prescribed *method*. Service, piety, personal times of prayer and Bible-reading, a high ethic—all of these were demanded of the club's members. Charles took the B.A. and then an M.A. from Christ Church College, was ordained in the Anglican Church, and anticipated what he thought would be the life of an academic at Oxford, committed to his holy club.

His brother had other plans for him. Very soul-troubled at this point in his life, John Wesley was driven by an unquenched desire for salvation. If he only tried harder, he would often tell himself. His brother Charles felt the same pangs. Consequently, when John asked his younger brother to go with him to the colony of Georgia as a missionary, he didn't have to plead very long. Both set sail from England in 1735, unconverted missionaries intent on converting the great masses of Native Americans to Christ. By their own accounts, the trip to Georgia was a resounding disaster. John served as minister at Savannah. After a failed courtship with Sophey Hopkey, the niece of a chief magistrate, John found himself facing charges. More than likely, the charges stemmed from John's rather impolitic refusal to perform the marriage of Sophey and refusal to give the newly married couple communion, an interesting if not convenient tool of revenge for a spurned minister suitor. Evading the charges, John quickly returned to London in 1738.

Charles served as secretary to the new governor, James Oglethorpe, a friend of his father, and as parish minister at Frederica. Charles's Oxford life had not well prepared him for the rough-and-tumble world and congregants of a rural town in a fledgling colony. Parishioners would cross the street to avoid even a casual greeting with their minister when they saw him coming toward them. Before long, Charles also returned to London. Both brothers were at their lowest ebb.

In May 1738, that would change. Charles was reading out loud, with friends, the preface to Martin Luther's commentary on Galatians. One of them, William Holland, was converted that night. Luther's words stuck with Charles. He later records, "I spent some hours that evening in private with Martin Luther, who was greatly blessed to me." Four days later, as he turned Luther's words over in his head, he was converted. Three days after that, John Wesley, unaware of what had transpired in his brother's life, was out for an evening walk on May 24, 1738. He stopped along Aldersgate Street, eavesdropping on a midweek Moravian service. He stood gripped by the words of Luther's preface to his Romans commentary, read aloud by a member of the congregation. John Wesley records what happened next in his journal:

> About a quarter of nine, while [the speaker who had read the preface] was describing the change which God works in the heart through faith in Christ, I felt my heart strangely warmed. I felt I did trust in Christ, Christ alone for salvation; and an assurance was given me that he had taken away *my* sins, even *mine*, and saved *me* from the law of sin and death.

Both John and Charles had relinquished their striving for grace, instead—borrowing a line from Charles's hymn "And Can It Be,"—finding that it is "immense and free," and confessing, "For, O my God, it found out me."

At about the same time, one of their fellow Holy Club members, George Whitefield, found himself out of favor with the Anglican Church, in which he was ordained. Barred from pulpits, Whitefield simply turned to the outdoors. He found a ready audience, and by 1739 revival waves were sweeping across England. The next year, a similar phenomenon would occur in New England, and Whitefield would take his first of seven transatlantic preaching tours of the American colonies. Both Wesleys agreed with Whitefield's assessment of the Anglican Church that the gospel had become eclipsed by formalism, and both Wesleys followed Whitefield out of the pulpit to the outdoors. The rift formally came as Whitefield and John Wesley called upon people for conversion, whereas the Anglican establishment thought that one's baptism as an infant sufficed for salvation. "Church or no church," John Wesley and Whitefield both thundered, "we must attend to the saving of souls." Over the decade of the 1740s, thousands would hear all three preach as they crisscrossed England. They proclaimed the gospel and the message of the new birth, and called their audiences to piety, or what the Wesleys referred to as "scriptural holiness."

John Wesley, however, was not in full agreement with George Whitefield on theological issues, parting company over Whitefield's Calvinist stance on the doctrines of grace. He also distanced himself from the Moravians, founded by Count Von Zinzendorf (1700–1760). The Moravians had greatly impacted the established church and both Wesleys. The Wesleys found themselves out of step with the Anglican Church. Consequently, the revivals

JOHN WESLEY

11.3 John Wesley

of the Wesley brothers soon transformed into a reform movement. Neither brother ever officially withdrew, or was withdrawn, from the Anglican Church, both retaining their ordination credentials until their deaths. Like Luther before them, they would have been much more content to reform within rather than start anew without. But also like Luther's, their reform attempts were not so welcome. Practically speaking, they established a new church, the Methodist Church, officially organized as a separate church just after John Wesley's death in the 1790s. Perhaps the best way to summarize this is that in the Wesleys' day it was the Methodist movement within the Anglican Church, and that by the time of their deaths it was the Methodist Church standing as an alternative to the Anglican one.

During the late 1740s and on into the next decades, the Wesleys devoted much energy to organizing and developing the movement called United Societies of the People Called Methodists. They organized lay and itinerant preachers for the various societies all around England, established a curriculum of reading as the means of training, and deftly carried out the duties of troubleshooting and problem-solving often demanded of leaders. Like the Anglican Church, the movement took on a distinct structure, eventually emerging as a hierarchy of bishops over local congregations. They constructed new meetinghouses, shorn of the trappings of the cathedrals and richly ornamented buildings of the Anglicans. Their simple structures mirrored their simple services, which, though retaining certain liturgical elements as the recital of the creeds and the Lord's Prayer, moved away from trappings of ceremony. They established midweek prayer meetings and encouraged the straightforward preaching of the Word over sophisticated homilies. All of this had great appeal for the large masses from the coal regions, who simply did not feel at home in the uppity Anglican Church. The marginalized and poor masses flocked to hear the Wesleys preach and quickly joined the growing ranks of the United Societies of the People Called Methodists. The movement of the two brothers also established schools, orphanages, and hospitals, and even developed a mechanism for granting small-business loans. Moreover, the Wesleys encouraged the involvement of women in the service, mostly consisting of leading prayers, which was unheard of among the Anglicans. And John Wesley, as evidenced in the last letter he ever wrote, publicly spoke out against slavery— England's, and for that matter young America's, original sin, condoned by the silence of the Anglican Church. At a physical height of merely five feet three inches, John towered over his world, a sort of religious Napoleon.

After numerous ministries, and countless miles on horseback, both brothers settled in London. A large, but simple structure was built for John in 1778, where he preached when he was in town. Simplicity marked the church: "perfectly neat, but not fine," according to John's estimation. Stately wooden pillars about to be discarded from a large ship served to hold up the balcony. Later centuries saw them replaced with marble ones. He had the pulpit elevated on four posts. Those sitting on the ground floor would be able to look straight through the pulpit to the communion table behind it. From this pulpit, John Wesley preached his last sermon.

Next to the church a Georgian-style home was constructed for him. Some of the tastes of his wife, Molly Vazeille Wesley, are evident in the formal dining room on the street level, where passersby looked in while diners looked out. John's imprint may be seen in his "prayer room," which, according to John's wishes, was part of the house's original construction plan. The house also testifies to his fascination with medicine—it contains the electric machine that John Wesley devised and used to administer electric shocks as a medical treatment. Across the street from the church is Bunhill Fields, which, as mentioned in chapter 9, is the famous Nonconformist burial ground for the likes of John Owen, John Bunyan, and Isaac Watts. Bunhill Fields also contains the grave of Susanna Wesley, who died in 1742, long before the church was built across the street for her son. Samuel, her husband, is buried in the Epworth rectory cemetery. But Susanna chose the connection with her Nonconformist past. Her gravestone bears the badge of honor for the Nonconformists: "She was the youngest daughter of the Rev Samuel Annesley D.D. ejected by the Act of Uniformity from the Rectory of St Giles's Cripplegate, Aug. 24, 1662."

An unfortunate chapter in the life of John Wesley concerns his marriage to Molly Vazeille in 1751. In her book *Good Christians Good Husbands?*, Doreen Moore chronicles the unhappy and tumultuous years of marriage between Molly and John Wesley. Ministry, John Wesley again and again argued, would not be compromised by his marital commitments. At one point, thinking his wife to be mentally ill, he thought his life in danger around her. She, fueled by jealousy of his correspondence with a number of women influential in the early Methodist movement, often accused him of adultery, though without any legitimate grounds. Conflict ruled in their home. John was absent when his wife died and did not hear of her funeral until a few days afterwards. His journal, in which he does not hesitate to editorialize on even the most trivial of events, coolly records, "I came to London and was informed that my wife died on Monday."

Long before he met Molly, John had been in love with Grace Murray. But Charles and others had intervened, thinking that his marriage to Grace at that particular time would derail the Methodist movement. The two brothers had made a pact to seek each other's approval of any potential mate. John had circumvented the pact, making Charles all the more suspicious. While John was traveling, Charles and some co-conspirators arranged for Grace's marriage to another suitor. One wonders at the impact on

John Wesley of these personal matters. Following his wife's death, John lived another ten years, dying in London on March 2, 1791, buried behind the large church built for him in London.

For Charles's part, he had long regretted his actions in the Grace Murray debacle and sadly observed his brother's unhappy marriage to Molly. His own marriage, however, took a much happier route. Marrying Sarah Gwynne, whom he called "my dearest partner," in 1749, he curtailed his extensive travel and lived a more settled life of parish ministry, first in Bristol and then in London. His letters to her clearly reveal the love that reigned in their relationship, and it helped that he was so poetic. "My heart is with you," he tells her during one of his many travels, continuing, "I want you every day and hour. I should be with you always, or not at all; for no one can supply your place. Adieu." After an eventful life, Charles died on March 29, 1788, preceding his elder brother by three years.

The Wesleys' Thought and Writings

Many of the figures considered so far in this tour of church history follow a certain trajectory from Augustine to the Reformers and Puritans and on through to Edwards. John Wesley certainly has affinities with this line of thought and theology, but he also marks out a different path. When it comes to the doctrine of the new birth, both John and Charles Wesley see themselves within this line. "A hair's breadth," John Wesley declared, was all that separated him from John Calvin on the doctrine of justification. And he and Whitefield, who disagreed on a number of things, felt that on the pinpoint doctrine of the new birth, each got it right. Yet as John Wesley developed his theology, substantial differences came into play on a number of levels. First, regarding sanctification, John Wesley charted new territory. Often referred to as "Wesleyan Perfectionism" or "entire sanctification," John Wesley advocated the notion that we can attain perfect love in this life. On the opposite end of the spectrum, he took seriously the biblical injunctions about "falling away," arriving at the position that believers may in fact fall from grace. An impulse toward human ability and free will underlies his theology of sanctification, which incidentally also affects his view of conversion.

Other significant features of John Wesley's theology have been summarized in what has come to be known as the "Quadrilateral," or the four proofs for doctrine and practice. These include Scripture, reason, tradition, and experience. Two worth noting here are tradition and experience. As for tradition, one of the ways that John Wesley trained his lay preachers was by having them subscribe to a self-study of the great classics of the Christian tradition, as well as contemporary texts. These works were selected by and edited by John Wesley himself and include a wide range of texts from the mystics, the Puritans, a few Anglicans, a smattering of Roman Catholics and Greek Orthodox, and even his contemporary Jonathan Edwards. John Wesley liked Edwards's *Faithful Narrative, Life of David Brainerd,* and *Religious Affections*—he just excised all of the Calvinistic elements of the text. In other words, John Wesley's use of tradition, as the Quadrilateral points to, was eclectic and selective.

As for experience, John Wesley saw this as a necessary validation of one's own religious commitments. He set it against the formalism and ritualism of the Anglican Church. Even as late as 1784, however, John Wesley could still speak of the Anglican Church as "the best constituted national church in the world," commending its liturgy. Where he parted company, however, concerned the emphasis on experiencing the realities of Christianity for oneself. This emphasis on experience led to what historians have termed "Enthusiasm," a zealous, emotional, and visible response to God's working in the human heart. As the tendency in movements is for the followers to outpace the leaders, so it was with Methodism. Both Wesleys at first tried to rein in and then eventually had to distance themselves from their overzealous followers. Cartoons in the papers depicted the Methodist services as a free-for-all of ecstatic convulsions in fits and trances—an unfortunate and inaccurate caricature of the movement in general, but not wide of the mark on its fringes. John Wesley once preached a sermon entitled "On Enthusiasm," differentiating between its healthy and deleterious versions.

John Wesley's tombstone bears the tribute that he sought to "revise, enforce, and defend the Pure Apostolical [sic] Doctrines and practices of the Primitive Church." This impulse, referred to as *primitivism*, is an ever-present idea that the institutional church has drifted from the simple, original practices and beliefs of the early church. This primitive impulse further found a welcome home as Methodism took root in America near the end of the Wesleys' lives, especially finding appeal in the frontier regions, where the Puritan or Congregational establishment made little headway while the circuit-riding preachers of Methodism thrived. John Wesley commissioned Thomas Coke (1747–1814) and the better known Francis Asbury (1745–1816) as "joint superintendents," taking Methodism to the young republic—Wesley spoke of the American Revolutionary War and the founding of America as occurring "by a very uncommon train of providences." In America, Asbury racked up miles on horseback and numbers of sermons that rivaled the Wesleys' statistics.

The Wesleys are also associated with *pietism*, taking its name from the Latin for "piety" or "holiness" and stressing religious devotion or spirituality. The term became associated with Phillip Jacob Spener (1635–1705) and August Herman Francke (1663–1727). Spener and Francke were reacting to the cold formalism of the German Lutheran state church, reformers seeking to restore warm, religious devotion as the hallmark of genuine Christianity. They had an impact on Zinzendorf and the Moravians, who in turn impacted the Wesleys. John Wesley employed the Moravian structure of small groups meeting for discipleship, rechristening it as the "class meeting," the staple of Methodism. In these class meetings stress lay upon personal Bible study and personal holiness as one actively sought to live a life of love for God and one's neighbor. Incidentally, this same dynamic is largely responsible for John Wesley's intense social action.

The Wesleys were men of both action and words. John Wesley's book selection for his ministers, entitled *A Christian Library*, is almost a book in itself when one considers the thought he put into the nearly fifty-volume selection and especially his work in editing the volumes. His primary genre, however, was not full-fledged books, but essentially tracts, sermons, journal entries, and formal and public (as well as informal and private) letters. John Wesley's writings have been collected in a scholarly edition by Abingdon Press, numbering twenty-six volumes so far. Charles Wesley also wrote prodigiously, but not quite as much as his elder brother. His primary genre was hymnody or poetry, leaving behind nearly 6,500 hymns, less than half of which were published in his lifetime. He is surpassed only by Fanny J. Crosby and her 8,000-plus hymns. Charles Wesley also wrote a number of sermons and manuscript works on select biblical books, and he kept an extensive journal. The sections below briefly explore these literary legacies.

John Wesley's Journals and Sermons

John Wesley started his journal in 1735, the year he went to Georgia, continuing it until the time of his death. He kept two journals, actually, one written in code, utilizing shorthand and ciphers, in which he recorded the struggles of his spiritual life. No material for a salacious novel, they rather record the tenor of his heart during a time of prayer or even the effect that a particular book he was reading had on him. His other journal, the much more extensive one, offers insight into his theology, his life, and his aims for Methodism. Historians are not left to guess at what John Wesley was thinking at crucial times in his life. Neither are they left to fill in the blanks of the influences on his thought. He tells all in his journals. They also serve to chronicle the revivals in England in the 1740s, as well as the establishment of Methodism. John Wesley carefully records his places visited, honestly depicts the crowd's response to his messages, and keeps track of all of those miles on horseback. Through the journals, the life of John Wesley can be reconstructed.

His journals also reveal the diversity of John Wesley's talents. In an entry during a stay at Londonderry, he converses with the gardener attending to the bishop's palace, which he thought "exceedingly pleasant." The next few days found him at Lisburn, where he records, "All the time I could spare here was taken up by poor [medical] patients. I generally asked, 'What remedies have you used?' and was not a little surprised . . . the grand fashionable medicine for twenty diseases (who would imagine it?) is mercury sublimate! Why is it not a halter and a pistol? They would cure a little more speedily." And at Londonderry and at Lisburn, as well as all over the rest of Great Britain, he preached, again and again.

His journal records that he preached to 20,000 people in a natural amphitheater in Gwennap in 1769, only to return in 1773, at the age of seventy, to a crowd of 30,000. Yet not all loved him. Along the road to Roosky, his carriage was met by a mob of "both men and women [who] saluted us, first with bad words and then with dirt and stones." He continues, "My horses soon left them behind, but not till they had broken one of the windows, the glass of which came pouring in upon me." The journal of John Wesley is certainly a unique work among classics of the Christian tradition. His humor and warmth, his breadth of knowledge and interest, and his utter devotion to Christ all shine through.

And so is the case with his sermons. John Wesley's preaching was certainly less than stellar. One member of his audience remarked that the only reason he knew he wasn't looking at a statue was that he saw a hand move. Charles, in fact, had the reputation for being the much better preacher of the two, though curiously Charles has long since been forgotten as a preacher, while the fame of John's revival preaching persists. But John Wesley moved his audience through the power of his words and the persistence of his pleas. He withstood mocking crowds. Even the throwing of rocks was met by a resolute John Wesley. Though not as theatrical or eloquent as Whitefield, John Wesley spoke from a deep inner conviction, palpably felt by his audience. As he preached, the jeering subsided and the crowds were drawn to his message. Those crowds heard one of his most famous and oft-repeated messages (the benefits of an itinerant ministry), "The Almost Christian."

"The Almost Christian" well represents John Wesley's sermons and reveals the heart of his theology and his contribution to modern evangelicalism. It was first preached "at St. Mary's, Oxford, before the University" in July 1741—the same month that Jonathan Edwards delivered "Sinners in the Hands of an Angry God" at Enfield. He was in the presence of the enemy as Oxford was the home of the Anglicans, and 1741 was the height of the controversy over Wesley and Whitefield and the revivals in England. And having spent a number of years at Oxford as a student, he well knew the territory and its inhabitants. He knew the way they thought, and he could anticipate their reaction to his sermon. His text was Acts 26:28, Agrippa's response to Paul: "Almost thou persuadest me to be a Christian." From this phrase, John Wesley extracted two classes of people: those who are almost Christians and those who are altogether Christians. Speaking of the first group, he goes right for the jugular of his Anglican audience, referencing those who have a *form* (he undoubtedly put emphasis on the word as he spoke) of godliness, of having merely "the outside of a real Christian." The almost-Christian partakes of the sacraments and "constantly frequents the house of God." He even possesses "sincerity."

So what is the almost-Christian lacking? Wesley answers, "First, the love of God." He adds that the second thing is love of neighbor before declaring, "There is yet one more thing that may be separately considered, though it cannot actually be separate from the preceding, which is implied in the being *altogether a Christian*; and that is the ground of all, even faith." This is a faith that is a true and sure conviction and confidence and trust. And this faith must be personal, must be one's own. John Wesley inquired, "Is the love of God shed abroad in your heart? Can you [in the second-person singular] cry out 'My God and my All'?" Here is John Wesley's contribution to the revivals and to the history of Christian thought in a nutshell: the emphasis on a personal conversion concurrent with a life of love, themes repeated throughout his sermon corpus. John Wesley sometimes ended his sermons with a poem. Sometimes the poem was his. Often it was his younger brother's. And often those poems would soon be sung as hymns.

Charles Wesley's Hymns

John Wesley did not pioneer preaching outdoors; Whitefield did. But John Wesley is just as associated with the practice. In a similar way, Charles Wesley did not pioneer English hymnody. That place belongs to Isaac Watts (1674–1748). But Charles Wesley, along with Watts, is just as associated with the practice. The tradition from the medieval church was that Latin was the language of choice for singing in the church, and that the laity looked on as the trained choirs lifted their voices. Martin Luther, among his many other restorations—he preferred that term over *innovations*—insisted that all people in the church lift their voices to praise God in words they understood. In his lifetime, Luther wrote thirty-eight hymns, while launching the great tradition of German hymnody and church music that would eventuate in one of the greatest musicians, Johann Sebastian Bach (1685–1750).

The British Reformation also returned singing to the laity. But it had yet to develop its tradition of hymnody. Following the lead of John Calvin, the English churches practiced exclusive psalmody. This was the case in Isaac Watts's church. Watts complained to his father that the psalms do not explicitly speak of Christ. His father challenged him to write one. In response to the challenge, Watts wrote his first hymn, "Behold the Glories of the Lamb,"

GEORGE WHITEFIELD

11.4 George Whitefield

based on Revelation 5, which was sung that next Sunday by the congregation. English hymnody was born. It would be brought to rapid maturity through Charles Wesley.

Most of Charles Wesley's hymns that are well known, which indeed constitutes the tiniest fraction of his total output, concern the theme that he and his brother preached on so often: the new birth and the life of gratitude and love that accompanies it. Charles Wesley was an effective preacher in his own right. His sermons, when published, outsold his brother's. John Wesley possessed inordinate skills as an organizer, as well as an indefatigable spirit. Charles Wesley's gift was a poet's way with words. Audiences hung on every word of his sermons. He applied that gift to his writing of hymns. His "Hark! The Herald Angels Sing," with the tune supplied by Felix Mendelssohn, is a Christmas favorite of all denominations, while "Christ the Lord Is Risen Today" appears in most Easter services. Many have one of Charles Wesley's hymns as their favorite, such as "O for a Thousand Tongues to Sing" or "Love Divine, All Loves Excelling." Recently, the President of the United States used the first line of a Charles Wesley hymn for his autobiography, *A Charge to Keep*.

Perhaps the most well known of Charles Wesley's hymns is "And Can It Be." The first stanza finds the sinner amazed by the love of God, evidenced in the death of Christ for my sin, for me. The second stanza declares the mystery of this strange design of Christ slain, leaving even the first-born seraph vainly trying "to sound the depths of love divine." Charles Wesley then recalls, poetically recasting Philippians 2:5–11, how Christ left the Father's throne above, to undo what Adam did. The fourth stanza follows:

> Long my imprison'd spirit lay, fast bound in sin and
> nature's night:
> Thine eye diffused a quick'ning ray; I woke; the dungeon
> flamed with light;
> My chains fell off, my heart was free; I rose, went forth,
> and follow'd thee.

A fifth stanza, sometimes omitted in contemporary hymnals, speaks of the "atoning blood that is near . . . the life his wounds impart." The hymn concludes with a rousing declaration:

> No condemnation now I dread; Jesus, and all in him, is
> mine!
> Alive in him, my living Head, and clothed in righteousness
> divine.

> Bold I approach th'eternal throne, and claim the crown,
> through Christ, my own.

In his journal entry at the time of his conversion, Wesley records that he commemorated the event by writing a hymn, which he refers to only as the "conversion hymn." Many Wesley scholars believe "And Can It Be" is indeed the conversion hymn, Charles Wesley's grateful response for Christ's work of redemption.

The Wesleys' Legacy

Open any hymnal and one is hard-pressed not to find numerous hymns by Charles Wesley. If you're looking for hymns by John, you'll more than likely need to look in a Methodist hymnal. In just about every town in America a Methodist church stands, and just about every single nation in the world has either Methodist missionaries or a Methodist national church. The impact of these two brothers is keen and undeniable. The obvious influence, however, is perhaps not the strongest aspect of the Wesleys' legacy. In more subtle, yet perhaps more deeply and acutely felt, ways the brothers Wesley have left their mark on modern religion and on evangelicalism.

The Wesleys were key figures, joined by Whitefield and Edwards, in the revivals that swept through England and across the Atlantic in New England in the 1740s. Those revivals shaped both nations—historians see links between the colonial revivals and the American Revolutionary War and the revivals and the emergence of the middle class in Britain. Those revivals continue to shape the psyche of contemporary evangelicalism. Revivalism is taken as the construct for understanding modern church history. Many structure American church history, for instance, around the different awakenings or revivals. Revivalism is also taken by some as the ordinary way to live the Christian life. Further, the revivals of the Wesleys and the movement of Methodism brought pietism (which had a strong presence on the European continent) to Great Britain, and from there, through the likes of Francis Asbury, to America. Finally, Primitivism, attested to by John Wesley's tombstone epigraph, continues to be a deep-felt drive among contemporary Christians.

In terms of the Wesleys' particular contribution to the history of the Christian tradition, they offered an alternative view of sanctification than that found in the Augustinian-Calvinist tradition. In the Wesleyan view, one can either rise to the height of a life of perfect love or sink to the depth of falling from grace. In both of these, we see that the Wesleys placed a great emphasis on the human side of the equation: on the human contribution both to conversion and to living the Christian life. They stressed the life of love in gratitude for the work on the cross. But, to use a gambling metaphor that neither of them would enjoy since from the days of the Holy Club they eschewed cards, they overplayed their hand; they were overzealous in their pursuit of love perfected.

Much, nevertheless, can still be gained by the lives and legacy of the brothers Wesley. In one of his letters to his wife, Sarah, Charles Wesley wrote what may be true for both men: "My prayer for my dearest partner and for myself is, that we may know him, and the power of his resurrection." Turning to one of Charles Wesley's hymns, we can see how both brothers made this prayer their life's ambition. We can see what motivated them through the thousands upon thousands of miles on horseback, the rock throwing and jeering of mobs, the slanderous cartoons, the troubled marriage, and the tiring work of building a church.

They were driven by the gospel: "Ye servants of God, your Master proclaim, and publish abroad his wonderful name."

A Note on the Sources

The tercentenary of John Wesley's birth in 2003 was marked by a number of biographies. Among them is Stephen Tomkins, *John Wesley: A Biography* (2003), and Iain Murray, *Wesley and Men Who Followed* (2003). For Wesley's complete works, including the journals and sermons, see *The Works of John Wesley* (1984–). See Doreen Moore, *Good Christians Good Husbands?* (2004), for an account of the marriage of John and Molly Wesley. See John R. Tyson, ed., *Charles Wesley: A Reader* (1989), for a very helpful introduction to and splendid selection of Charles Wesley's writings. For a discussion of the Wesley brothers' influence and impact, see Mark A. Noll, *The Rise of Evangelicalism: The Age of Edwards, Whitefield, and the Wesleys* (2003).

12

WILLIAM CAREY
AN ENQUIRY INTO THE
OBLIGATIONS OF CHRISTIANS
TO USE MEANS FOR THE
CONVERSION OF THE HEATHENS

> Expect great things; attempt great things.
>
> William Carey

I f God wants to convert the heathen," someone once told William Carey, "he can do it without you." These words were not entirely out of step with the thinking of the day. In fact, at the time there were actually anti-missionary hymns:

> "Go therefore into the world," is what the apostles of old
> did say,
> Here is where God has put you, and here is where he
> wants you to stay.

In response, William Carey wrote his eighty-seven-page book, which is not only a classic text, but a revolutionary one as well. Credited as the founder of the modern missions movement, Carey was certainly not the first missionary. The apostles, as the anti-missionary hymn at least acknowledges, took the command to spread the gospel seriously, as did the early church, and as did many in the medieval church, such as St. Patrick (c. 386–c. 460), the legendary missionary to Ireland.

The Reformers were not to be outdone when it came to missions, either. Martin Luther trained hundreds of nationals and sent them back to their homelands to spread the doctrine of justification by faith alone. In fact, his first hymn, "A New Song Shall Here Be Begun" (1523), commemorates the martyrdom of his former students who were proclaiming the gospel in the Netherlands. As noted in chapter 8, John Calvin and the city of Geneva sent hundreds of missionaries into Roman Catholic–dominated France, even managing, in the 1500s, to send missionaries all the way to the shores of Brazil. In seventeenth- and eighteenth-century New England, some viewed their purpose for being in the colonies to bring the gospel to Native American tribes. John Eliot (1604–1690), British-born and Cambridge-trained, immigrated to the Massachusetts Bay colony in 1631. By 1646, after having acquired a little of the Algonquin language, he began preaching. Eventually, he helped establish the Society for the Propagation of the Gospel in New England, which then became the Society for the Propagation of Christian Knowledge (SPCK). By 1663, Eliot had published his translation of the Bible into Algonquin. As a result, a few thousand Indians came to Christ. These converts were called Praying Indians.

A century later, Jonathan Edwards would minister to a congregation of Praying Indians at Stockbridge, Massachusetts, from 1751 to 1758, under the support of the SPCK. Just before he began his role as a missionary for seven years,

Edwards wrote the classic missionary biography *The Life of David Brainerd* (1749). This work, the most popular of his books during his lifetime and one that profoundly affected Carey, chronicles the short but adventurous missionary work and the intense spiritual life of David Brainerd (1718–1747), as he worked among the Delawares in the New Jersey and Pennsylvania colonies. John Wesley, himself briefly a missionary to the colony of Georgia, commissioned Francis Asbury to take the gospel to the frontier regions of the American colonies. Elsewhere in the colonies and around the world, the Moravians were very busy doing missionary work of their own. When the New England Congregationalists began to pursue missions among the Native Americans in earnest, they were playing catch-up with the firmly established work of the Moravians. And this is not to mention the mission work of the Jesuits throughout Europe and the Americas.

William Carey, in other words, was not the first missionary. He himself acknowledges "the success of former undertakings." But there remains something extremely significant, even epochal, about his book and his life. Probably of all the books surveyed so far in this tour of church history, William Carey's *Enquiry* (a severely abbreviated title) stands out as the least known and least read. Yet its influence simply cannot be underestimated. Much of what has occurred in the Modern Age of church history may very well be considered bad news, missteps. Deism turned out a domesticated God while elevating humanity. Science trumped faith and the Bible and pointed generations away from the mythological worldview to the modern one. The Enlightenment enthroned human reason and further pushed Christianity to the margins. But there is another side to the story of the Modern Age; there is some good news against all the bad. On the good-news side of things, certainly the modern

THE LIFE

OF

REV. DAVID BRAINERD,

CHIEFLY EXTRACTED FROM HIS DIARY.

BY PRESIDENT EDWARDS.

———

SOMEWHAT ABRIDGED.

———

EMBRACING, IN THE CHRONOLOGICAL ORDER,

BRAINERD'S PUBLIC JOURNAL

OF THE MOST SUCCESSFUL YEAR OF HIS

Missionary Labors.

———

PUBLISHED BY THE

AMERICAN TRACT SOCIETY,

NO. 150 NASSAU-STREET, NEW-YORK.

D. Fanshaw, Printer.

View of the Parsonage in Cranbury, New-Jersey, July, 1833,
Occupying the ground where Brainerd preached to the Indians, 1746.

12.1 Jonathan Edwards's
Life of David Brainerd, often
reprinted as seen here,
influenced William Carey
and many others in the
modern missions movement.

mission movement takes prominence. And at the center of this movement stands William Carey and his book, the full title ambitiously exclaiming:

An Enquiry into the Obligations of Christians, to Use Means for the Conversion of the Heathens, into which the Religious State of the Different Nations of the World, the Success of former Undertakings, and the Practicability of further Undertakings, are Considered.

Published in England in 1792, the book was met with wide readership. Not everyone cheered it, the old sentiment of the anti-missionary hymns holding sway against Carey's argument. Many, however, found Carey's challenge compelling. A few even went so far as to take his book's charge for further undertakings to heart. Among the latter group is the book's own author. In 1793, Carey left England for Bengal, India, under the auspices of the newly formed Baptist Missionary Society, originally named the Particular Baptist Society for Propagating the Gospel among the Heathen. The modern missionary movement was born. In the pages to follow, we'll explore this man and his book and the movement that they started.

Carey's Life and Times

"He is short; his hair white; his countenance benevolent," runs the description of William Carey by two English visitors at Serampore in 1826. Carey offered his own self-study: "I am a plodder. I will persevere in a definite pursuit." He arrived in India as an illegal alien; his papers never came through. He endured seven long years of absolutely fruitless ministry near Malda before settling in at Serampore and walking the first convert from Hinduism to

Christianity, Krishna Pal, to the river for baptism. Shortly after arriving in India, his five-year-old son died, which plunged his wife into depression, and eventual mania and mental illness. He buried his first wife in 1808, his second in 1821. On two occasions he mourned the deaths of his closest associates in his work. In 1812, fire destroyed his beloved manuscripts and printing press. Infighting and conflict threatened to rip apart the mission and college at Serampore. Financial challenges dogged Carey most of his life, but by the end of his life thousands of pounds sterling

FIG. 12.2

Timeline of William Carey's Life

1761	Born at Paulurspury, Northamptonshire, England, August 17
1775	Begins apprenticeship as shoemaker
1781	Marries Dorothy Plackett
1783	Baptized by John Ryland Jr.
1785	Serves as Baptist lay pastor, Moulton
1789	Serves as Baptist minister, Harvey Lane, Leicester
1792	Publishes *Enquiry*; helps establish Particular Baptist Society for Propagating the Gospel among the Heathen (later renamed Baptist Missionary Society)
1793	Sails to Bengal, India, with family and John Thomas, June 13
	Arrives at Calcutta, India, November 11
1794	Settles near Malda; begins working at indigo plantation

would have passed through his hands. He founded a college, served as a professor, and translated the Bible into numerous languages, though he never went beyond a basic elementary education himself formally. Born and baptized Anglican, Carey eventually migrated to the dissenting Particular Baptists and become one of that group's leading figures in England before setting sail for India. William Carey's is a complex life, worth unraveling.

His life began in the midlands of England in the county of Northamptonshire on August 17, 1761. Carey began his life

1800	Settles at Serampore; baptizes first Hindu convert
1801	Publishes Bengali New Testament
1807	Publishes Sanskrit New Testament; receives D.D. degree from Brown University
1808	First wife, Dorothy, dies; marries Charlotte Emilia Rumohr
1812	Manuscripts and printing press destroyed by Serampore fire
1820	Organizes Agricultural and Horticultural Society of India
1821	Founds Serampore College Second wife, Charlotte, dies
1823	Marries Grace Hughes
1834	Dies at Serampore, June 9

as an Anglican and destined for a trade. As a fourteen-year-old, he watched some of his fellows go off to college, but himself became apprenticed to a cobbler (shoemaker), Clark Nichols. That same year, in 1775, he met John Warr, a fellow apprentice, a meeting that would eventually lead him away from both the Anglican Church and his career path. Warr was a dissenting Baptist, the "dissenting" part meaning he dissented from the state church, Anglicanism. Warr and Carey passed the time in the shop debating theology, and Carey spent the evenings reading books supplied by Warr. Carey had been an avid reader from the beginning. His grandfather had been a village schoolmaster, and his father, a weaver by trade, made sure that reading was part of William's life. Some of those early books included works on geography. Young William was learning about the world beyond his village. He also hung on the stories of the travel exploits of an uncle, Peter Carey, who had been to Canada fighting for the British against the French. And he devoured the tales of Captain Cook. Carey also enjoyed learning languages. Being self-taught in Latin, Greek, and Hebrew, he would later, while in India, add many more languages and dialects.

In 1779, Clark Nichols died, causing Carey to move his apprenticeship to Thomas Old. Old had an unmarried sister-in-law, Dorothy Plackett. And on June 10, 1781, Carey married her. Carey's biographers are quick to point out the mismatched nature of the relationship. Only a few offer a sympathetic reading of the couple or of Dorothy, and then typically the blissful years are rather limited to the few early years of their life together. She was illiterate; Carey loved his books. Finances were always a challenge for them. Once Old died, following custom, Carey had to provide not only for his own family but also for Old's widow and family. In later years, especially with Carey's decision to embark for India, tensions increased in the marriage.

In those early years, however, Dorothy, or Dolly, was one of a stream of influences on Carey taking him away from Anglicanism and to the Particular Baptist community. The designation *Particular* comes from this group's Calvinistic commitments, stressing their belief in a limited atonement or, as it was sometimes alternatively referred to, particular redemption. On October 5, 1783, William Carey was baptized by John Ryland, signaling Carey's full move to the Baptists. In 1785, he became ordained as a lay preacher among the Baptists, and by 1789 he was beginning his first full pastorate at Leicester. The 1780s were a formative decade in many ways. Carey was now married with a family, he had moved from being a cobbler to a minister, and he was becoming more and more impressed with a global burden. During this time, he was reading Jonathan Edwards's biography of David Brainerd. Eventually, his curiosity of the world beyond the villages of his landlocked province and the inspiration from the life of Brainerd would merge into an intense missionary fervor.

Three things resulted from this merger in the decisive year of 1792. He published his book in May and that same month preached his sermon with the now-famous line, "Expect great things; attempt great things." This phrase is better known in its alternative form, "Expect great things from God; attempt great things for God." Timothy George, one of Carey's biographers, points to the controversy over this saying, noting that the fuller version, which is the much more well-known version, was more than likely a later embellishment. But George also points out that Carey is in every way in synch with the fuller version. What is seen in this phrase are both Carey's ambition and zeal; these led to the third result, the establishment of the Particular Baptist Society for Propagating the Gospel Among the Heathen on October 2, 1792. The society then looked around for a missionary. The minutes from the society's November meeting pick up the story from here:

> At the meeting at Northampton, Nov. 13, 1792, the Committee was informed that Mr. John Thomas (a Baptist minister, who for years past has been learning the Bengalese language, and preaching to the natives), was then in London, and that he much wished, by a subscription, to return to his work, and to take some fellow-labourer with him. The committee then agreed to make inquiry into Mr. Thomas's character, principles, etc.

In January, Thomas met with the society, had a successful interview, and, alongside the society, began laying out plans to embark in the spring. The unresolved issue of the "fellow-labourer" remained. By the end of the day, however, that, too, was decided upon. The minutes record simply: "Mr. Carey, of Leicester, who was present, at the same time, engaged to go with him." Carey was the ideal choice as a fellow-labourer. He had written the book that started it all, he was an accomplished linguist and autodidact, and he had already evidenced qualities of administration. There is no evidence, however, that he ever discussed the decision with his wife, who was pregnant at the time. She refused to go.

Their plans were delayed a few months, with finances, traveling visas, and foul weather all conspiring against them. In the interim, Dorothy gave birth to their child. Now, she reluctantly consented to go along. On June 13, 1793, they were finally on their way from Dover to Calcutta, a full six-month sea voyage ahead of them, arriving on November 11, 1793. For the next forty-one years, until his death, Carey would remain in India.

Shortly after the Careys arrived, their five-year-old son died of dysentery. This exacted a heavy toll on an already disenchanted Dorothy. She became delusional and even abusive. Carey once confided in a letter to his sisters in England that "I have been for some time past in danger of losing my life." Carey had Dorothy confined to a room, for both of their sakes. In fact, as Ruth Tucker points out, for years Carey would sit in one room doing his translation work while his wife would literally rant and rave in the room next door. Dorothy died in 1808. Causing quite a scandal, Carey was remarried five months later, to Charlotte Rumohr. She was a wealthy Danish woman of identical age with Carey who had come to Calcutta for the climate. Well educated, she was an accomplished linguist in her own right. This was a happy marriage. In the words of Carey, "We had as great a share of happiness as ever was enjoyed by mortals." They enjoyed only thirteen years together, as Charlotte died in 1821, a devastating blow to Carey. He spoke of his house as a wilderness. Over a year later, he married Grace Hughes, herself widowed twice. She would outlive him by a year.

When Carey first arrived in India, he began work at an indigo factory in the heartland at Mudnabatti. John Thomas had used the bulk of their funds to establish his own surgical practice, and little if any money was being sent from England. While Carey was deeply discouraged by these disastrous beginnings, he threw himself into language studies. In a short time, he established a Baptist church at Malda, all the while working on a Bengali translation of the New Testament. In 1800, after a seven-year "apprenticeship" as a missionary, he moved to Serampore, a Danish settlement town bordering Calcutta, where the mission work took off in earnest. That year he baptized his first convert. In 1801, he was appointed lecturer of Sanskrit and Bengali languages at Fort William College in nearby Calcutta, a post he held for twenty years. The college served mostly the British governmental officials, providing Carey with many contacts that would prove useful in the decades to come.

At Serampore, Carey was joined by William Ward, a printer, and Joshua Marshman, an educator. With Carey, they formed the famous "Serampore Trio," establishing a network of boarding schools and churches and a printing press and business. The press was the instrument to accomplish Carey's chief goal of Bible translation. As early as 1801, the Bengali New Testament rolled off the press, the first of many Bibles in India's indigenous languages and dialects. When fire destroyed the Serampore compound in 1812, the press and much translation work in progress was destroyed. This setback was matched by Carey's determination. "I am a plodder," we remember he once said of himself. His singular, defining characteristic was to persevere, especially in the face of intense challenge.

As a child, Carey had dreamed of being a gardener. He suffered, however, from allergies, sending him on a different path in life. Ironically, as a missionary to India he could fulfill his early dreams at least in part. The different climate in India allowed him to garden, and in 1820, he organized the Agricultural and Horticultural Society of India. By 1821, Carey and his associates at Serampore were able to establish their own college, still in existence to this day. Eventually, however, this led to a conflict with the missionary society, and in just a few short years the Serampore Mission and College broke with the Baptist Missionary Society.

In truth, conflict between Carey and the board had been brewing for years. He once wrote "except for Mr. Burls and Ryland, no person belonging to the Committee has, since Fuller's death, written me a single letter of friendship." Part of the conflict entailed politics. Britain's wars with France in the early 1800s, in part to control the Asiatic regions, resulted in a series of decisions and policies that had an adverse effect on India, policies that Carey sometimes criticized. In return,

Carey was villainized by certain governmental officials. The aftermath of the war also led to the collapse of banks and business ventures in India, cutting off funding sources for the Serampore mission. Mary Drewery, in her biography of Carey, expresses it well: "Wars create as many problems as they solve." All of these problems threatened the Serampore mission. Again, Carey plodded. He endured much as he worked at Serampore for thirty-four years, forty-one in total in India—and all without ever leaving that country once. Carey died on June 9, 1834. He left his wishes that his grave bear only his dates and a couplet from one of his favorite hymns by Isaac Watts, "A wretched, poor, and helpless worm, on Thy kind arms I fall."

Carey's Thought and Writings

Unlike many of the other figures considered in our tour of church history, William Carey did not leave behind a massive literary legacy. His *Enquiry* is his main book. That, however, may be a little deceiving. Carey established the Serampore College to train ministers, mostly nationals, before sending them back into India to plant churches. The work at Serampore alone saw hundreds of converts. His chief labor at Serampore, and even at Malda, consisted of his translation work. By the time of his death, Carey had been the chief contributor to and overseen the translation of the complete Bible into Bengali, Oriya, Marathi, Hindi, Assamese, and Sanskrit. In addition, he translated parts of the Bible into twenty-nine other languages. Along with his translation work, he also produced grammars of Bengali and Sanskrit, and a polyglot dictionary. Most of this work was destroyed by fire in 1812. Carey, who had been away traveling at the time, heard the devastating news and took the whole incident as a judgment of God, writing, "The Lord had smitten us, he had a right to do so, and we deserve his corrections. I wish to submit to his sovereign will, nay, cordially to acquiesce therein, and to examine myself rigidly to see what in me has contributed to this evil." Carey's sense that God was judging him may or may not have been on the mark; nevertheless, his commitment to the sovereignty of God in light of this dark trial demands notice.

Even the fire and the destruction of literally years of work did not keep Carey down. When he returned to Serampore, he was right back to work. His Bibles and his grammars not only served the needs of missionaries in India and other parts of Asia in Carey's own day, but also became the basis for other translation work. As John Wycliffe and William Tyndale had done for the English Bible, and Luther for the German Bible, Carey's work laid the foundation for translations in an entire region of the world. His translation work went two ways: he devoted many years to translating the *Vedas*, the sacred texts of Hinduism, into English. This enabled the missionaries to have a much better understanding of the religion and worldview of those they would be encountering. It no doubt gave Carey a much better understanding of the people to whom he ministered. Further, Carey's translation work extends beyond missions. Literary scholars speak of a nineteenth-century renaissance in Indian literature, and most credit Carey's work as lying behind it.

Carey, however, did not remain secluded in his study carrying out his translation work. His mission at Serampore also entailed medical services, relief work, general education, and horticultural and agricultural instruction and training. His estate, at the time of his death, did not consist of much. Of course, there was his library, which was of significant value, but beyond that not much was passed on, except a large and meticulously classified collection of stones, minerals, and shells. His will directed the collection to the Serampore College. Carey, in other words, was a man of diverse interests, and he brought all of it to bear upon his mission work. This is most conspicuous in his work in establishing the Agricultural and Horticultural Society of India.

In Carey's day in India, large masses were threatened by poverty and malnourishment. Carey thought the natural resources were far too underutilized. With a little planning and vision, he argued, the whole situation could be turned around. In his prospectus for the society, he wrote of the "abject and degraded state" of agriculture in one of "the finest countries in the world." He proposed irrigation, crop rotation, composting, and fertilizing. He also saw the aesthetic angle, calling for well-laid-out fields in the rural areas and gardens and trees in the urban areas. His efforts gained the support of the governor-general's wife, and experimental farms and trial fields were established, backed by government grants.

Carey's missionary work was multidimensional. He preached and taught and translated the Bible. He oversaw schools and colleges, hospitals and medical missions. And he sought solutions to the problems of poverty and starvation. In many ways, he followed the medieval model of some of the monastic missionary endeavors, summed up in their motto, "Cross, book, and plow" (*Cruce, libro, et atro*). At the center of Carey's thought and writings, however, clearly stands his book, the *Enquiry*.

Carey's *Enquiry*

Recently, American historian Scott Liell published *Forty-Six Pages: Thomas Paine, Common Sense, and the Turning Point to Independence,* a study of a truly revolutionary text, originally published in 1776. Paine, with a rhetorical flair—he was the one who wrote, "These are the times that try men's souls"—sounded the battle cry for independence, marshaling a series of compelling arguments to make his case. Liell sees the book not only as going a long way to contributing to the Revolutionary War, but also as marking a new era of government and political philosophy. Paine's book, short as it was, changed the course of history and left a lasting mark. If we were to tell the story of the Modern Age from a different angle, we could easily argue for the same place to be accorded the eighty-seven pages of Carey's book published in 1792. These are eighty-seven pages that truly changed the world.

On the title page, Carey quotes Romans 10:12–14, which contains Paul's series of rhetorical questions asking how people may believe if they never hear, how they can hear unless they have a preacher, and how they can have a preacher unless they are sent. Carey's use of this text demonstrates the book's aim. Entitled *An Enquiry*, the book enquires about the obligations of the church to preach the gospel. Of course, this requires being sent to those who have never heard, or in nineteenth-century parlance, the heathen. Carey's book consists of a brief introduction and five sections or chapters.

Carey states his point of enquiry more directly in the first section. He cites the Great Commission from Matthew 28:19-20, asking if that commission, given to the disciples, is "still binding on us." He further relates how he will go about answering that question in the next four chapters. He first looks at "former undertakings" of missions. Next, he offers a survey of the world, cataloging nations by size, population, and religion. This section consists mostly of charts, gleaned from numerous sources and reflective of Carey's longtime interest in geography and the peoples of the world. The next section, having just identified the overwhelming task before the church, asks of "the practicability of something being done." The final section, rather brief, looks at "the duty of Christians in general, and what means ought to be used, in order to promote this work."

The genius of the *Enquiry* is twofold. First, there is the simplicity of the argument; Carey knew not to overplay his hand. Second, he fills his book with impassioned pleas on behalf of those who have never heard, "who have no Bible, no written language (which many of them have not), no ministers, no good civil government, nor any of those advantages which we have. Pity therefore, humanity, and much more Christianity, call loudly for every possible exertion to introduce the gospel amongst them."

Carey's brief survey of missions, section 2 of his book, starts with the apostles, moves through the book of Acts, and continues on to the early church. Carey briefly speaks of the recovery of the gospel by the Reformers and turns his attention to Britain and the missionary work in the American colonies, citing John Eliot's work among the Algonquin and David Brainerd's work among the Delawares. He concludes by looking at the work of the Danish in the East Indies, Moravian missions—a work that he says "none of the moderns have equaled"—and John Wesley's efforts in sending missionaries to the West Indies. Carey's underlying point is clear: the church through the ages has understood the Great Commission as binding.

Chapter 3 presents a statistical analysis of the needs and state of the world, consisting mostly of tables listing countries by size, population, and religion in the four categories of Europe, Asia, Africa, and America. Carey lists "India, *beyond the Ganges*," as being 200 miles long by 1,000 miles in breadth, with a population of fifty million, and consisting of Mahometans (Muslims) and pagans. He offers the following summary in a brief narrative conclusion to this section: "The inhabitants of the world according to this calculation amount to about seven hundred and thirty one million; four hundred and twenty million of whom are still in pagan darkness." He continues, noting the vast numbers of adherents of non-Christian religions. He underscores the ignorance of the Bible and the gospel of Christ among the hundreds of millions. He then pleads to his reader that this picture of the world will "enlarge" all Christians. He was especially hopeful that it would impact ministers. Someone once wrote of Carey that he knew the weight of the word *world*. In these eighty-seven pages, Carey attempts to share his burden with others.

Faced with such overwhelming statistics, Carey raises the question of whether anything practical can be done in the next section. He outlines what he sees as the impediments: "Their distance from us, their barbarous and savage manner of living, the danger of being killed by them, the difficulty of procuring the necessities of life, or the unintelligibleness of their languages." He then knocks down each apparent impediment. "It was no impediment to an Eliot or a Brainerd," he declares at one time; "I greatly question whether most of the barbarities practiced by the savages upon those who have visited them have not originated in some real or supposed affront, and were therefore more properly acts of self-defence than proofs of ferocious disposition," he says at another. Let missionaries simply "engage in the work," he concludes, with his usual grit and determination, "and we shall see that it is not impracticable."

In the final section, Carey turns to some guidelines in carrying out the church's duty of missions. He emphasizes prayer, the "first and most important" means. He then envisions a missionary society, consisting of persons contributing from their various stations to the work of missions. This society, he continues, might appoint a committee, and the committee might appoint missionaries. The members of the society will contribute funds, some of their wealth, some of whatever they can. This mission work can begin, Carey continues, right in the villages of England, where there are "those who sit in darkness," and eventually the society could spread the "gospel amongst the heathen." On the eighty-seventh page, he concludes, "Surely it is worthwhile to lay ourselves out with all our might, in promoting the cause, and kingdom of Christ."

Carey's Legacy

When Christianity began, it was a regional phenomenon, but it was never intended to be so, nor did it remain that way. The well-known text of Acts 1:8 declares that Christianity is to be proclaimed to the end of the earth, and the Old Testament prophets consistently speak of the spread of the knowledge of God as the waters cover the sea (Isa. 11:9). By the end of the eighteenth century, however, Christianity was limited primarily to Europe and parts of the Americas. The nineteenth century, hailed as the "Great Century" as far as missions goes, saw that trend reversed. It was a century of great missionary expansion into India, China, Africa, and beyond. It was the century of Adoniram Judson (1788–1850), David Livingstone (1813–1873), J. Hudson Taylor (1832–1905), and Amy Carmichael (1867–1951). England and then America led the way in sending missionaries around the world. In 1910, a gathering of missionary statesmen at Edinburgh symbolized the concerted efforts to see the gospel spread as the waters cover the sea. And behind it all in no small way was the cobbler and his book.

Carey not only inspired missions through the *Enquiry*, he also modeled many of the conventions of the modern missionary enterprise. We see in Carey the formation of missionary societies as sending agencies. His work in translation, church-planting, and ministerial training offers a blueprint for mission work. In other ways, Carey influenced the modern missionary movement. Many have observed the significant role that women have played in missions. Most Protestant denominations, especially in the nineteenth century and earlier, had not offered women much in the way of leadership roles in the institutional church. Missions afforded women an opportunity for service.

While Carey's first marriage is not in view here, his second marriage to Charlotte sees him in many ways working in partnership with his gifted and capable wife as he carried out his translation work and administration at Serampore. Ann Judson (1789–1826) followed similarly in her work with her husband Adoniram at Burma. She lost a son, and while she was expecting another child, her husband was arrested during the war between Burma and Britain. All the while, she also helped her husband in his translation work and ran a school for girls. Soon single women began pouring onto the mission field. The labors of Amy Carmichael in India are legendary. She risked her own life rescuing boys and girls from being sold into temple prostitution and then established a school that taught and cared for as many as nine hundred such children at a time. Mount Holyoke Seminary in Massachusetts, founded by Mary Lyon, trained and sent out nearly two hundred female missionaries in the nineteenth century. The 1800s also gave rise to numerous women's missionary societies.

Carey's legacy is also deeply felt in India. The Serampore College still exists. Amidst sometimes painful memories of the colonial past, William Carey's life and work continues to be honored in his adopted country. He is credited with having significant impact on modern Bengali language and writing. He also helped a number of English speakers to better understand Hinduism as he translated Hindu scriptures into English. He once wrote, "My heart is wedded to India." Some who write of Carey speak of the inordinate amount of credit given him. It was he, after all, who accompanied John Thomas when they first went to India. At Serampore, it was really the Serampore Trio that accomplished so much, not Carey alone. There were missionaries before him. Many who came after him encountered much more success than he. Nevertheless, he retains his place as the founder of modern missions. Carey looked at a world in need. Others, in his day, didn't look. And others still looked and grew callous to its need.

In the famous nave of Westminster Abbey stands a wooden lectern, used for Scripture-reading for all the services, from the daily evensong to state funerals and weddings and the coronations of queens and kings. On the base of the lectern reads an inscription: "The Gift of the Baptist Missionary Society in Honour of William Carey, 1761–1834, missionary in India and translator of the Bible." Across the top runs "Attempt Great Things for God"—the longer version of Carey's famous quote. A lectern used in the most significant assemblies of the Anglican Church may seem an odd place for a tribute to a Baptist missionary. But the location could not be more fitting. The nave of Westminster immediately draws one's eyes upward. As the light bursts in, the grandeur of the building seamlessly points to the grandeur of God. Carey knew that he could attempt great things for God on no other basis than the greatness of God. Putting it differently, because God is great, we can attempt great things. William Carey learned that during his life, and the modern missionary movement is a continual reminder of it.

A Note on the Sources

Recent reprints of William Carey's *Enquiry* include William Carey, *An Enquiry into the Obligations of Christians to Use Means for the Conversion of the Heathens*, ed. John L. Pretlove (1988), and a facsimile edition published in 1961 by Oxford University Press. Among the many biographies of William Carey, see Timothy George, *Faithful Witness: The Life and Mission of William Carey* (1991). For a history of missions, see Ruth A. Tucker, *From Jerusalem to Irian Jaya: A Biographical History of Christian Missions* (1983). For a reference work on missions and its history, see A. Scott Moreau, ed., *Evangelical Dictionary of World Missions* (2000).

13

DIETRICH BONHOEFFER
THE COST OF DISCIPLESHIP

When Christ calls a man, he bids him come and die.

Dietrich Bonhoeffer, 1937

It is only by living completely in this world that one learns to have faith.

Dietrich Bonhoeffer, from Tegel Prison, 1944

On February 1, 1933, two very different individuals addressed German audiences over the radio. The one would end in ignominy, his name synonymous with one of the most atrocious events in all of human history. On that day, Adolph Hitler offered his first radio broadcast to the German nation, and that year he became Chancellor of the Third Reich. Troubled by the recent developments of Hitler's national socialist program, Dietrich Bonhoeffer, pastor and theologian, offered his own radio address that same day. He titled his talk "The Leader and the Individual in the Younger Generation." He proceeded, "The leader must be responsibly aware of this clear limit to his authority. If he understands his function differently, then the image of the leader slips into that of the misleader." And there his speech came to an abrupt halt, the transmitter having cut out. While Bonhoeffer had particular insight into the dangers of Hitler, insight not shared by all of his colleagues in the church, little did he know just how intertwined his life would be with Hitler's. Both men would die in a dozen years: Hitler, presumably, by his own hands, while Bonhoeffer would be put to death, martyred. Hitler himself gave the order over lunch.

There is certainly an irony in the life and martyrdom of Dietrich Bonhoeffer. Living in the modern world, he had much in common with those early Christians long in the past who met their end at the hands of a hostile Roman Empire. We began our tour of church history with one of them, Polycarp. We now come full circle, as it were, finding Bonhoeffer (as so many others in the twentieth and now twenty-first century) at odds with the powers that be due to his Christian commitment. Bonhoeffer once said that Christ came into this world and offered himself to a sinful humanity, only to be met with rejection. Humanity pushed him out of the world, Bonhoeffer lamented, and right onto the cross. So a similar fate met Bonhoeffer and his message of hope and life and of suffering and of the cross. He, too, was rejected, pushed out of the way and onto the gallows. On April 9, 1945, in his thirty-ninth year, Dietrich Bonhoeffer joined the growing ranks of martyrs at the Flossenbürg concentration camp, just days before the Allied Forces liberated Germany from the Third Reich. Hitler's orders for the execution were among his last deeds. Bonhoeffer's legacy is not restricted to the final testimony of his death; it also entails his life. In the pages to follow, we will see how full and rich his short thirty-nine years were and what a lasting legacy they are for the church.

Bonhoeffer's Life and Times

To understand Bonhoeffer, one must see him in connection with those around him, within his community. The theme of community would come to dominate his writings, from his first doctoral thesis, *Sanctorum Communio* (*The Communion of Saints*), to his meditation on Christian fellowship, *Life Together*. The first community that he was a part of, and one that remained significant throughout his life, was his family. Born on February 4, 1906, along with a twin sister Sabine, he was the sixth of eight children of Karl and Paula Bonhoeffer. On his mother's side, the von Hases, there was a great-grandfather who, as a professor at Jena, had written a textbook on the history of doctrine—a textbook that would still serve students when the great-grandson prepared for examinations. Bonhoeffer's maternal grandfather was also a professor at Breslau and had numerous political connections. His mother trained as a teacher, earning her degree from the Imperial Provincial Teachers College at Breslau. His father was an academic as well, studying medicine at Tübingen and then psychiatry under Carl Wernicke, the famous German pioneer in neurology.

Karl and Paula Bonhoeffer began their life together at Breslau, where he taught at the university and ran a psychiatric clinic. His career would take him to Berlin, where, by the time of his retirement in 1938, he would have established himself as a leading neurologist and psychiatrist. His connections made along the way would later serve to help his family as they stood against the Nazi regime and as Dietrich and another son and two sons-in-law were imprisoned. His place at Berlin also opened the doors for Dietrich as he made his own way in the theological halls of academe.

The Bonhoeffer home was one of gentility, culture, and moderate wealth. A large and bustling house with children and extended family, with nannies, servants, and a chauffeur, was complemented by bookshelves and portraits lining the walls and a formal living room that doubled as music conservatory. Music was such a part of Bonhoeffer's life that, for a time, at least, it vied with theology as young Dietrich's career choice. Once, while in college, Dietrich would write to his twin sister, "This is just a quick note to tell you that I was able to buy a beautiful guitar with an adjustable bass string for 27 marks." Summers were spent in the country home. Children played in treehouses and with peashooters in the

FIG. 13.1

Timeline of Dietrich Bonhoeffer's Life

1906	Born in Bereslau, Germany, February 4
1921	Confirmation, Grunewald Church, Berlin
1923	Studies at Tübingen University
1927	Defends doctoral thesis, *Sanctorum Communio* (*The Communion of Saints*)
1928	Takes assistant pastorate, German congregation, Barcelona, Spain
1929–1936	Begins teaching at Berlin; disqualified in 1936
1930	Completes second doctoral thesis, *Act and Being*; studies at Union Theological Seminary, New York
1935	Becomes director of the Confessing Church Seminary at Finkenwalde
1937	Finkenwalde closed by Gestapo; publishes *The Cost of Discipleship*

backyard, and they were assembled often for family pictures. Karl routinely brought his work home, and his colleagues frequently joined around the family table. Evenings were spent listening to him read as the family gathered around. Not all was ideal, however. Due to a plummeting economy, inflation soared and everything was rationed. The family moved to a new home, with a garden to grow food. Tragedy struck the family in 1918 as Walter, the second son, died of complications from war wounds he had received while fighting in the First World War—that war hailed to end all wars. Two years later, at the age of fourteen, Dietrich announced to his family that he would be a minister.

1939	Travels to London and New York; returns to Germany
1940	Under watch of Gestapo
1943	In January becomes engaged to Maria von Wedemeyer; arrested April 5
1943-1944	Imprisoned at Tegel
1944-1945	Imprisoned in Berlin
1945	After a series of moves to concentration camps, arrives at Flossenbürg on April 8; martyred April 9
1986	Publication of sixteen-volume *Dietrich Bonhoeffer Werke* begins; publication of English edition begins in 1996

Dietrich Bonhoeffer began his studies at Tübingen in 1923, clearly standing out among his peers. By 1927, he had completed his doctoral thesis, *Sanctorum Communio* (*The Communion of Saints*), which was published in 1930. With the title borrowed from a line in the Apostles' Creed, Bonhoeffer's first book was a sociological and philosophical investigation of the Christian community united in fellowship in the church—an ambitious project for a twenty-one-year-old. Having successfully defended his thesis, he was licensed in theology, a credential enabling him to teach. He opted, instead, however, to try his hand briefly in the pastorate, taking an assistant pastoral position in a German congregation in Barcelona, Spain. "Starting from the beginning," he wrote in his diary as he faced a new world of preaching sermons and the routines of the pastorate. Bonhoeffer focused on youth work, presumably putting his guitar to good use, and he drank deeply of life in Spain. He read *Don Quixote* in the original language and attended a bullfight. He felt called in a different direction, however, and returned to Germany and academic life in the fall of 1929.

Bonhoeffer began lecturing in theology at Berlin University, a place quite familiar to him as it was his father's university as well. In 1930, he traveled for study at Union Theological Seminary in New York City, just on the heels of the stock-market crash and the Depression. Not much impressed by his studies, except for Reinhold Niebuhr, he soon took to skipping morning chapels. He found Union's warmed-over liberalism wanting. He, however, forged some deep and abiding friendships, on one occasion taking a road trip with friends all the way from New York to Mexico and back. He was also deeply impressed with his work in black Harlem, again among youth, at Abyssinian Baptist Church on 138th Street. One of his seminary colleagues, Paul Lehmann, noted how Bonhoeffer had an insatiable curiosity that had led him to Harlem and its unique Christian experience. Though having aristocratic tendencies and upbringing, which he wore "comfortably" and not pretentiously, he achieved "a remarkable kind of identity with the Negro community, so that he was received there as though he had never been an outsider at all." His lessons learned of sacrifice and sorrow and alienation fully mingled with joy in the gospel would accompany him the rest of his life. While in New York, he amassed a collection of phonographs of spirituals, which he would take back to Germany with him and play for his students at Berlin.

And then came Hitler. His meteoric rise was due in small part to the promise of deliverance he offered to the German nation. Kept underfoot as a result of the conditions of the negotiations to end World War I, Hitler fueled the embers of the German nationalistic spirit. Soon his zeal would turn to hatred for the enemies of the German people, embodied in the Jewish population, and soon his maniacal craze for power would force the hands of Europe's leaders and plunge the world into another season of war. Bonhoeffer was deeply troubled not merely by Hitler, but also by the national church's—the Lutheran Church's—reluctance to criticize and by its tacit approval of Hitler's national socialism. In response, Bonhoeffer and others were instrumental in the establishment of the Confessing Church in 1934. And also in 1934, he was instrumental in drafting the Barmen Declaration, which attempted to have Lutheran, Reformed, and United churches affirm their unity and identity in their confession of Christ, not in national government and interests. He led the seminary established to train its pastors at Finkenwalde, then Germany and now Poland.

By 1936, Bonhoeffer's opposition to the Nazi party had led to his dismissal from Berlin University. He kept teaching in the seminary for the Confessing Church at

Finkenwalde, until the Gestapo closed it in 1937. That same year he published *Nachfolge*, known in English as *The Cost of Discipleship*. The seminary went "underground." By 1939, a number of Bonhoeffer's colleagues in theology and ministry had left Germany for the United States or Switzerland. Reinhold Niebuhr tempted Bonhoeffer to visit New York, trying in vain to get him to stay. As soon as Bonhoeffer arrived in New York, he knew that he was doing the wrong thing. Niebuhr and others made a final plea for him to stay. Bonhoeffer recorded the following in his diary: "The decision has been made. I have refused [to stay]. They were clearly disappointed, and rather upset. It probably means more for me than I can see at the moment. God alone knows what."

Before he returned to Germany, he visited his twin sister, Sabine, and her husband in London. She had escaped Germany via Switzerland. There are many photographs of Bonhoeffer, but perhaps none more moving than the one of Dietrich and Sabine sitting in the garden of her boarding house in London. He is in a suit with his pocket-watch chain on his vest, and she is wearing a dress and a tiny pearl necklace, both oblivious to the camera, warmly smiling at each other. This would be the last time they would see each other. Perhaps they sensed it, but for the moment the trials that the whole family would face in the coming war were distant.

Upon his return to Germany, Bonhoeffer became a member of the *Abwehr*, the German resistance movement to Hitler and Nazism. Politics had been in the background for Bonhoeffer the theologian. Now, his life and his theology would be inextricably linked to politics. The *Abwehr* plotted to overthrow the government. Containing members of the German military, it planned a coup and an internal purging of the Nazi regime. Bonhoeffer was sent to Sweden and to Norway to relay messages intended for the British government seeking support for the resistance. "Undoubted interest, but deeply regret no answer possible," came the reply. Eventually, a group within the *Abwehr*, Bonhoeffer and his brother-in-law among them, reluctantly embraced the idea that Hitler must be stopped. It was time to plot his assassination.

Hans von Dohnanyi, who had married Dietrich's sister Christine, brought Dietrich into a highly secretive group of conspirators, among them a major general, Hans Oster, and one with close ties to Hitler himself, Admiral Wilhelm Canaris. Dohnanyi was to put a briefcase loaded with explosives onboard a plane in which Hitler would travel. Hitler visited the Russian front at Smolensk on March 13, 1943. The explosives were placed on the plane waiting to return him to Berlin. The bomb never went off; the assassination failed. A suicide bomber made another attempt on March 21. Bonhoeffer waited in the family home to hear of the news, but a last-minute change of plans by Hitler thwarted the attempt. Bonhoeffer's phone never rang.

Bonhoeffer hoped for the success of the movement and longed for a time of peace. So much so that he became engaged on January 17, 1943, to Maria von Wedemeyer. At eighteen years old, she was many years his junior, and she was well aware of his dangerous activities in the *Abwehr*. But love prevailed. Their time together did not last long. On April 5, 1943, Bonhoeffer was arrested by the Gestapo, his name uncovered as a conspirator in the attempted overthrow and assassinations. He was sent to Tegel Prison, his home for the next eighteen months. Through bribes paid by his parents and the sheer force of his personality, Bonhoeffer won over the prison guards, who smuggled out letters and smuggled in such luxuries as paper and books. From his cell, he wrote letters to his family and Maria, sermons for marriages and baptisms of cousins and nieces and nephews, haunting poems, and even drama, short stories, and a novel. And here he contemplated suicide: "suicide," a fragment reads, "not because of consciousness of guilt but because basically I am already dead."

That was written early on at Tegel. Soon, however, any thoughts of suicide left him completely. He would be resigned to his sentence and his six-by-nine-foot cell, and if need be, he would die for the cause of peace and justice and righteousness. During this dark night of his soul, he grasped the meaning of the cross and suffering, and from here he did some of his best work as a theologian. Bonhoeffer once wrote, thinking of his time in Barcelona, that his theology now had a touch of humanity to it, and was forever different, deeper and more alive. His time at Tegel would take him deeper still. It was only in Tegel that he could say:

> When we have completely renounced trying to make something of ourselves—be it a saint or a converted sinner or a cleric (a so-called priestly figure), a righteous or unrighteous person, a sick or healthy person . . . when we have done this, then we completely throw ourselves into God's arms, take God's own suffering in the world seriously rather than our own, and keep watch with Christ in Gethsemane. That, I think, is faith. That is conversion, and it is this way that one becomes a human being, a Christian.

Bonhoeffer was removed from Tegel in the fall of 1944 and taken to a military prison in Berlin for interrogation, where he would remain until February 1945. He was imprisoned so long because a solid case could never be built against him. Through a series of ciphers and coded messages, all orchestrated by Bonhoeffer's father, the coconspirators concocted false stories and covered their involvement, even withstanding intense times of individual interrogations. It worked, until the so-called Zossen files were discovered, which contained reports of their activities and their names. A report of the case went to Hitler himself, who ordered the execution of Bonhoeffer and the others on April 5.

During Bonhoeffer's Berlin imprisonment, the freedoms of writing letters and receiving books that he enjoyed at Tegel were cut off. The long stream of letters was choked to a mere trickle. Only three letters were sent: a Christmas letter to Maria, a birthday letter to his mother, and one final letter to his parents in January. In prison it is he who offers fortitude. His Christmas letter to Maria: "We've now been waiting for each other for almost two years, dearest Maria. Don't lose heart."

Bonhoeffer was moved from Berlin to the concentration camp at Buchenwald on February 7, 1945. In April, after Hitler signed his execution orders, he was moved to Flossenbürg, one of the so-called death camps. The prison doctor records his final moments on April 9, 1945:

> On the morning of that day between five and six o'clock the prisoners . . . were taken from their cells, and the verdicts of the court martial read out to them. Through the half-open door in one room of the huts I saw Pastor Bonhoeffer, before taking off his prison garb, kneeling on the floor praying fervently to his God. I was most deeply moved by the way this lovable man prayed, so devout and so certain that God heard his prayer. At the place of execution, he again said a short prayer and then climbed the steps to the gallows, brave and composed. His death ensued after a few seconds. In the almost fifty years that I worked as a doctor, I have hardly ever seen a man die so entirely submissive to the will of God.

Bonhoeffer's own last words were spoken to a captured British officer: "This is the end—for me the beginning of life." In a few weeks, Germany would be liberated. Maria would not learn of Bonhoeffer's death until June; his parents would not know of it until July—and then when they heard a broadcast of a memorial service held for him in London on July 27, 1945.

Bonhoeffer's Thought and Writings

Bonhoeffer was profoundly influenced by Martin Luther. He writes of Luther as if they were friends; he reads his books as if they are in conversation. Perhaps the idea of Luther's that Bonhoeffer cherished most was the theology of the cross. Luther once remarked that when we come to God, we come to him in the person of Christ on the cross. And, he added, this is not where we should expect to find God. Here is God in the person of Jesus Christ on the cross, suffering and shamed and brought low by sin. The cross, thundered Luther, is God's "no" to all the vain attempts of humanity to merit God's favor. It is, he countered, God's "yes" to our sinfulness, to our frailty, to our inability. For Bonhoeffer, like Luther, the cross is at the center of everything. "The figure of the reconciler," Bonhoeffer wrote in 1940, "of the divine human Jesus Christ, steps into the middle between God and the world, into the center of all that happens." At the cross, God at once declares the guilt of the world for sin and extinguishes that very guilt. From another perspective, Bonhoeffer continues, "The world takes out its rage on the body of Jesus Christ. But he, tormented, forgives the world its sin." At the cross, God answers the hatred with love.

These words come from Bonhoeffer's *Ecce Homo*, Latin for "Behold the Man"—from John 19:5. He continues, "It is a secret for which there is no explanation that only part of humankind recognizes the form and shape of its redeemer. To this very hour, the yearning of the Incarnate to acquire shape and form in all human beings does yet remain unful-filled. He who bore the form of *the* human being can acquire form only in a small host, and that host is his church." This is a dense statement that needs some unpacking, but one that perhaps gets at the heart of Bonhoeffer's thought. On the cross, Christ was establishing a new humanity, a new people, the church (Eph. 2). Bonhoeffer preferred to speak of this as community, as genuine Christian fellowship. This idea of community first took shape in his mind during his theological studies, finding expression in his first doctoral thesis, *Sanctorum Communio* (*The Communion of Saints*), which, as mentioned earlier, came about in his twenty-first year. It permeates his second doctoral thesis, *Act and Being*, published in 1931. It finds further expression in his lectures on Genesis 1–3, published as *Creation and Fall* (1937). Fi-nally, he offered a more popular treatment of the idea in his work *Life Together* (1939).

Distilling his thought on community into a short treat-ment, especially since it takes such a circuitous route through most of his writings, is no small task indeed. Per-haps a sampling will whet the appetite. Bonhoeffer grounds his idea of community in Christ and the cross. In *Sancto-rum Communio*, he points out that we are not reconciled by Christ, we are reconciled *in* Christ, drawing heavily from Ephesians 1. And, as he tells us in *Life Together*, this new community is the divine reality: "I have community with others and I shall continue to have only through Jesus Christ. . . . We have one another only through Christ, but through Christ we do have one another, wholly, for all eter-nity." At this point, however, Bonhoeffer takes a surprising turn as he repudiates what he terms a "wish dream." We might call it naive thinking that because of our union with Christ, all is well in the Christian community. "By sheer grace," Bonhoeffer interjects, "God will not permit us to live even for a brief period in a dream world." He then calls us to an authentic fellowship that faces "disillusionment, with all its unhappy and ugly aspects." He continues, "The sooner this shock of disillusionment comes to an individual and to a community the better for both. A community which cannot bear and cannot survive such a crisis, which insists upon keeping its illusion when it should be shattered, permanently loses in that moment the promise of Christian community." He challenges the unrealistic expectations placed on ourselves and placed on others. He calls the church to be a community of grace.

In Bonhoeffer's prison letters, he speaks of another significant idea that seems counter to his thought in *The Cost of Discipleship*. He speaks of it as *this-worldliness*. Writing to Eberhard Bethge on July 21, 1944, Bonhoeffer recalls a conversation he had with a Frenchman while they were both studying at Union Theological Seminary in New York in 1930. As young men, they were naturally asking each other what they wanted to make of their lives. Jean Lasserre, the Frenchman, replied that "he would like to become a saint." Bonhoeffer answered, "I should like to learn to have faith." Then in his letter, thirteen years and a world of experience after that conversation, he adds, "I discovered later, and I'm still discovering right up to this moment, that it is only by living completely in this world that one learns to have faith. . . . By this-worldliness I mean living unreservedly in life's duties, problems, successes and failures, experiences and perplexities." By living this way, we take the focus off ourselves and off our own suffering. Instead, we look to Christ and his suffering. This idea of Bonhoeffer's stems from Luther's notion of *incurvitas*, the tendency of the self to look inward due to sin. Faith forces us to look outward to Christ, not inward to ourselves. In fact, Bonhoeffer concludes that this looking to Christ on the cross *is* faith.

Bonhoeffer's this-worldliness, then, is not at all what we might initially think. Further, it very much speaks to what he writes in *The Cost of Discipleship*. It is, in fact, a radical way of thinking about living the Christian life—one that vies between escapism from the world, on the one hand, and conformity to the world, on the other. It is a call to a lived Christianity, a theme pulsing through Bonhoeffer's writings.

Decades after Bonhoeffer's death, Eberhard Bethge, who married Bonhoeffer's cousin and who corresponded with him throughout his imprisonment, undertook the publication of his collected writings, *Dietrich Bonhoeffer Werke*, which is currently being published in English. Filling no fewer than sixteen volumes, these works include all of Bonhoeffer's published books, as well as his letters, lectures, shorter treatises, sermons, poems, and manuscript fragments. Among those works is his *Ethics* (published posthumously, 1949), which, along with other related writings, addresses the issues of the Christian and the Christian community in the world and in relation to the state. Among his many writings, two works stand out: the posthumously published *Letters and Papers from Prison*, edited by Eberhard Bethge (1953), and *The Cost of Discipleship* (1937). In the pages that follow, we'll explore his masterly treatment of what it means to be a disciple, especially for one in the modern world.

Bonhoeffer's *The Cost of Discipleship*

In the first line of the first chapter, Bonhoeffer has us hooked: "Cheap grace is the mortal enemy of our church. Our struggle today is for costly grace." He continues, "Cheap grace means grace as bargain basement goods, cut-rate forgiveness, cut-rate comfort, cut-rate sacrament." Then he builds up to this: "Cheap grace means justification of sin but not of the sinner," before the crescendo, "Cheap grace is preaching forgiveness without repentance. . . . Cheap grace is grace without discipleship, without the cross, grace without the living, incarnate Jesus Christ." Now comes costly grace, "the hidden treasure in the field." He continues, "It is costly, because it calls to discipleship; it is grace, because it calls us to follow *Jesus Christ*. It is costly, because it costs people their lives; it is grace, because it thereby makes them live." And then he crescendos again: "Above all, grace is costly, because it was costly to God, because it costs God the cost of God's own son—'you were bought with a price'—and because nothing can be cheap to us which is costly to God."

Bonhoeffer then turns to the rediscovery of grace in the time of the Reformation at the hands of Luther. But Bonhoeffer addresses the challenge that Luther is somewhat responsible for the rise of cheap grace. After all, Luther was the one who said, "Sin boldly, but believe and rejoice in Christ even more boldly." And Luther was the one who laid such a stress on justification and grace that he eclipsed obedience and law and discipleship. Bonhoeffer steps in by noting that "Luther's teachings are quoted everywhere" in support of the apostles of cheap grace. But, Bonhoeffer counters, those quotes are "twisted from their truth into self-delusion." Understanding Luther aright will not lead to cheap grace. The German Lutheran Church, Bonhoeffer's milieu, had gotten its founder, Luther, wrong. Consequently, Bonhoeffer saw the church getting both grace and discipleship wrong. For Bonhoeffer, getting grace and discipleship right, especially in relationship to each other, is decisive in the "question of how we are to live as Christians today." The rest of the book, after the first chapter on "Costly Grace," takes up that question.

The Cost of Discipleship consists of two parts. The first part looks at discipleship from the perspective of the individual, while the second part addresses discipleship within the new community of the church. These are not two different books, however, but one and the same. Bonhoeffer does not want us to read the two parts in isolation but together. One is a disciple only within the body of Christ, the community of the church. Bonhoeffer puts it this way as he starts the second part: "If we want to hear his call to discipleship, we need to hear where Christ himself is present. It is within the church that Jesus Christ calls through his word and sacrament."

In the first part, Bonhoeffer addresses various elements of discipleship before turning to an extensive discussion of Matthew 5–7. It makes sense that Bonhoeffer spends time on this text, the Beatitudes. Those advocating cheap grace can easily point to Matthew 5–7 as merely ideal; its commands are not to be taken seriously, especially in the modern world. But Bonhoeffer sees Matthew 5–7 posing a fundamental challenge to the assumptions of the modern world. Self-centeredness is checked by Christ-centeredness, evidenced in others-centeredness; materialism is checked by simplicity; false security is checked by faith; and arrogance is checked by humility. Bonhoeffer ends his discussion of Matthew 5–7 by pointing out that "Jesus does not permit his listeners to simply walk away, making whatever they like of his discourse, extracting what seems to them to be useful in their lives, testing how his teaching compares to 'reality.'" The response, Bonhoeffer adds, is not to "interpret or apply, but do it and obey."

As mentioned, the second part turns to discipleship within the community of the church, Bonhoeffer's ubiquitous theme. More than one commentator has pointed to the tendency of the modern toward individualism. Germans in Bonhoeffer's day suffered from it at the hands of Friedrich Nietzsche and his concept of the *Übermensch*, or "Superman." And

no shortage of evidence reveals its presence in most of
the rest of the Western world. Consequently, Paul's statement
of being part of the body of Christ "sounds very strange and
incomprehensible to us." Bonhoeffer begins with baptism,
making the point that "all who are baptized are 'one in
Christ' (Gal. 3:28; Rom. 12:5; 1 Cor. 10:17)." This "Body of
Christ takes up physical space here on earth," he tells us in
the next chapter. The church becomes, as it were, the con-
tinuation of the incarnate Christ. And the Word becomes visible, Bonhoeffer continues, as the church preaches and pro-
claims the gospel and as the church administers the
sacrament: "The body of Christ becomes visible in the
church-community that gathers around word [preaching]
and sacrament." Bonhoeffer's next step views the church as
living "its own life in the midst of this world, continually bearing witness in all it is and does that 'the present form of this
world is passing away' (1 Cor. 7:31)." Like John the Baptist,
the church points to the reality of the kingdom of God to
those content with living in its shadow.

Two more chapters round out the book. The first explores
what it means to be a communion of *saints*, noting this does
not mean that the church is populated by perfect people,
but that it is to be populated by those who have tasted of
grace and forgiveness and are striving to live lives "worthy
of their calling and of the gospel (Eph. 4:1; Phil. 1:27; Col.
1:10; 1 Thess. 2:12)." Bonhoeffer then ends by looking at
the church and the image of Christ. As human beings, Bonhoeffer reminds us, we bear the image of Adam. This is our
shared humanity. As Christians we bear and are ever being
transformed into the image of Christ. This is our shared new
and true humanity. He writes of our state in Adam, "Human beings live without being truly human. They must live
without being able to live. That is the paradox of our existence and the source of all our woes." And into this, "God

sends the divine Son in the likeness of sinful flesh (Rom. 8:2f.).” And, as if the whole book has been leading up to this, “Since we have been formed in the image of Christ, we can live following his example.” We can live as disciples.

Bonhoeffer published *The Cost of Discipleship* in 1937, the same year the Gestapo shut down the Confessing Church’s seminary at Finkenwalde. Bonhoeffer, his students, and his fellow colleagues in the Confessing Church all had firsthand experience of the cost of discipleship. The Confessing Church faced opposition from the German Reich Church, which supported Hitler’s Third Reich and the Nazi party. The Confessing Church, meeting at Barmen in 1934, declared, “We repudiate the false teaching that the church can turn over the form of her message and ordinances at will or according to some ideological and political convictions.” Instead, the Confessing Church affirmed, “with her faith as well as her obedience, with her message as well as with her ordinances, [the church] has to witness in the midst of the world of sin as the church of forgiven sinners that she is his alone.” For taking such a stand, the Confessing Church was driven to found new seminaries, like the one at Finkenwalde in 1935. It had a short life, closed by the Gestapo on September 28, 1937. “Cheap grace,” writes Bonhoeffer, “is the mortal enemy of our church. Our struggle today is for costly grace.”

Bonhoeffer’s Legacy

In his novel, written in Tegel Prison, Bonhoeffer’s main character, Frau Karoline Brake, rattles off, “You mustn’t confuse Christianity with its pathetic representatives.” The context is important. They were words that “perhaps she could have said” to her grandson, who was quite nonplussed by the church service and the hollow phrases trickling from the pulpit. Frau Brake knew authentic Christianity to be different.

But not everyone in her congregation shared her insight or her predilections. They were quite content with the pathetic representatives, passing on the authentic original. Scholars of Bonhoeffer are quick to point out that Bonhoeffer's first and only novel is not a detached one; it has a good dose of memoir. And like his other writings, it also has a good dose of exhortation and sermon in it. For Bonhoeffer, watering down or sweetening up Christianity to make it more palatable to modern tastes does not help Christianity but destroys it. In fact, as one looks at Bonhoeffer's life and the value of his legacy, rising right to the surface is the line, "You mustn't confuse Christianity with its pathetic representatives." Bonhoeffer's life is his character's line.

Perhaps by now, having taken our tour through church history, we have seen the various pressures and challenges as well as opportunities facing the church in every age. The Reformers contended with centuries of theological missteps. The early church fathers contended with a hostile empire, while Augustine and those who followed contended with a friendly one. Many in the twentieth century practiced Christianity with little or no repercussions, while others, such as Bonhoeffer, paid with their very lives. There is a tendency to prioritize such experiences, to attribute a higher value to one over the other. Bonhoeffer himself would likely be suspicious of such a tendency. He would certainly not condone the denial of one's faith to escape persecution. But neither would he be likely to advocate that physical persecution and martyrdom are a higher form of discipleship. His life, however, reminds us that whether or not the state is hostile to Christianity, the modern mind in many ways has set itself at odds with the gospel. He stands as a testimony that discipleship in the modern world, just as it has been throughout the centuries, is costly.

Bonhoeffer also speaks poignantly to some of the most troubling issues of the twentieth century: racism and xenophobia. Such attitudes led to countless atrocities in that century, from civil-rights abuses to lynchings, from unfair trade policies to genocide. It was while serving in a Baptist church in Harlem that Bonhoeffer first confronted the problem of race. He also saw how it was fundamental to Hitler and the Nazi program. Bonhoeffer's theological commitments, his understanding of basic human identity, gave him a biblical perspective on the race issue that allowed him to speak and act courageously.

He founded no church and was at the center of no new movement. Yet merely his name and his act of martyrdom make him one of the most singular influences on contemporary Christianity. He was a Lutheran minister and an academic theologian, but his appeal transcends denominations as he is read by scholars, clergy, and laity alike. *The Cost of Discipleship* and the posthumously published *Letters and Papers from Prison* are classics. His genius is exposed in his doctoral thesis at age twenty-one. His gift of expression reveals itself in just about everything he wrote. But above all, the sheer force of his personality compels us to listen. We see him in his numerous photographs with thinning hair and rimless glasses. Smiling with students and sleeves rolled up, he looks, in the words of one Bonhoeffer biographer, more like a prize-fighter than an academic. He was at ease with himself. He was a sprinter. He was a musician. He was a poet. He was a theologian who once wrote, "The young theologian should be aware that his theology is in the service of the true church of Christ, which unerringly confesses its Lord and lives in the consciousness of this responsibility." He was a martyr.

Perhaps, however, he can tell us the most about himself. One of his many prison poems begins:

> Who am I? They often tell me
> I would step from my cell's confinement

> calmly, cheerfully, firmly,
> like a squire from his country-house.

He continues:

> Am I really that which all other men tell of?
> Or am I only what I know of myself,
> restless and longing and sick, like a bird in a cage,
> struggling for breath, as though hands were compressing
>   my throat,
> yearning for colours, for flowers, for the voices of birds,
> thirsting for words of kindness, for neighborliness,
> trembling with anger at despotisms and petty humiliation,
> tossing in expectations of great events,
> powerlessly trembling for friends at an infinite distance,
> weary and empty at praying, at thinking, at making,
> faint, and ready to say farewell to it all?

Then he ends:

> Who am I? They mock me, these lonely questions of mine.
> Whoever I am, thou knowest, O God, I am thine.

A Note on the Sources

The comprehensive, monumental biography of Dietrich Bonhoeffer is by his friend and prison correspondent, Eberhard Bethge, *Dietrich Bonhoeffer: A Biography*, rev. ed. (2000). Dietrich Bonhoeffer, *Letters and Papers from Prison*, ed. Eberhard Bethge (1971), is indispensable. Numerous editions of *The Cost of Discipleship* are available. See the English edition of the authoritative, scholarly collection of his writings, *Dietrich Bonhoeffer Works* (1996–). Eight of the sixteen projected volumes have been published; *Discipleship* is volume 4 (2001).

Continuing the Journey: A Guide for Further Reading

> Beware of the man of one book.
>
> Thomas Aquinas

This tour through church history began with the notion, drawing from Langston Hughes, that we are enriched as we make meaningful connections to our past. I hope this has been shown to be true indeed. My goal in this tour, however, is to leave you unsatisfied. My hope is that it only starts you on your journey through church history—or, as I suspect for most of you, pushes you a little further along. Fortunately, we have an embarrassment of riches when it comes to the literary legacy of our past.

First, there are a number of single-volume surveys that serve for the next step. Mark A. Noll's *Turning Points: Decisive Moments in the History of Christianity* tops the list. His survey employs the notion of selective attention, though instead of focusing on classic texts as here, he looks to events or, as he terms them, "decisive moments." Earle E. Cairns, *Christianity Through the Centuries: A History of the Christian Church*, 3rd ed., continues to be a classic textbook on the subject. For a single volume treating the history of theology and doctrinal development, see Alister McGrath, *Historical Theology: An Introduction to the History of Christian Thought,* as well as John D. Hannah, *Our Legacy: The History of Christian Doctrine.*

Standard multivolume works include the classic eight-volume *History of the Christian Church* by Philip Schaff, America's first serious Christian historian. His eight volumes, however, get you only to the Reformation. Picking up where Schaff leaves off, the five-volume *History of Evangelicalism* (InterVarsity Press) promises a transatlantic reading of the church in the Modern Age. A new series with volumes that span the whole of church history is the *Baker History of the Christian Church,* with Tim Dowley as the series editor.

These works are what historians refer to as secondary sources, which means that they are about the subject. They provide the necessary context and help us interpret what are referred to as primary sources, texts by the subject. Amassing the various primary texts from church history can be both overwhelming and bank-breaking. One of the most affordable sets, from which one can pick and choose volumes of personal interest, is the Library of Christian Classics: Ichthus edition (Westminster John Knox Press). These provide helpful introductions and scholarly texts. One way to gain exposure to primary sources is through readers. There are many such readers available that focus on a particular age, person, or denomination. Some readers focus on a particular genre, such as Philip Schaff's classic three-volume *The Creeds of Christendom* or John H. Leith's one-volume *Creeds of the Churches.* Simple Internet searches will reveal a wealth of material online. One significant site is the Christian Classic and Ethereal Library, www.ccel.org. Other sites offer numerous sources for a particular era or person. Some examples of helpful sites include: www.earlychristianwritings.com for the early church and www.yale.edu/wje for an online source of the writings of Jonathan Edwards.

For further sources on the individuals and texts discussed in this survey, see the Note on the Sources section that concludes each chapter. One of the challenges of this book, however, was leaving many worthy individuals out. Athanasius would have well represented the early church. John Owen would have been just as good a representative of the Puritans as John Bunyan. C. S. Lewis makes as worthy a candidate for the twentieth century as Bonhoeffer. And the list goes on. Again, if this book leaves you unsatisfied, it will have accomplished its goal. For those who do wish to explore further, there is no shortage of subjects and no shortage of books.

A note, however, is in order on how to read historical figures and their texts. Our tendency is to go to one extreme or the other. On the one hand, we tend to nearly idolize our heroes. Historians call this hagiography, the turning of our heroes into saints who can do no wrong. On the other hand, we can unduly judge them against modern standards, or standards developed later in time. The technical term is *anachronism*, meaning in this context that we read current standards back in time. Succumbing to either tendency causes us to misread and misapply history. Instead, just as the biblical scholar will remind us that we need to read Scripture in its historical context, so, too, we need to be careful to read historical figures in the context of their own times. Of course, this cannot be used to excuse inexcusable behavior. We cannot, however, miss the application to us. We are quick to point out blind spots and shortcomings of ages previous to ours, all the while oblivious to our own. Yet another lesson we can learn from church history.

The study of church history may be best viewed as a second-order discipline. It is subservient to our study of the Bible and the central and defining figure unfolded in its pages—Christ. It is, however, a significant story. It reminds us that the community of believers (those united to Christ) is a group of people who are, in the words of Augustine, simultaneously sinners and saints, who have experienced triumphs and challenges, victories and setbacks. It reminds us that we in the twenty-first century are not alone, that we belong to something much bigger than we, even in our collective, global strength. Again, church history is a second-order discipline. Nevertheless, it is one that we neglect to our own disservice, for we are a people with a past. And as we connect with our past, our souls grow deeper like a river, carving its contours as it runs.

BIBLIOGRAPHY

Augustine. *Confessions.* Ed. R. S. Pine-Coffin. New York: Penguin, 1972.
———. *Confessions.* Ed. Henry Chadwick. Oxford: Oxford University Press, 1982.
Barker, William S. *Puritan Profiles: 54 Puritans.* Ross-Shire: Mentor, 1996.
Bethge, Eberhard. *Dietrich Bonhoeffer: A Biography.* Minneapolis: Fortress Press, 2000.
Bonhoeffer, Dietrich. *Letters and Papers from Prison.* Ed. Eberhard Bethge. New York: Simon & Schuster, 1971.
———. *Dietrich Bonhoeffer Works.* Gen. ed. Wayne Whitson Floyd Jr. Minneapolis: Fortress Press, 1996–.
Bunyan, John. *Pilgrim's Progress.* Ed. N. H. Keeble. Oxford: Oxford University Press, 1998.
Calvin, John. *The Institutes of the Christian Religion.* Ed. John T. McNeill. Louisville: Westminster John Knox Press, 1960.
Carey, William. *An Enquiry into the Obligations of Christians to Use Means for the Conversion of the Heathen.* Oxford: Oxford University Press, 1961.
Chadwick, Henry. *The Early Church.* New York: Penguin, 1967.
Charlesworth, M. J. *St. Anselm's Proslogion.* Notre Dame: Notre Dame University Press, 1979.
Collinson, Patrick. *The Reformation: A History.* New York: Modern Library, 2004.
Cross, F. L., ed. *The Oxford Dictionary of the Christian Church.* Oxford: Oxford University Press, 1997.
Dickens, A. G. *The English Reformation.* University Park: The Pennsylvania State University Press, 1989.
Edwards, Jonathan, *History of the Work of Redemption.* Edinburgh: The Banner of Truth Trust, 2003.
Elwell, Walter, ed. *The Evangelical Dictionary of Theology.* Grand Rapids: Baker, 1984.
Elwood, Christopher. *Calvin for Armchair Theologians.* Louisville: Westminster John Knox Press, 2002.

Evans, G. R. *Anselm.* Wilton, CT: Morehouse-Barlowe, 1989.

——, ed. *The Medieval Theologians.* Oxford: Blackwell, 2001.

Fairweather, A. M., ed. *Aquinas on Nature and Grace.* Louisville: Westminster John Knox Press, 1954.

Fairweather, Eugene R., ed. *A Scholastic Miscellany: Anselm to Ockham.* Louisville: Westminster John Knox Press, 1961.

Ferguson, Everett. *Backgrounds of Early Christianity.* Grand Rapids: Eerdmans, 2003.

Fitzgerald, Allan D., ed. *Augustine through the Ages: An Encyclopedia.* Grand Rapids: Eerdmans, 1999.

George, Timothy. *Faithful Witness: The Life and Mission of William Carey.* Alabama: New Hope, 1991.

Hannah, John D. *Our Legacy: The History of Christian Doctrine.* Colorado Springs: Navpress, 2001.

Hart, D. G., Sean Michael Lucas, and Stephen J. Nichols, eds. *The Legacy of Jonathan Edwards: American Religion and the Evangelical Tradition.* Grand Rapids: Baker, 2003.

Helm, Paul. *Calvin and the Calvinists.* Edinburgh: The Banner of Truth Trust, 1982.

Kapic, Kelly M. and Randall C. Gleason, eds. *The Devoted Life: An Invitation to the Puritan Classics.* Downers Grove: InterVarsity Press, 2004.

Lieth, John. *Creeds of the Churches.* Louisville: Westminster John Knox Press, 1982.

Lull, Timothy, ed. *Martin Luther's Basic Theological Writings.* Minneapolis: Fortress Press, 1989.

Luther, Martin. *Luther's Small Catechism and Explanation.* St. Louis, Concordia Publishing House, 1991.

McGrath, Alister. *Historical Theology: An Introduction to the History of Christian Thought.* Oxford: Blackwell, 1998.

——. *A Life of John Calvin.* Oxford: Blackwell, 1990.

Marty, Martin. *Martin Luther.* New York: Penguin, 2004.

Moore, Doreen. *Good Christians, Good Husbands?* Ross-Shire: Christian Focus, 2004.

Moreau, A. Scott, ed. *Evangelical Dictionary of World Missions.* Grand Rapids: Baker, 2000.

Mouw, Richard. *Calvinism at the Las Vegas Airport.* Grand Rapids: Zondervan, 2004.

Murray, Iain. *Wesley and the Men Who Followed.* Edinburgh: The Banner of Truth Trust, 2003.

Needham, N. R. *The Triumph of Grace: Augustine's Writings on Salvation.* London: Grace Publications Trust, 2000.

Nichols, Aidan. *Discovering Aquinas: An Introduction to His Life, Work and Influence.* Grand Rapids: Eerdmans, 2002.

Nichols, Heidi L. *Anne Bradstreet: A Guided Tour of the Life and Thought of a Puritan Poet.* Phillipsburg, NJ: P&R, 2006.

Nichols, Stephen J. *Jonathan Edwards: A Guided Tour of His Life and Thought.* Phillipsburg, NJ: P&R, 2001.

——. *Martin Luther: A Guided Tour of His Life and Thought.* Phillipsburg, NJ: P&R, 2002.

Noll, Mark A. *The Rise of Evangelicalism: The Age of Edwards, Whitefield, and Wesley.* Downers Grove: InterVarsity Press, 2003.

——. *Turning Points: Decisive Moments in the Shaping of Christian History.* Grand Rapids: Baker, 1997.

Parker, T. H. L. *Calvin: An Introduction to His Thought.* Louisville: Westminster John Knox Press, 1995.

Pelikan, Jarislov. *The Christian Tradition: A History of the Development of Doctrine.* Chicago: Chicago University Press, 1975.

Percy, Ray C. *Late Medieval Mysticism.* Louisville: Westminster John Knox Press, 1995.

Piper, John and Justin Taylor, eds. *A God-Entranced Vision of All Things: The Legacy of Jonathan Edwards.* Wheaton: Crossway, 2004.

Renick, Timothy M. *Aquinas for Armchair Theologians.* Louisville: Westminster John Knox Press, 2002.

Southern, R. W. *Saint Anselm: A Portrait in a Landscape.* Cambridge: Cambridge University Press, 1990.

Steinmetz, David. *Calvin in Context.* Oxford: Oxford University Press, 1995.

Thomas à Kempis. *The Imitation of Christ.* Ed. Leo Sherley-Price. New York: Penguin, 1972.

Thomas Aquinas. *Selected Writings.* Ed. Ralph McInerney. New York: Penguin, 1999.

Tomkins, Stephen. *John Wesley: A Biography.* Grand Rapids: Eerdmans, 2003.

Tucker, Ruth A. *From Jerusalem to Irian Jaya: A Biographical History of Christian Missions.* Grand Rapids: Zondervan, 1983.

Tyson, John R., ed. *Charles Wesley: A Reader.* Oxford: Oxford University Press, 1989.

Wills, Gary. *Augustine.* New York: Penguin, 1999.

Wilson, John F., ed. *The Works of Jonathan Edwards, Volume 9: A History of the Work of Redemption.* New Haven: Yale University Press, 1989.

Zahl, Paul F. M. *Five Women of the English Reformation.* Grand Rapids: Eerdmans, 2001.

INDEX OF PERSONS

INDEX OF SCRIPTURE

Stephen J. Nichols (M.A., West Chester University; M.A.R. and Ph.D., Westminster Theological Seminary) is a professor at Lancaster Bible College and Graduate School. He is the author of numerous books, most recently including *J. Gresham Machen: A Guided Tour of His Life and Thought* and *Heaven on Earth: Capturing Jonathan Edwards's Vision of Living in Between*. He lives with his wife, Heidi, and two sons in Lancaster, Pennsylvania. He was recently elected to the Board of Supervisors for Caernarvon Township.

Also in the GUIDED TOUR *series*

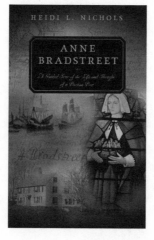

by Heidi L. Nichols
Price: $13.99
To order, visit
www.prpbooks.com
or call
1(800) 631-0094

"This book does a masterful job of performing the task identified in the subtitle—it is a guided tour of the life and work of Anne Bradstreet, conducted by a wonderfully talented tour guide. For anyone wishing to acquire or renew an acquaintance with Anne Bradstreet, this is the book of choice."

— LELAND RYKEN

"Puritan pioneer Anne Bradstreet, solid believer, ardent wife, faithful mother, wise woman, and gifted poetess, is a lady well worth meeting. Dr. Nichols arranges that meeting beautifully in these pages, and merits our gratitude for doing so."

— J. I. PACKER

"Nichols not only illuminates the poet's life and social context, she makes it possible for a new generation to savor Anne Bradstreet's own words and to share the sorrows, joy, and hope of her inner journey."

— CHARLES HAMBRICK-STOWE

Also in the Guided Tour *series*

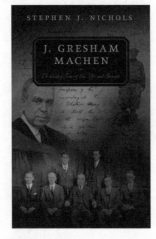

by Stephen J. Nichols
Price: $13.99
To order, visit
www.prpbooks.com
or call
1(800) 631-0094

"Nichols has done a fine job of presenting an accessible introduction to the life and thought of J. Gresham Machen. Nichols offers lucid expositions and fresh interpretations based on his own research."

—George M. Marsden

"J. Gresham Machen's writing was as clear as his arguments were persuasive. Nichols has accomplished the rare feat of making Machen even more accessible. For readers unfamiliar with Machen, this is the perfect appetizer to the feast of further study in Machen's writings. For those more knowledgeable, this will be a reliable reference."

—D. G. Hart

"Nichols has provided an accessible gateway to conservative Presbyterianism's most stalwart defender in the tumultuous 1920s. His admiring portrait reminds us of Machen's probing scholarship, his trenchant analysis of modernism, and his attempts to further the Christian world and life view in American culture.

—Andrew Hoffecker

Also in the GUIDED TOUR *series*

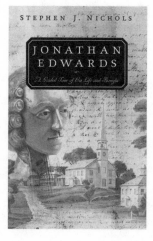

by Stephen J. Nichols
Price: $13.99
To order, visit
www.prpbooks.com
or call
1(800) 631-0094

"A lively and vivid introduction to America's greatest theologian—
the best one yet for use in most churches and Christian colleges."
—DOUGLAS A. SWEENEY

"Nichols is an enthusiastic, experienced, and reliable tour guide
to the theology of Jonathan Edwards. If your experience is like
mine, these pages will make you want to visit Edwards on your
own for frequent and extended periods. An excellent introduction."
—SINCLAIR FERGUSON

"Edwards is still America's greatest theologian, and his works
remain of lasting value to the church. This book is a useful introduction to the great man's message and ministry. Nichols has chosen his material carefully to help readers begin to understand
Edwards's most important writings."
—PHILIP GRAHAM RYKEN

Also in the GUIDED TOUR *series*

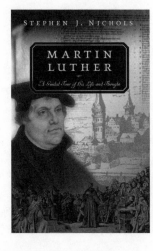

by Stephen J. Nichols
Price: $13.99
To order, visit
www.prpbooks.com
or call
1(800) 631-0094

"For over half a century Roland Bainton's *Here I Stand* has been the best popular introduction to Luther. Stephen Nichols's engaging volume is in many ways better than Bainton's for this purpose. It deserves to be widely read, and as an unashamed Luther-lover I hope it will be."

—J. I. PACKER

"How do you do a book on everything from training children to hymns to preaching to political conflict—and have it running over with the glorious gospel? Nichols has done it. Be alert: people forget how life-changing the gospel really is—and then are astonished to remember it again as they read Luther."

—D. CLAIR DAVIS

"Since Luther published a printed work about every two weeks of his adult life, there is a lot of ground to cover. But Nichols knows the terrain well and opens up its treasures with a deft touch."

—MARK NOLL

"A marvelous mixture of biography, history, theology, and anecdote. If you don't feel the heartbeat of the Reformation in these pages, check your pulse!"

—SINCLAIR FERGUSON

"Those who know nothing of Luther will benefit greatly from such a readable introduction, while those more familiar with him will find Nichols's enthusiasm infectious."

—CARL R. TRUEMAN

"Nichols has a gift for making a complex subject simple without being simplistic."

—MICHAEL A. ROGERS